THE FIELD GUIDE TO NORTH AMERICAN HAUNTINGS

Also by W. Haden Blackman

The Field Guide to North American Monsters

THE FIELD GUIDE TO NORTH AMERICAN HAUNTINGS

Everything You Need to Know About Encountering Over 100 Ghosts, Phantoms, and Spectral Entities

W. Haden Blackman

Three Rivers Press
New York

Copyright © 1998 by W. Haden Blackman

Published by Three Rivers Press, a division of Crown Publishers, Inc., 201 East 50th Street, New York, New York 10022. Member of the Crown Publishing Group.

Random House, Inc. New York, Toronto, London, Sydney, Auckland
www.randomhouse.com

THREE RIVER PRESS and colophon are trademarks of Crown Publishers, Inc.

Printed in the United States of America

Library of Congress Cataloging-in-Publication Data
Blackman, W. Haden.
   The field guide to North American hauntings: everything you need to know about encountering over 100 ghosts, phantoms, and spectral entities / by W. Haden Blackman. — 1st ed.
      p.   cm.
   Includes bibliographical references.
   1. Ghosts—United States. 2. Haunted houses—United States. 3. Haunted places—United States. I. Title.
BF1472.U6B57   1998
133.1'0973—dc21   98-4086
                                                                                        CIP

ISBN 0-609-80021-3

10   9   8   7   6   5   4   3

For Hope and Matt

May your home always be haunted

by only the kindest of spirits

and the sounds of laughter and love.

And for Anne-Marie,

who is hauntingly beautiful in every way.

CONTENTS

ACKNOWLEDGMENTS

While ghost hunting itself is a fairly solitary endeavor, a ghost hunter must look to those around him for support and encouragement. In both these respects, my entire family excels. I warmly thank my mother, Nancy, for inspiring me with her personal ghost story when I was young. Bill and Cheryl Blackman, Greg and Shirley Cravens, Barbara and Tom Blackman, Steve Cravens, Dave and Jan Bonfilio, Tony, and Matt and Hope also deserve credit for, if nothing else, putting up with me for so long.

For sharing friendship and spirits, I am grateful to Michael Braley, Melanie Stamps, Kim Carlson, Matt Brophy, James and Rose Ann Lang, Brian Bixby, Lara Thompson, Todd Platt, Molly Fisk, Joe Harrop, and Michelle Bonfilio. My deep appreciation to Matt Ragland for accepting (and often enjoying) my eccentricities.

Thanks also to my agent, Candice Fuhrman, who made this possible; to my insightful (and patient) editor, Jessica Schulte; and to Wendy Hubbert, who first suggested the book.

Once again, I have discovered that numerous people have taught me certain skills that have allowed me to see this project to fruition. I consider David Swanger, Kate Toll, Anne Busenkell, John Barnes, Lorraine Gayer, Dr. Cross, and John McManus excellent teachers all because they not only instruct, but share their own experiences and enrich the lives of their students.

And for helping me through my most desperate dry-spell moments, I am indebted to Tom Petty and the Heartbreakers, whose shows at the Fillmore kept me inspired for months.

INTRODUCTION

ALMOST EVERYONE KNOWS AT least one ghost story. We learn them at summer camps and slumber parties and trade them around campfires. Swapping tales of ghostly terror has become an art form, perpetuated in novels and on film. But ghost stories are not a new phenomenon; they have existed since the beginning of recorded history. Hundreds of years before European settlers arrived, Native Americans reported encounters with disembodied voices, demonic phantasms, and living corpses in caves, forests, and mountains across the continent. The early colonists also detected powerful spirits in the New World. As they built their homes, churches, and schools, ghosts began to appear in these edifices as well. Over the centuries, ghosts have been sighted consistently in all areas of the continent, in a variety of locations ranging from dank caves to the **White House.** And today, hundreds of people across the continent are convinced that they share their homes with some sort of phantom or spirit.

From the huge collection of firsthand accounts, **supernaturalists**—people who study the world of the **paranormal**—have been able to define the term **"ghost"** and have learned to recognize a site haunted by these restless dead. In general, a ghost is the life force of someone who has died but, for any number of reasons, has not ceased to exist in this realm. In many cases, ghosts are the souls of those who have died violently or well before their time. Other people become ghosts simply because they cannot accept the fact that they are dead, become lost on their way to the afterlife, or retain abnormally strong ties to the living and cannot bear to leave the mortal plane.

Ghosts fall into several categories depending upon the manner in which they manifest. The most recognizable ghosts are **phantoms,** spirits that appear as fairly normal humans. They are often identified as ghosts by a strange glow, unusual voice, or special powers, such as the ability to walk through walls. Because they are completely visible, they are often recognized by their loved ones.

Another prominent ghost type is the mischievous invisible spirit known as the **poltergeist.** Rarely seen but extremely common, poltergeists interact with humans by throwing dishes, slamming doors, and stealing small items. Many poltergeists become evil and loathsome over time, escalating in violence until they begin smashing windows, setting fires, and assaulting their living neighbors.

The third most common form of ghostly manifestation are **ghost lights.** These spirits appear as bobbing, glowing orbs wandering through the air. They frequently change color or size and seem to move through objects at will, but they cannot be caught or cornered. Because ghost lights appear most often along beaches or in deep swamps, they are often blamed for drowning deaths. However, most evidence shows that ghost lights are relatively harmless, although they may occasionally lead the curious wanderer astray.

Aside from phantoms, ghost lights, and poltergeists, ghosts manifest in numerous other ways as well. Some are simply disembodied voices that scream, wail, cry, or whisper in empty rooms. Other ghosts can cause temperature changes throughout a haunted site, making certain spots suddenly very cold or very warm. More unusual ghosts even manifest through disturbing odors or persistent stains. A small percentage of ghosts appear as horrific visions with missing heads, severed limbs, or rotting flesh.

A haunted site is any location inhabited by one or more ghosts and displaying at least one of the ghostly phenomena described above. Although they range from open fields to exquisite mansions, haunted sites tend to share a few common characteristics. Almost all haunted sites, for example, are surrounded by strong **auras,** invisible fields of energy that convey emotions to particularly sensitive people, such as **psychics** and children. The auras cloaking most haunted sites usually engender feelings of sadness, fear, or loss. Animals, including domestic dogs and cats, are extremely susceptible to the auras of haunted sites and will often refuse to enter such places. An aura might also emit a strange odor, an array of col-

ors, or even bizarre noises, all detectable by **sensitives.**

Haunted locales usually have some dark secret or tragic history as well. The vast majority were once the site of at least one heinous murder, accidental death, or suicide. Forms of bad luck, such as sudden financial or romantic troubles, may also afflict those living near or within a haunted site.

Because they are inhabited by restless spirits, haunted sites are plagued by unexplained noises, voices, shadows, and other unnerving effects. Creaking stairs, the sounds of laughter and screaming, mysteriously vanishing keepsakes, electrical problems, plumbing mishaps, and random fires are all common to haunted sites. Those who live in haunted houses may be prone to the psychic energy generated by their ghostly neighbors and begin suffering from nightmares and the sensation of being watched. Prolonged exposure to the ghostly phenomena at a haunted site can cause eating disorders, insomnia, paranoia, apathy, fits of uncontrollable sobbing, depression, ulcers, and outright insanity.

However, it must also be noted that many haunted sites are inhabited by peaceful ghosts who interact amiably with their human neighbors and never exhibit the slightest sign of hostility. While these ghosts do not attract the attention of novelists or storytellers, they enrich the lives of those around them, offering the living insight into a world that they seldom glimpse.

HOW TO USE THIS BOOK

THE FIELD GUIDE TO NORTH

American Hauntings is divided into five major sections, each covering a specific type of haunted locale. Chapter 1 describes the variety of haunted sites with which we are all most familiar: the true haunted house, human dwellings occupied by one or more restless spirits. Chapter 2 explores haunted vessels, including many ghost ships and other phantom craft; while chapter 3 discusses haunted cemeteries and burial sites. Chapter 4 deals with natural haunted sites, such as caves, rivers, and forests. Finally, chapter 5 focuses on an assortment of haunted sites that do not fit easily into any other category, including haunted villages and possessed objects. It must be remembered that there are virtually thousands of haunted sites within North America and it would be impossible to catalog all of them here with any great detail. Therefore, each chapter includes some of the most exciting haunted sites indicative of the particular type discussed. Ghost hunters must be aware that for each site contained in this book, there are hundreds of similar spirit-infested locations.

Each chapter begins with a broad overview of the characteristics common to the particular type of haunted site discussed and then gives detailed accounts of specific hauntings. Each chapter save chapter 5 also ends with a brief mention of other haunted sites that fit into the category.

Because finding and interacting safely with ghosts requires quick action and clear thinking, each individual entry begins with a "Vital Statistics Box" that sums up the site's prevalent and important characteristics. The Vital Statistics Box contains the following information:

LOCATION: The address or general location of the site, including city and state.

NUMBER OF GHOSTLY RESIDENTS: The estimated number of ghosts inhabiting the site.

IDENTITIES OF GHOSTLY RESIDENTS: Names, occupations, and other pertinent information on the spirits.

TYPE OF ACTIVITY: A brief description of the prominent ghostly activities, including **ghost lights, poltergeists, phantoms,** disembodied voices and screams, unexplained noises, and inexplicable temperature changes.

DEMEANOR OF GHOSTLY RESIDENTS: An overview of the personalities of the ghostly residents, including proclivity for violence and attitude toward the living.

ENCOUNTERING THE SITE'S GHOSTS: The number of RIP appearing immediately after this heading reflects the likelihood of encountering a spirit or ghostly phenomenon while visiting the haunted site, ranging from one (the chance of an encounter is unlikely, except under specific conditions) to four (the chance of an encounter is probable at all times).

The Vital Statistics Box is followed immediately by a detailed description of the haunted site and its ghostly inhabitants. Each entry then ends with advice for successfully exploring the haunted site and observing the ghost found therein.

After the five major chapters is a bonus chapter meant for novice ghost hunters. The chapter first describes the process for identifying a haunted site, then offers tips for dealing with ghosts in general, including those with violent personalities.

The supplemental information found at the back of the book consists of three appendices, a glossary, and a selected bibliography. If you come across an unfamiliar word or concept, refer to the glossary, which contains many terms important to the fields of supernaturalism and ghost hunting. Throughout the book, words that appear in **boldface** are discussed in greater detail elsewhere in the text; refer to the glossary for more information on these terms or sites. Appendix A is a sample questionnaire to be used when interviewing ghost witnesses, while Appendix B is a questionnaire that may be helpful in discussions with the ghosts themselves. Finally, Appendix C organizes the haunted sites by U.S. state and Canadian province.

THE FIELD GUIDE TO NORTH AMERICAN HAUNTINGS

1. TRUE HAUNTED HOUSES

WE ARE ALL familiar with the term "haunted house," the most common form of ghostly habitat.

A haunted house is basically any conventional building occupied by humans and restless spirits. This definition obviously allows for a huge variety of locations, but fortunately many haunted houses do share a number of other similarities.

First, most haunted houses have been the site of violence or tragedy. The notorious history of a haunted house may include a brutal murder (or, in many cases, double, triple, or even mass murder), suicide (or group suicide), or some other disaster, such as a fire or sweep-ing sickness, that claimed the lives of the previous residents.

Not surprisingly, the ghosts present in a haunted house are generally former inhabitants. Many experienced terrible deaths within the home or lived at the site for decades before dying. Those ghosts who only lived in the house for a short time (such as the ghosts haunting the **White House**) have returned because the building was either their favorite home or the place where they experienced the greatest joy or most profound sorrow. Some ghosts may also be former employees of the household or laborers who built the home and died during its construction.

If the haunting is limited to certain areas, these are usually the rooms or locations within the house that were most important to the spirit in life. For example, the ghost of a murdered cook will come back to haunt the kitchen, while a little boy felled by pneumonia may wander his playroom or continually return to the bed where he died. It often seems as if ghosts are drawn to attics or basements, but this is not because these places are dark and infested by cobwebs; rather, both attics and basements often serve as storerooms for family heirlooms, old furniture, scrapbooks, forgotten toys, and other objects that may be important to the spirits of the dead. It is also interesting to note that in the majority of haunted houses, some sort of supernatural phenomenon is reported to occur in the bathroom.

From the outside, haunted houses generally appear to be distinguished, venerable homes. Many are at least two stories tall, with several bedrooms, an attic, basement, and some sort of garden or large yard. Quite a few were originally constructed in isolated areas, often near some other type of haunted site, such as a haunted forest or graveyard.

When haunted houses are first purchased or entered, the haunting does not always become readily apparent. In fact, new owners may live in a home for months, or even years, before they realize that they are sharing the house with a spook. While a haunted house is usually in pristine condition at the time of purchase, it eventually undergoes unsettling cosmetic changes. Bursting pipes, mysterious fires, and inexplicable hot and cold spots are the most common attributes displayed early on by a haunted house. The walls or floors may also be marred by strange stains that cannot be removed, and those visiting the house are likely to detect an unpleasant odor or feel uneasy in certain rooms. There may also be an unusual proliferation of flies, cockroaches, rats, or other pests despite the owners' best efforts to keep the house spotless.

Oddly enough, most haunted houses only manifest spectral activity in certain areas of the home, as ghosts often limit themselves to specific rooms or hallways. It seems that the greater the ghostly population within a particular house, the more likely it is that each spirit will contract its range as the ghosts attempt to "share" the home. Conversely, if a dwelling is haunted by a single spirit, that ghost may feel it has the run of the house and will appear everywhere.

Haunted houses usually have a profound effect on animals. Even the most independent of dogs will often become timid and nervous when brought into a haunted house and will often seem to bark at empty rooms and corridors. Cats will continually bolt from the building or seek out hiding places.

The impact of living in a haunted house can

also be detectable in children. Obvious signs are recurrent and persistent nightmares or a deep and abiding fear of certain rooms. However, not all children are terrified of ghosts; in fact, an introverted, intelligent, and/or only child may actually enjoy a ghost's company. Therefore, the sudden appearance of a new imaginary friend can be especially telling. Children who are aware of a ghost and its activities may also seem paranoid, fearing that they will be blamed for the spirit's mischievous antics.

Aside from befriending one another, ghosts and children are connected on many other levels as well. In fact, when full-fledged hauntings finally manifest, the home is likely to be occupied by a family with at least one child (most likely a daughter) between the ages of five and fifteen. The psychic energy discharged by children, particularly girls entering puberty, seems to attract spirits of all kinds, although poltergeists appear most fascinated by this lure.

While extensive hauntings often begin with the appearance of children in a house, other factors may also "awaken" a home's resident ghosts. Something as simple as an impulsive outburst on the part of a new occupant can invoke the spirits, but ghosts are more commonly aroused by lengthy emotional experiences. Domestic violence, depression, prolonged sickness, adultery, and even a pregnancy can cause ghosts to manifest. Loud music, incessantly noisy children or animals,

drug or alcohol abuse, new construction, or any disrespect toward the home or its former occupants can also provoke the ghosts. Finally, ghosts can be drawn from hiding by a living occupant's exploration of black magic or the occult: burning certain types of candles, experimenting with Ouija boards, attempting to communicate with the dead in any way, reading satanic literature, or killing small animals while inside a haunted house is almost certain to drum up any local spirits.

Once a haunting is under way, haunted houses are likely to have a high turnover of owners and occupants, as few people have the patience, courage, or desire to spend any length of time in a haunted house. Unless new owners can learn to live with the spirits or the ghosts are chased away (see chapter 6), a haunted house may remain on the market for years. Some eventually become bed-and-breakfast inns that cater to the morbid or eccentric, or they are purchased by city governments and preserved as historic landmarks. With only a few exceptions, all of the haunted sites listed below are, in fact, open to the public. While there are literally thousands of privately owned haunted houses in America, this chapter focuses on public buildings to facilitate the novice ghost hunter's research: most homeowners who have experienced ghostly phenomena do not wish to be disturbed by curiosity-seekers and are unlikely to open their doors for ghost hunters.

THE AMITYVILLE "HORROR" HOUSE

VITAL STATISTICS

LOCATION: 112 Ocean Avenue, Amityville, Long Island, New York 11701. This home is a private residence and, although easy to find and extremely recognizable, should only be investigated with the permission of the current owners.

NUMBER OF GHOSTLY RESIDENTS: Between six and ten

IDENTITIES OF GHOSTLY RESIDENTS: Ronald DeFeo, Sr., and his wife, two daughters, and two sons, all murdered by Ronald DeFeo, Jr. A hooded figure and something described as a "demon" have also been reported.

TYPE OF ACTIVITY: Apparitions, inexplicable auras, disembodied footsteps, strange odors, poltergeists, and numerous other manifestations

DEMEANOR OF GHOSTLY RESIDENTS: Definitely evil and prone to attacking, possessing, and terrorizing humans

ENCOUNTERING THE AMITYVILLE GHOSTS:

the case are extremely well documented.

The Amityville House was built in 1928, and by the early 1970s it was occupied by Ronald DeFeo, Sr., his wife, and his five children, including twenty-four-year-old Ronald Jr. According to police, at approximately three o'clock on the morning of Friday, November 13th, 1974, Ronald Jr. rose from his bed, picked up a gun, and methodically executed his parents, his two brothers, and his two sisters. Despite his early claims that a Mafia hit man killed his family, local authorities easily connected DeFeo to the crimes and he was charged with six counts of murder.

The first indication that the supernatural may have been involved with the events at Amityville surfaced during the trial. DeFeo eventually confessed to murdering his family and admitted that he felt little remorse, but Ronald also argued that his family home was inhabited by spirits that urged him to kill.

The prosecution dismissed the notion that the house was haunted and instead argued that Ronald, an alleged heroin addict, had killed his family while stealing jewelry and some $200,000 in cash, loot that was never recovered. The jury accepted this theory and found Ronald DeFeo guilty, sentencing him to six consecutive life sentences in Dannemora prison.

Few haunted houses in America have received as much attention as the infamous Amityville House, a site seemingly plagued by a host of malevolent entities bent on causing murder and mayhem. The ghostly activity that occurred within this stately Dutch Colonial became the basis for a wildly successful book, *The Amityville Horror,* and a film of the same name, and the facts of

Despite the house's gruesome history, George and Kathy Lutz moved into the house on December 18, 1975, a little over a year after the murders. Almost immediately, they began experiencing strange phenomena. As in many cases, the hauntings began with a mysterious, foul odor that permeated the house. This was followed soon after by the arrival of a swarm of flies in one of the bedrooms and the appearance of a disgusting black ooze in the bathroom.

Over the next few weeks, the haunting intensified. George began hearing the disembodied footsteps and brass horns of a marching band invading his house, and woke several times to the sight of his wife levitating above their bed. Both the front door and the heavy garage door were nearly torn from their hinges on separate occasions, and the family once found a disturbing trail of cloven footprints in the snow outside their home. Before they had lived in the house for a full month, the ghostly activity escalated into full-fledged assaults. Kathy was attacked more than once, her body seemingly encircled by invisible arms that left huge red welts all over her body.

Finally, apparitions began to appear in the house. On various occasions, family members encountered a towering, hooded figure in

UPI/Corbis-Bettmann

The DeFeo home, Amityville, New York.

white and a demonic creature with horns and a mangled face. One night, George and Kathy's five-year-old daughter directed the couple's attention to a window, where they spied the flaming red eyes of some evil, feral piglike creature. After this instance, which occurred only a month after the family had moved in, the terrified Lutz family abandoned the house forever.

> "Every moron knows the difference between human footsteps . . . and the normal noises of an old house settling slowly and a little at a time on its foundation."
>
> —Hans Holzer, *Ghosts: True Encounters with the World Beyond*

Almost immediately, rumors of a haunting at the former DeFeo residence began to circulate, stories that George Lutz confirmed in articles in the *Long Island Press* and *Good Housekeeping*. In 1977, the Lutzes hired author Jay Anson to record their story, which became the best-selling book *The Amityville Horror* (1978). The success of the book, which spawned five films, has led some researchers to believe that the Lutzes concocted the hauntings in order to profit from the DeFeo killings and escape the huge mortgage on the house.

However, on January 15, 1977, ghost hunter Hans Holzer brought a psychic, Ethel Johnson Meyers, to the site. Together, they found evidence that seems to suggest that the house is indeed haunted. First, Meyers sensed that the house had been built on a Native American burial ground, which in itself is often the sole cause of a haunting. According to Meyers, the Native American spirits are angry because of some past transgression, causing a great deal of rage to build within the house. This collective anger and hatred may have possessed Ronald DeFeo, Jr., causing him to attack his family. According to many reports, Lutz also began to feel this rage and had dark thoughts about slaughtering his own family.

As is to be expected, the spirits of the murdered DeFeo family apparently reside within the house as well. Holzer took several photographs while in the house and discovered that white haloes appeared on the images taken in the rooms where the shootings occurred.

Today, there have been few reports of ghostly activity at the Amityville House. Recent owners have not encountered any spirits, demons, or evil auras. Some hauntings inexplicably cease when new owners move in or when the ghost seemingly tires of this plane of existence, and the Amityville House may in fact be an example of such phenomena. However, if the ghosts of Amityville persist, ghost hunters should be extremely careful. The influences at 112 Ocean Avenue have proven extremely strong and could conceivably possess the unwary.

If you enter the Amityville house, *by invitation only*, remember that there could be several different forces at work within its walls. Bring a priest to combat any demonic influences you might encounter. If you begin to feel enraged, frustrated, or violent, leave the home immediately and never return. Also, take copious photographs, as the spirits of the slain DeFeos may appear as white, amorphous shapes in pictures taken in the various bedrooms.

THE BELL HOUSE AND THE BELL WITCH

VITAL STATISTICS

LOCATION: The original Bell farmhouse was built in Robertson County, Tennessee, near the Kentucky state line and the Red River. Today, the house is gone, but the Tennessee Historical Commission has placed a marker along U.S. Highway 41 identifying the edge of the Bell property. A gravel road leads from the highway to the former site of the home, where a monument in memory of the Bell family has been erected. A cave on the property, also believed to be haunted, can be found overlooking the Red River.

NUMBER OF GHOSTLY RESIDENTS: At least one, and possibly as many as four

IDENTITIES OF GHOSTLY RESIDENTS: The Bell Witch, also known as Kate or Kate Batts. Other ghosts may include John, Betsy, and Richard Bell

TYPE OF ACTIVITY: Classic poltergeist activity of every kind, including invisible attacks, and a disturbing disembodied voice. More recent phenomena have included ghost lights and at least one apparition.

DEMEANOR OF GHOSTLY RESIDENTS: Incredibly vengeful and potentially dangerous. The central ghost, the Bell Witch, attacks specific individuals with a terrible fury. The other ghosts are probably harmless.

ENCOUNTERING THE BELL HOUSE GHOSTS:
RIP RIP RIP

The Bell haunting is one of the most important cases in the field of supernaturalism, because it is perhaps the most thoroughly documented example of poltergeist activity and one of few recorded instances in which a poltergeist has actually committed murder. The ghostly happenings affected the entire Bell family—John, Lucy, and their nine children—and were witnessed by many family friends and other outsiders, including President Andrew Jackson.

The hauntings began in 1817 after John Bell noticed a strange doglike creature lurking in his cornfields. When he fired upon the animal, it simply vanished before Bell's eyes. Soon, however, the Bell household was plagued by an invisible stranger who rapped and scraped against the walls of the house, as if trying to gain access. Eventually the spirit did find its way into the home, where it gnawed on bedposts, kicked the ceiling, knocked over furniture, and pulled unseen chains across the floor. Within a year after the spook's arrival, the Bell house was constantly under siege by a din of unexplained noises.

Eventually, the poltergeist escalated to committing unpredictable and sudden acts of violence, such as striking visitors directly in the face. Several of the Bells' nine children reported that as they tried to sleep at night, the spirit slapped them or pulled their hair. Furthermore, whenever the Bell brood left for school, they found themselves caught in a hail of rocks and sticks. The poltergeist especially enjoyed tormenting twelve-year-old Betsy Bell, who experienced convulsions and fainting spells as the haunting grew more intense. She also began hearing a disembodied voice, which seemed to grow closer each day.

Finally, the poltergeist announced itself to the entire family, introducing itself as simply "the Witch" and promising to plague poor John Bell forever. Almost immediately, it began to carry out this oath. John experienced a long succession of beatings, at least one of which left his jaw and tongue too swollen for speech. The Witch's voice filled the house at all hours, screaming, quoting Scripture, or threatening to murder John.

Throughout the hauntings, the ghost was never conclusively identified, although the family eventually began calling her Kate. It was suspected that the spirit was the tormented soul of Kate Batts, a native of Halifax, North Carolina. Although Kate was surly and disagreeable, Bell had fallen in love with her while living in Halifax. He even proposed marriage, but for unknown reasons the wedding never occurred. In the late 1770s, Kate's lifeless body was found alongside a well near her home. Her mysterious death was never adequately explained, but John Bell recovered fairly quickly from the loss and married Lucy soon after Kate's funeral. The newlyweds promptly relocated to Tennessee, where their troubles with the poltergeist began. It is possible, although unlikely, that Kate was murdered by Bell after he realized that he could not possibly spend the rest of his life with the moody woman. If this theory is true, Kate returned from the grave in search of vengeance. However, it is more probable that Kate died of natural causes but became even more cantankerous after death. Thus, she felt obliged to deprive Bell of any happiness simply out of pure malice.

Regardless of her true identity or motives, news of the Bell Witch spread and witnesses from all over the county began to visit the home. Many experienced the bizarre happenings and were often punched or kicked by the Witch. In desperation, John Bell implored his family minister, James Johnson, to perform an exorcism on the house. Johnson agreed, but the ritual seemed to have little effect and Kate continued to plague the home. Unable to admit defeat, Johnson encouraged his parishioners to stand vigil within the Bell home and document any ghostly encounters. The God-fearing folk agreed, but their presence did little to deter the Witch. During the following weeks, Kate's activities only intensified until few of Johnson's flock would dare set foot inside the house. Even President Andrew Jackson arrived on the scene to confront the spirit, but he too fled after dishes and large pieces of furniture were hurled at him.

> "I am a spirit from everywhere. I am in the air, in houses, any place at any time. . . . I was once very happy, but I have been disturbed and made unhappy."
>
> —The Bell Witch, speaking through Betsy Bell

Slowly, John Bell began to unravel. He suffered from uncontrollable twitching and was bedridden for months at a time. Meanwhile, his wife Lucy was pelted by fruits and nuts that hailed down from the empty air, and three of his sons endured nightly attacks. When Betsy turned fifteen and became engaged to a neighbor, the Witch whispered to her endlessly until she was forced to call off the marriage.

The Bell Witch's campaign against John Bell became even more murderous when the spirit switched his tonic with poison. This assassination attempt was thwarted, but on December 19, 1820, John was found in a mysterious stupor from which he could not be roused. The attending doctor heard the Witch announce that Bell would soon be dead, and in fact he passed away the very next day. At the funeral, the sadistic Witch's lilting voice was heard singing "Row me up some brandy, O."

About a month after John's death, the Witch mysteriously disappeared, but not before swearing to return in seven years. In 1828, the spirit did visit the house again, when only Lucy and two of her sons, Richard and Joel, remained in the home. It made a halfhearted attempt to torment the trio for about two weeks, then announced its departure. However, it again made an oath to continue haunting the site, swearing to reappear once every 107 years. This arbitrary number seems ill-suited to the ghost, for it was reported in 1852 and 1861. In 1935, when it should have actually revealed itself again, no one caught sight of the spirit, although several Bell descendants did suffer tragic deaths.

Today, the Bell House is no more—it was burned to the ground by frightened neighbors long ago—but the site is still overrun by ghostly activity. Where the house once stood,

visitors sometimes spot floating ghost lights or hear eerie screams and the sounds of chains rattling. The 1980s brought a series of encounters with a raven-haired woman, who silently floats over sections of the property before disappearing into the mist. The portion of U.S. Highway 41 nearest the Bell House site is said to be haunted by a young female ghost who suddenly appears in front of panicked motorists and passes through their cars. The ominous Bell Witch Cave, which overlooks Red River from a cliff on the Bell property, is also rumored to possess a strange aura and play home to at least one active spirit, perhaps Kate herself.

Like the Bell Witch, the current ghosts have not been identified. It is highly likely that the malevolent presence known as Kate is still lurking at the site. John Bell, deprived of a long and happy life by his tormentor, has probably found his way back home as well. One of the specters could also be Betsy Bell, who died in Mississippi at eighty-six, but seemed to suffer the most from her family's ghostly visitor. Richard Bell was profoundly disturbed by the hauntings and his father's untimely death, as revealed in his book *Our Family Troubles*, and he too may visit the site from time to time in ghostly form.

Finding the Bell House is relatively easy. Simply take U.S. Highway 41 north from Nashville until you reach Adams. As you near the Kentucky state line, you will encounter a road marker near a gravel road, which signals the start of the Bell property. Follow the gravel road to a monument commemorating the Bell family, and you will find yourself standing at the very site where John Bell was tormented. Spooky tours of the Bell Witch Cave can also be arranged.

Once you have reached the property, you can attempt contact with the Bell Witch by calling for its attention, either verbally or through a Ouija board or similar device. You might attract and befriend the spirit by loudly condemning John Bell as an evil, hateful man (although this will do little to endear you to locals). In addition, if the spirit's promise holds true, it will reappear in 2042, and those ghost hunters who have yet to join their quarry would do well to visit the site numerous times that year. Addressing any other Bells, espe-

cially by reminiscing about the life and great deeds of John Bell, may also prove useful when exploring the property. As with many other cases, any attempt to contact these ghosts should be made at night and be accompanied by the burning of candles or incense.

If a ghost does appear, be on guard. The Bell Witch has shown considerable contempt for human life and possesses powers that far exceed those of normal poltergeists. If you engender this spirit's wrath, you could be forced to endure a most horrible haunting.

THE CONFERENCE HOUSE

VITAL STATISTICS

LOCATION: Conference House Museum, Hylan Boulevard, Tottenville (Staten Island), New York 10307. Contact the museum at (718) 984-2086 for hours of operation.

NUMBER OF GHOSTLY RESIDENTS: Between two and ten

IDENTITIES OF GHOSTLY RESIDENTS: Presumably Captain Christopher Billopp, his jilted fiancée, his grandson, numerous British soldiers buried in unmarked graves on the grounds, and a murdered slave

TYPE OF ACTIVITY: Disembodied laughter and screams, cold spots, frightening auras, apparitions, and mysterious knocks and footsteps

DEMEANOR OF GHOSTLY RESIDENTS: Mostly sad and angry. While capable of inflicting lasting psychological damage, the ghosts have yet to commit acts of physical violence.

ENCOUNTERING THE CONFERENCE HOUSE GHOSTS:

To those uninterested in the ghostly, the Conference House museum is most notable because it hosted Benjamin Franklin, Edward Rutledge, and John Adams when they met with British commander Lord Howe on September 11, 1776, to

discuss a possible peace treaty to end the Revolutionary War. Such a treaty was never signed, and the revolutionaries ultimately won America's freedom—but some say the British still inhabit the Conference House.

What is today known as the Conference

House was once the Bentley Mansion, a stately home built on Staten Island by Captain Christopher Billopp. Since the time of its construction, it has been a place of death and tragedy. Early on, the settlers of Staten Island were plagued by Native American raids. Many were murdered and, according to sensitives who have visited the place, still roam the grounds of Conference House. Personal tragedy also followed Billopp: In the late 1600s, he allowed his fiancée to live in the house, but shortly before their wedding, he abandoned the poor woman. She died of grief a few days later. Today, her weeping can still be heard, and a sadness pervades certain bedrooms of the house where she is said to have spent her last days. After his retirement, Billopp returned to the mansion. He too died in the home he had built, and he may still lurk in the hallways.

Decades after Captain Billopp's death, his grandson, also named Christopher, took over ownership of the house. One night, he began arguing with one of his female slaves, with whom he may have been romantically involved. When she attempted to walk away, he was consumed by a fit of uncontrolled rage. He attacked her at the top of the staircase and drove a knife into her chest. The young girl tumbled to the foot of the stairs, where she bled to death. She and Billopp, who often appears as a portly man in dark clothes and a fur coat, are destined to repeat the crime over and over again until the end of time. At night, their laughter can be heard drifting through the hallways, followed shortly after by Billopp's furious shouts and the girl's terrified screams, after which the house is overcome by an uncanny silence.

During the Revolutionary War, Conference House was ruled by the British. While they occupied the site, the bodies of the British soldiers killed in skirmishes or felled by sickness were buried in unmarked graves in the cellar. Perhaps enraged that they have not been returned to their native land, these soldiers still lurk in the basement, their presence causing visitors to feel chills and inexplicable anxiety. Outside, members of the Billopp family are also interred, and they too may rise at night to wander the area.

Today, Conference House has been converted into an historical museum celebrating the Revolutionary War and such patriots as Ben Franklin. But it is also considered premier ghost hunting ground by supernaturalists and psychics.

To visit Conference House, take a ferry from Manhattan to Staten Island and then travel by train to Tottenville. Initially visit the house at night, when it is closed and visitors aren't about. While you will not be able to enter, you may be able to wander the perimeters of the property and peer into ground-level windows, where you may catch a glimpse of some ghostly activity. Pay special attention to a crooked window above the porch; many witnesses have reported feeling as if they were being watched by some presence hiding just inside that particular window.

Once inside the house, begin your tour by wandering the entire basement. There you will find a small archway, which many sensitives report carries a strong aura. You may feel chills or sense the presence of Captain Billopp. Also explore the front wall, which is near the site where the British soldiers are said to be buried. Again, you may notice extreme and sudden temperature changes at this spot.

After leaving the cellar, visit the upstairs hallway. Although relatively inactive during the day, this hallway reportedly echoes with the cries of the murdered slave. Next, wander from the hallway to the attic stairs, where legend maintains the actual stabbing occurred. If you are allowed to stay into the late afternoon (or even through the night), you may hear the reenactment of the murder, which has been reported in the past by the house's caretakers and their relatives.

THE HOTEL DEL CORONADO

VITAL STATISTICS

LOCATION: 1500 Orange Avenue, Coronado (San Diego), California 92118. The most haunted room is room 3502, although rooms 3505 and 3312 have experienced ghostly phenomena as well. Call (800) HOTEL-DEL for reservations.

NUMBER OF GHOSTLY RESIDENTS: At least one

IDENTITY OF GHOSTLY RESIDENT: Kate Morgan, also known as Mrs. Lottie Anderson Barnard, killed on Thanksgiving Day in 1892

TYPE OF ACTIVITY: One apparition in a black lace dress, strange choking noises, unexplained footsteps, and disturbing cold spots

DEMEANOR OF GHOSTLY RESIDENT: Tragic and miserable, but unlikely to be hostile. Regardless, the haunting is often unsettling to novice ghost hunters.

ENCOUNTERING THE GHOST OF HOTEL DEL CORONADO:

Hotel del Coronado, ca. 1912.

The haunting of Hotel del Coronado represents a classic ghost story filled with tragedy and untimely death. Kate Morgan was born in Dubuque, Iowa, in 1868. By the time she was twenty-four, she had married a disreputable gambler named Tom Morgan. The two migrated to California, where they set up their home in Visalia. Unfortunately, Tom was not a family man, and when Kate became pregnant, the gambler left home. A few days later, Kate received a letter from her husband in which he ended their relationship.

Distraught, Kate tracked Tom to the Hotel del Coronado, where she registered under the assumed name of Mrs. Lottie Anderson Barnard and checked into room 302. On her first night in the upscale hotel, she spied her husband in the card room, engaged in a romantic interlude with another woman. After a brief argument, Kate stormed from the card room, and was found dead in her room one or two days later, having been killed on Thanksgiving Day.

Initially, it was reported that Kate left the hotel after her confrontation with Morgan and immediately purchased a gun with intent to murder Tom and his new lover. This version of the tale concludes that Kate had a change of heart and committed suicide, alone in her room, killing both herself and her unborn child. However, new evidence uncovered in 1989 suggests that Tom Morgan actually invaded his wife's hotel room, shot her dead, and staged the scene to appear as a suicide.

Whatever the case, Kate Morgan still haunts the room in which she died. Now known as room 3502, the site is plagued by disembodied footsteps, mysterious temperature changes, and a persistent gurgling noise. Animals brought into the room have become overwhelmed with terror, and guests have reported that objects seem to disappear or move on their own. Kate has also been spotted by guests and hotel employees alike as she wanders the room in a black lace dress. Most dramatic, perhaps, is a report that a study of the room using computers and infrared cameras detected thirty-seven abnormalities in temperature, humidity, electrical output, and magnetic emission.

Kate Morgan's influence, or the presence of other ghosts, has also been sensed in room 3505 and room 3312. Spectral apparitions, a host of noises, and cold spots have been encountered in these rooms as well.

Hotel del Coronado is on the island of Coronado, which is connected to the city of San Diego by the Coronado Bridge. Although the hotel usually does not rent room 3502 unless absolutely necessary, the persistent ghost hunter should be able to request the room for an evening. Bring a Polaroid instant camera and take pictures of every object in the room repeatedly throughout the night, then compare these photographs to determine if anything has been moved by a ghostly presence. Walk the perimeter of the room several times each hour, searching for sudden cold spots. Also listen for the sound of Kate's footsteps. If possible, bring a cat into the room and watch the creature for any signs of anxiety or agitation, which could signal Kate's approach. If the ghost actually appears, try to communicate with her. Specifically, ask whether she was murdered by Tom Morgan or took her own life, a question that must be answered before the controversy can finally be put to rest.

THE COX HOUSE AND THE AMHERST ATTACKS

VITAL STATISTICS

LOCATION: 6 Prince Street, Amherst, Nova Scotia, Canada. A tire store now occupies the site where the Cox house once stood.

NUMBER OF GHOSTLY RESIDENTS: One

IDENTITY OF GHOSTLY RESIDENT: Bob, a previous resident of the house who gained vast supernatural powers in death

TYPE OF ACTIVITY: Unexplained noises and poltergeist activity, including attacks on residents, mysterious fires, and objects moving on their own

DEMEANOR OF GHOSTLY RESIDENT: Malicious and patently dangerous, but only on a limited scope. Bob singled out an individual victim to torment and did not directly attack others. However, Bob's pranks involving fire could have directly caused the deaths of others.

ENCOUNTERING THE AMHERST GHOST:

The Amherst poltergeist, which manifested between 1878 and 1879, is one of the most famous cases of those hauntings that revolve around a single individual. In this instance, the victim was nineteen-year-old Esther Cox, who lived with her two older sisters and a brother-in-law in a quaint two-story house in Nova Scotia.

The hauntings began in August of 1878, shortly after Esther was almost raped by a local boy named Bob McNeal. As has been noted, emotional turmoil often awakens nearby ghosts, and this may have been the case in the Amherst attacks, which affected Esther alone. First she sensed the ghost's presence as a light touch on her leg as she tried to sleep. The next night, however, she awoke screaming as her face and body swelled dramatically. Her cries for help attracted her family, who watched in horror as Esther's eyes nearly erupted from her head. As the girl writhed in agony, the family suddenly heard a loud thunderclap, after which Esther's body returned to normal.

Only four days later, the ghost returned again, this time pulling the sheets from the bed that Esther shared with her sister, Jennie. Esther's brother-in-law, Daniel, could do nothing to stop the spirit and called in a local physician named Dr. Carritte to study the case. While Carritte was present, the poltergeist knocked and scratched on the walls, and then slowly carved a message on the bedroom wall. The chilling note read: "Esther Cox, you are mine to kill." The poltergeist then spent the bulk of the night shaking the walls and ceiling so violently that plaster fell onto the horrified witnesses.

The day after the horrible message appeared, Esther and Dr. Carritte were in the basement, where the family stored firewood and piles of potatoes, when the spirit attacked again. Both Esther and Dr. Carritte were caught in a storm of potatoes and wood and forced to flee. Soon after, Esther was stricken with diphtheria, but while she was bedridden the ghost disappeared. When she was well enough to leave her bed, she was sent to live with another sister in New Brunswick, and her torment seemingly ended.

Unfortunately, as soon as Esther returned to Amherst, so too did the poltergeist. During this new round of hauntings, the spirit began whispering to Esther and identified itself as "Bob." On one occasion, it threatened to set the house afire. The moment Esther heard this, lighted matches began falling from the air and onto her bed. This hail of matches lasted a full ten minutes. Over the next few days, dresses, curtains, and sheets spontaneously caught fire, and Daniel was forced to ask Esther to leave the house before the spirit burned his home to the ground.

Throughout the following months, Esther was passed around between family friends, some of whom reported strange ghostly activity within their homes while Esther was present. Eventually, though, it seemed as if Bob had left Esther's side and she was allowed to return to the family home. Yet again, the poltergeist reappeared.

At this point, a quirky stage magician named Walter Hubbell approached the family and asked permission to study Esther's case. After he was pelted by paperweights, furniture, and other objects, he became convinced that he could showcase Esther's personal poltergeist for profit. Daniel agreed, and a performance was arranged in the house. Bob proved reluctant to appear, and the customers demanded their money back, at which point a frustrated and angry Daniel banished Esther and Hubbell from his home forever. Esther wandered for some time, but was still plagued by the poltergeist wherever she went. She was even briefly imprisoned after an employer accused her of burning down his barn. Eventually, however, Esther escaped Bob's influence and lived out her remaining days in peace. In 1907, thirty years after the attacks, she confirmed the details of the hauntings to investigator Hereward Carrington, but claimed that the ghost had not reappeared after her short stint in prison.

Today, the Cox house no longer stands, having been replaced by a tire store long ago. No ghostly activity has been reported at the site since Esther permanently left the house. Yet if Bob's claims hold true and he was indeed a former resident, he may still be trapped on the grounds. It is interesting to note that Esther's sister Jennie once claimed to have established communication with Bob, but was only allowed to ask him "yes" or "no" questions; he would answer through a series of raps that the two had agreed upon. Today, a brave ghost hunter might take a Ouija board to the site and ask simple "yes" or "no" questions as well, allowing Bob to answer through the board if he still lurks nearby.

THE HAW BRANCH PLANTATION

VITAL STATISTICS

LOCATION: Amelia, Virginia. The plantation is located along U.S. Highway 360, about twenty-six miles west of Richmond. It is a private residence, but is open to visitors. Contact the plantation at Box 188, Amelia, VA 23002 or call (804) 561-2472.

NUMBER OF GHOSTLY RESIDENTS: Unknown, but at least two

IDENTITIES OF GHOSTLY RESIDENTS: The Woman in White, the apparition of a young girl, along with the spirit of Florence Wright, a relative of the family who experienced the hauntings. A giant white bird and several male phantoms have also been reported but never identified.

TYPE OF ACTIVITY: Apparitions, disembodied screams, and mysterious scents

DEMEANOR OF GHOSTLY RESIDENTS: Extremely enigmatic, only mildly psychologically disturbing, and completely harmless in all other aspects

ENCOUNTERING THE HAW BRANCH PLANTATION GHOSTS:

In 1964, Cary McConnaughey and his wife Gibson purchased the dilapidated remains of the Haw Branch Plantation, which was once the home of Gibson's grandmother. The McConnaugheys moved into the 15,000-acre plantation on August 13, 1965, and began working hard to restore the house to its former glory. Unfortunately, just three months after arriving at the house, on November 23, 1965, a night of well-earned rest was shattered by bloodcurdling shrieks emanating from the attic. The screams woke the entire family and terrified the family dogs, but no source could be found. The invisible banshee was quiet the following nights, but exactly six months later, its wails could be heard throughout the house again. The spirit continued to wake the family with its screeching at regular six-month intervals until the summer of 1967, when an apparition began to appear in the house.

The ghost, known only as the Woman in White, was the spirit of an attractive young woman wearing a flowing white skirt. Cary and Gibson spotted the wraith standing before the fireplace in the drawing room, but the phantom always disappeared before any contact could be made. The couple later discovered that the McConnaugheys' great-grandmother, Harriett Mason, had also reported an encounter with the ghost; decades before Cary and Gibson moved into the house, Harriett had reported that the spirit once awakened her from a deep sleep with a gentle touch.

On a night in May of 1968, the McConnaugheys' son and daughter witnessed a giant white bird with a wingspan of over six feet standing in the yard. The bird vanished, but soon afterward, the Woman in White's horrible screams echoed through the house.

The most dramatic and unusual ghostly manifestations began in 1969, when the family inherited a portrait of a deceased ancestor named Florence Wright. According to the painting's previous owner, Florence had died shortly before the completion of the portrait, but he promised that the work was beautifully colored. Yet when the McConnaugheys received the painting, they discovered that it was a somber piece that appeared to have been done in charcoal. Undaunted, they mounted the portrait in the library. Only days later, they began hearing female voices whispering in the library, although no visitors appeared.

The voices in the library continued unabated, and in February of 1970, Cary McConnaughey noticed that the portrait had begun a startling transformation: a portion of the painting containing a rose was slowly taking on color. Over the course of the following months, the portrait gradually regained all of its original hues. When the process was complete, the voices in the library were no longer reported. A local psychic called in to investigate the portrait claimed that Florence Wright's spirit had been imprisoned in the painting as a

> "I could plainly see the silhouette of a slim girl in a floor-length dress. . . . I could see no features but she was not transparent, just a white silhouette. I saw her for perhaps ten seconds. In the next instant she was gone."
>
> —Woman in White witness Gibson McConnaughey

result of her untimely death. While hanging in the library, she had enlisted the aid of other ghosts (the voices the McConnaugheys had heard) in order to restore the portrait to its former glory. It is unknown whether she remains within the painting to this day.

Since the 1970s, there have been numerous sightings of other spirits in and around the Haw Branch Plantation. Among the ghostly visitors is a male phantom who exits the barn bearing a brightly glowing lantern; when approached, he vanishes, but his lantern can still be seen hovering in the air for several moments. Other spirits include a dapper gent who screams "Help me!" before disappearing and a gaunt man who walks with a noticeable limp.

When visiting the Haw Branch Plantation, devote your energies to exploring the library. Pay close attention to the painting of Florence Wright and take careful stock of any strange emotions you might experience. Specifically, be sure to record if you sense that you are being watched. Temperature changes or the faint sound of someone whispering could also indicate that the portrait still holds Florence's spirit.

If you are permitted, also spend time in the attic, where the Woman in White seems to originate. Before your visit, call the plantation and ask if her disembodied screaming has been heard of late; if it has, plan to arrive at the site exactly six months after the last reported shriek.

HULL HOUSE AND THE DEVIL BABY

VITAL STATISTICS

LOCATION: 800 S. Halsted Street, Chicago, Illinois 60607. Hull House is now a public museum located on the corner of Halsted and Post Streets. Call (312) 413-5353 for more information.

NUMBER OF GHOSTLY RESIDENTS: At least five, including a group of four hooded phantoms and a deformed "Devil Baby." Other ghosts are suspected as well.

IDENTITIES OF GHOSTLY RESIDENTS: One of the ghosts may be the spirit of an orphaned child. Other spirits may include Charles Hull, who constructed the house, and Jane Addams and Ellen Starr, who converted it into a social services center.

TYPE OF ACTIVITY: Ghost lights, ectoplasmic mist, and at least five phantoms

DEMEANOR OF GHOSTLY RESIDENTS: Largely unknown. If the ghost of a Devil Baby does exist in the house, it is likely to be quite violent. In contrast, the other ghosts may be particularly benevolent.

ENCOUNTERING THE GHOSTS OF HULL HOUSE:

Hull House was first built in 1856 by Charles Hull as a shelter for immigrants struggling to find a new life in America. In the 1880s, patrons of the poor Ellen Starr and Jane Addams converted the large building into a settlement house to serve Chicago's most impoverished residents. Despite a steady stream of people coming and going, no ghostly activity was reported until the early 1900s.

The first supernatural event surrounding Hull House took place in 1913, when the so-called Devil Baby arrived at the home. According to legend, the child was born to a God-fearing Italian woman who had unwisely married an atheist; as punishment, their baby was cursed with the Devil's appearance: it had cloven hooves, scaled skin, horns, pointed ears, and a sinuous tail. The couple tried to raise the infant for a short time, but when it became unruly the father entrusted it to the care of Jane Addams and Hull House.

Within days, news of the Devil Baby leaked into the immigrant neighborhoods surrounding Hull House, causing widespread panic. Throughout the uproar, Addams maintained that no such creature existed, although many reports indicate that she was hiding the mon-

Hull House, ca. 1894.

strosity in the attic in an attempt to protect it from mob violence.

Eventually, the panic subsided, leaving the mystery of the Devil Baby unsolved. But years later, the legend of the creature reemerged. For decades now, people passing the house have spotted a wild, bestial creature peering from one of the attic windows. This apparition has been tentatively identified as the ghostly remains of the Devil Baby, which may have died in the house while still a child.

Aside from the creepy Devil Baby, Hull House has several other phantoms in residence. Ghost hunters exploring the site have reported encounters with floating balls of light that wander down the attic staircase. The apparitions, along with a strange ectoplasmic mist, have been caught on film by a number of researchers. In addition, four hooded phantoms, often described as monks, have also been sighted and photographed in recent years.

All of Hull House's ghosts, other than the Devil Baby, have yet to be identified, largely because the list of candidates is so long. Virtually anyone who ever visited Hull House, including a great many impoverished immigrants, could have returned to the site in death. The home's founder, Charles Hull, is also a prime suspect in the current hauntings, as is Jane Addams, who eventually received a Nobel Prize for her efforts on behalf of the poor and the women's movement.

In 1963, the settlement house relocated to a larger facility. At that time, the original building was converted into a historic museum, which is now open to the public. The current staff denies all knowledge of any hauntings and has reported no unusual phenomena. Ghost hunters, however, are convinced that Hull House remains one of the most haunted sites in America.

Hull House is one of the few haunted houses that is arguably more rewarding (and probably much safer) to study from the *outside*. Begin your search for ghosts at the site by observing the upper left attic window, where the Devil Baby most often appears. Once inside, spend your hours repeatedly wandering the attic staircase, which often plays host to a parade of ghost lights. The attic should also be thoroughly searched, especially if you managed to glimpse the Devil Baby before you entered the house. Throughout your visit, snap several rolls of photographs, devoting a large number of exposures to both the staircase and the corners of the attic. While some of Hull House's ghostly manifestations may not appear to the naked eye, they often reveal themselves on developed film.

THE LALAURIE HOUSE

VITAL STATISTICS

LOCATION: A private residence at 1140 Royal Street, New Orleans, Louisiana 70116

NUMBER OF GHOSTLY RESIDENTS: Probably six or seven, but perhaps two dozen or more

IDENTITIES OF GHOSTLY RESIDENTS: Murdered slaves and servants and the deranged spirit of Madame Delphine Lalaurie herself

TYPE OF ACTIVITY: Disembodied screams, the rattling of invisible chains, and several phantoms

DEMEANOR OF GHOSTLY RESIDENTS: Tormented, confused, and, in at least one case, sadistic and murderous. The atrocities that occurred at this house have had a lasting effect and are capable of psychologically scarring those who enter the site. Lalaurie's ghost, in particular, still holds to a love of death and torture.

ENCOUNTERING THE LALAURIE HOUSE GHOSTS:
RIP RIP RIP RIP

The Lalaurie House, one of New Orleans' most haunted sites, has a tragic and sordid history, even in comparison to the tales told of other ghost-infested homes. The stately mansion was built in 1832 by wealthy socialite Madame Delphine Macarty Lalaurie. Throughout the early 1830s, the elegant home served as the playground for the social elite. Lalaurie displayed her financial status by furnishing her house in the most expensive and elegant manner possible and by purchasing an enormous number of slaves. In fact, Lalaurie's guests often quipped that it seemed as if the matriarch owned one slave for every chore imaginable.

The house's gruesome troubles began in 1833, when Lalaurie's slaves began mysteriously vanishing. At the time, no one questioned these disappearances, assuming that the slaves either escaped, had been set free, or were sold for profit. But eventually, a servant girl named Lia escaped from her room in the Lalaurie mansion and fled onto the rooftop, where she screamed for help. Witnesses watched as Lalaurie herself confronted the girl, beating her severely with a whip, until the poor girl leaped from the building in order to escape her enraged mistress. Lia did not survive the fall, and Lalaurie quickly collected the body, attempting to conceal it in a well.

Police were notified of the murder and easily found Lia's corpse. To punish Lalaurie, authorities levied a fine against her and demanded that she sell all of her slaves at public auction. Unfortunately, Madame Lalaurie's friends purchased each of her slaves and secretly returned them to the wicked woman.

The extent of Madame Lalaurie's dementia became evident on April 10, 1834, when a fire brigade responded to a blaze at the mansion. When they arrived, they found an elderly black cook chained to the kitchen floor. She confessed to lighting the fire in the kitchen, claiming that she had suffered unconscionable abuse at the hands of Madame Lalaurie. To corroborate her story, she directed her rescuers to a small attic apartment, where Lalaurie's other slaves were imprisoned. There, the fire brigade was greeted with a horrible, mind-wrenching site.

The attic, which was rank with decay and the smell of death, had been converted into a torture chamber, where Lalaurie kept nude victims shackled to crude and barbaric devices. A number of long-dead slaves, surrounded by flies and maggots, littered the room. Other victims were unconscious or weeping uncontrollably as they endured tremendous agony. Among the atrocities found in Lalaurie's attic was a woman gutted and tied down by her own intestines. Another woman was found with her mouth sewn shut; when rescuers cut the stitches, they discovered that her mouth was filled with feces. Most of the male victims were missing fingernails, eyes, ears, and portions of their buttocks. At least one man had had a hole drilled into his head to allow Lalaurie to "stir" his brains with a stick. Other victims were doused in honey and covered in black ants or had been starved to near-death after their mouths were painfully pinned shut. Lalaurie's victims were freed immediately, but most died within days.

The Lalaurie death toll has never been accurately reported. Some accounts maintain that only seven bodies were discovered in the attic, while other sources cite far higher numbers. In addition, no one has been able to estimate the number of slaves who mysteriously disappeared while in Lalaurie's service, nor were these bodies immediately located. Around the turn of the century, workmen refurbishing the house uncovered several skele-

tons in makeshift graves hidden beneath the floorboards. These corpses were attributed to Madame Lalaurie, bringing the estimated number of murders to at least a dozen.

When the depth of her depravity was revealed, a mob convened at Madame Lalaurie's home and threatened her life. She fled to Paris, and most reports claim she died some years later after she was gored to death by a wild boar while hunting in southern France. However, local legends hold that Madame Lalaurie surreptitiously returned to New Orleans, living on the outskirts of town under the pseudonym "Widow Blanque" until she died in obscurity.

In the decades since Lalaurie's occupation of the home, it has been refurbished several times. It served as a school for girls, and was then converted into a barbershop, an antique shop, and finally an apartment building. In all its incarnations, the building's tenants have confirmed that the Lalaurie House's horrible history has resulted in an epic haunting.

The first ghostly phenomena were noted in the early 1900s, when a range of phantoms began manifesting in the building. Madame Lalaurie has been sighted numerous times in all areas of the site. The apparition of a tall black man mounting the stairs has also been observed quite frequently, and a host of less tangible spirits are said to float through the house. Strange and frightening noises are also commonly reported: The sobbing of the slave girl Lia can be detected outside the house, while tortured screams descend from the attic. The rattling of unseen chains is reported in the kitchen and on the staircase as well.

Today, the Lalaurie House is still considered quite haunted and pedestrians often claim to hear the ghosts' agonized shrieks when they pass by the house. The building has

A. Bonfilio

The LaLaurie Mansion, New Orleans.

been remodeled yet again and is now part of many French Quarter tours, which are recommended for novice ghost hunters beginning their exploration of New Orleans. As with the **Hull House,** you can search for ghosts at the Lalaurie site from outside: simply stand in the shadow of the building and listen intently for screams of any kind. Once inside the property, pay special attention to the courtyard's cherub fountain, which is said to be near the site of Lia's death. Her cries often seem to emanate from this location.

Within the Lalaurie House, concentrate your efforts on the attic and the main staircase. There, the spirits of the slain slaves may be contacted through a psychic, a Ouija board, or some other device. If you do establish contact with any of the house's dead, try to determine the exact number of people murdered by Madame Lalaurie, as this is key information currently missing from the house's case history.

Be warned that the ghost of Madame Lalaurie is likely to be even more demented and barbaric in death than the woman ever was in life. Only experienced ghost hunters should attempt to establish any form of communication with this spirit, whose evil nature cannot be ignored. She appears in all areas of the house, but will probably be present most often in either the attic or on the roof, the two locations where she committed murder. In fact, there is the strong possibility that Lalaurie's ghost and the spirit of Lia may act out the slave's death from time to time. If you do manage to communicate with Lalaurie, again ask her about the number of murder victims she can claim, but also try to determine how and where she really died.

THE PHELPS MANSION AND THE STRATFORD KNOCKINGS

VITAL STATISTICS

LOCATION: 1738 Elm Street, Stratford, Connecticut 06497

NUMBER OF GHOSTLY RESIDENTS: Two

IDENTITIES OF GHOSTLY RESIDENTS: Unknown, but possibly Goody Bassett, who was hanged as a witch in 1661, and Anna Phelps

TYPE OF ACTIVITY: Every conceivable type of poltergeist manifestation from the simple movement of small objects to children being thrown from their beds. Unexplained knocks, disembodied whispers, and the sudden appearance of phantoms, cryptic mirages, and life-sized figures made out of clothing have also been reported.

DEMEANOR OF GHOSTLY RESIDENTS: Once unrelenting and vicious, but today somewhat benign, if disturbing

ENCOUNTERING THE PHELPS HOUSE GHOSTS:

The case of the Phelps Mansion is a perfect example of the horror caused when untrained mortals foolishly conjure up the dead. The terror that took hold of the mansion started in March of 1850, shortly after a Dr. Eliakim Phelps and his family moved into the home. Dr. Phelps was a Presbyterian minister, but he was also fascinated by the occult and spiritualism. This hobby led him to attempt communication with the dead, and he held numerous séances at his home. Eventually, he must have succeeded, but the spirit he summoned proved uncontrollable and eventually took full control of the house.

The first signs of a haunting at the Phelps Mansion appeared on March 10, 1850, when the family returned from church to find black cloth draped over their open front door. Moments later, they all encountered a phantom corpse laying on their parlor table. The body disappeared in minutes, but was eventually identified as Goody Bassett, an alleged witch murdered by the local populace near the site in 1661.

By afternoon, the spirit had struck again, this time arranging each family member's clothes on his or her bed in a position emulating final repose. In the weeks following, the Phelps began to stumble across lifesize and lifelike "bodies" constructed from stuffed clothing. Strange puppets and dolls made of cloth scraps also began appearing, as if from nowhere. These were often placed on tables with their heads bowed and hands clasped, which Phelps construed as a mocking insult toward his occupation.

Other, more common poltergeist manifestations also began to overwhelm the Phelps household. Chief among these was a constant barrage of strange knocking noises, the source of which could never be determined. Then, small objects began moving of their own accord, and two of the Phelps children, twelve-year-old Harry and four-year-old Anna, began suffering nightly attacks. Both children were thrown from their beds and struck by an invisible assailant.

Frustrated, Dr. Phelps invited a fellow clergyman to visit the house and serve as the family's witness to the strange happenings. Phelps's contemporary was not disappointed and reported that furniture, including tables and chairs, levitated without apparent cause. On another occasion, a candlestick beat itself against the ground until it snapped, and a set of fireplace pokers flew around the living room.

As the haunting intensified, the case began to attract widespread attention and made international headlines. Visitors flocked to the house, and many reliable witnesses supported the Phelpses with their own testimony. Observers beheld furniture leaping through windows or waltzing across the floors, all the while listening to the eerie, incessant knockings which filled the house.

Psychics attracted to the house could not identify the ghost, or ghosts, but many began to suspect that the hauntings revolved around Harry and Anna. Dr. Phelps's other son and daughter, who were three and sixteen respectively, were practically ignored by the poltergeist. And in fact, when Dr. Phelps eventually sent Harry and Anna away to boarding school, the haunting all but ceased, ending six months of terror. This type of preoccupation with specific members of a household is common in poltergeist cases. For whatever reason, this particular spirit was drawn to Harry and Anna, perhaps even incited to violence by the

energy released by the children's mere presence.

Almost one hundred years later, however, ghosts returned to the Phelps Mansion. In 1947, the building was converted into a convalescent nursing home, and for the next twenty years the staff consistently reported strange voices whispering in the shadows and heavy doors opening or closing on their own. By 1968, the site was abandoned and became a refuge for vagrants and drug addicts. Still, the hauntings did not cease: In 1971, police responding to reports of vandalism spotted a little girl in the house. They pursued her into a bedroom on the third floor, where she vanished. Although it can never be proven, the phantom child may be the ghost of Anna Phelps, who could have returned to her childhood home (and childlike appearance) after death.

At last report, the Phelps Mansion was saved from demolition to be assimilated into a hospital being built next to the site. Before visiting the location, call the Stratford Chamber of Commerce or City Hall to find the mansion's current status. If it is still a derelict building, be wary of vagrants, criminals, or other unsavory characters who may be lurking within the house's walls. If you feel it is safe to enter, spots of special interest include any of the larger rooms on the lower level and any of the bedrooms upstairs, all of which have recorded numerous spectral manifestations during the past 150 years. Also listen very carefully for the oft-reported knocks or whispers, and bring along a tape recorder to preserve any noises you may encounter. To date, the ghosts of the Phelps Mansion have proved relatively harmless, but if you should see objects moving, prepare to duck, as poltergeists have a nasty habit of hurling household items at intruders.

THE SHUE HOUSE AND THE GREENBRIAR GHOST

VITAL STATISTICS

LOCATION: A private residence in Greenbriar, West Virginia. The haunting is commemorated by a marker near the town, which is located along I-64 in south central West Virginia.

NUMBER OF GHOSTLY RESIDENTS: One

IDENTITY OF GHOSTLY RESIDENT: Zona Heaster Shue

TYPE OF ACTIVITY: Phantom

DEMEANOR OF GHOSTLY RESIDENT: Unknown. The ghost is not currently active, but in the past attempted to find peace by seeing her killer convicted of his crime.

ENCOUNTERING THE GREENBRIAR GHOST:

I n a great number of hauntings, the ghosts of the murdered return to finger their killers and ensure that justice is served. In some instances, such spirits are detected by psychics or other sensitives, who may even relive the events surrounding the murder in order to advise authorities on the case. Sometimes, a murdered phantom torments the killer until the offender breaks down and admits to the crime. However, in most examples of this type of haunting, the victim's ghost manifests before a relative and reveals the slayer's identity. The most dramatic of these cases, and the only one on record in which a ghost's testimony actually appeared in a court of law, involved the Greenbriar Ghost of West Virginia.

The weird tale begins on January 23, 1897, when authorities discovered the body of Zona Heaster Shue on the kitchen floor of her home in Greenbriar. Zona lived with her husband, Edward Shue, the local blacksmith, who was considered an upstanding citizen and a kind man. Although family members are always suspects in a mysterious death, the physician who studied Zona's body declared that she had not met with foul play. Rather, the doctor informed authorities, Mrs. Shue had suffered an "everlasting faint."

However, shortly after Zona's funeral, her ghost returned from the land of the dead. Mary Jane Heaster, Zona's mother, encountered the phantom on several occasions. In each instance, Zona insisted that she had been beaten to death. Furthermore, the apparition revealed that the killer was none other than Edward Shue, who had attacked Zona when he discovered that she had not prepared meat for dinner that fateful January night.

After conversing with her daughter's ghost at least four times, Mary was convinced of Edward's guilt and sought justice. She implored authorities to resume the investigation, and they finally agreed. Zona's body was exhumed and subjected to an intense autopsy that revealed the woman had endured a severe attack resulting in a broken neck and collapsed windpipe. Almost immediately, Edward Shue was arrested and forced to stand trial.

During the proceedings, the prosecution called Mary Heaster to the stand. She was asked to publicly name anyone she felt could have murdered her daughter. Of course, she identified Edward Shue. There was no mention of Zona's ghost during this part of the trial. However, the defense knew that Mary was driven to find the girl by visions of her daughter. Attempting to discredit the witness and her testimony, Edward's defense team asked Mary about her four meetings with Zona's ghost. In doing so, they inadvertently allowed Zona's own words to be introduced as evidence. Clearly, the defense attorneys hoped that the court would scoff at any tales of the supernatural and view Zona's phantom as nothing more than a mirage created by an unstable and possibly senile mind. However, the jury believed Mary's testimony and understood that Zona's manifestation was only further proof that Edward Shue had savagely attacked his wife.

Edward Shue was convicted of murdering Zona Shue and received a life sentence. As he was being transported to prison, a lynch mob rallied behind the words of Zona's phantom and attacked the blacksmith. Edward barely escaped unharmed, only to die of natural causes in his cell three years later. Zona Shue's phantom never reappeared, her soul finally at peace after Edward's conviction.

Because she has returned to the land of the dead, it is probably impossible to actually encounter Zona Shue's phantom in modern times. However, the case should be remembered by ghost hunters who meet other spirits with similar agendas.

THE SISE INN

VITAL STATISTICS

LOCATION: 40 Court Street, Portsmouth, New Hampshire 03801; (603) 433-1200. The inn is located in Portsmouth, a small seaport town about sixty miles north of Boston along Route 95. The most haunted room appears to be suite 214.

NUMBER OF GHOSTLY RESIDENTS: At least two

IDENTITIES OF GHOSTLY RESIDENTS: Unknown, but possibly the victims of a murder-suicide that may have occurred at the house, the ghost of John E. Sise or his family, or the spirits of departed mental patients

TYPE OF ACTIVITY: Poltergeists and cold spots

DEMEANOR OF GHOSTLY RESIDENTS: Relatively playful, for the most part. In some instances, the ghosts have physically confronted female guests. Although such harassment has never resulted in physical injury, the encounters are extremely unsettling.

ENCOUNTERING THE GHOSTS OF THE SISE INN:

Any home that has gone through several transformations and uses, such as **Hull House** or the **Lalaurie Mansion** described previously, is likely to host at least one ghost simply because so many people with a variety of backgrounds and personalities have passed through the front doors. A perfect example of this phenomenon is New Hampshire's Sise Inn, which was built in 1881 as the personal residence of the wealthy John E. Sise. The home remained with the Sise family until the 1930s, and then went through a series of owners and served a variety of functions. The Sise House spent stints as business offices, a beauty parlor, a fashion shop, a doctor's office, apartments, and a halfway house for mental patients beginning a new life. Finally, in 1986, it was converted into an inn.

Today, the inn is the site of an amazing haunting with many unusual spectral manifestations. Aside from cold spots and common poltergeist activity, including elevators and rocking chairs that move of their own accord, the ghosts of the Sise Inn have been known to use the ice machine, lock doors, steal keys, grab maids, and hop into bed with female visitors. Suite 214, in particular, has recorded a huge number of ghost reports. The keys to this room constantly vanish, only to reappear in the mailbox some days later. In other instances, the door has remained locked despite the best efforts of the Inn's owners. Piles of ice mysteriously appear in the room, and on at least one occasion, a ghost tried to pull a cleaning woman into the suite's main closet.

The identity of the spirits plaguing the Sise Inn are unknown, but the clues to their identities rest in the house's complex history. While under the ownership of the Sise family, the home may have been the site of at least two deaths. According to local legend, the Sises' butler and one of the family maids began a torrid affair. Unfortunately, the maid eventually tired of the relationship and snubbed her lover. Devastated, the butler killed the maid and then hanged himself in one of the upstairs bedrooms. This story has never been confirmed, but it would certainly explain the haunting. Another report indicates that the murder-suicide actually occurred in a home down the block from the Sise Inn, but it is unlikely that such ghosts would migrate up the street to haunt a house other than the one in which they died.

Of course, a number of homes are haunted by their original owners. In this case, the spirit of John Sise, who devoted time and money to the construction of his family home, may have returned. His offspring and loved ones could also be among those present in the house.

The Sise Inn's other applications may have attracted ghosts to the site as well. Possibly most important is the fact that the building housed mental patients, who were newly released from their respective hospitals and preparing to begin life in the open world. The stress and excitement of this environment could have been strong enough to bring these patients back to the house after death, and the theory certainly explains some of the spirits' odd behavior. In addition, many dead people

become ghosts simply because they do not realize that they have died; certainly, any type of mental defect could result in this type of ignorance.

While the building served as a doctor's office, it is quite reasonable to assume that a series of sick patients streamed into the former Sise home. As an apartment complex, the house hosted dozens of individuals, who undoubtedly lived and loved and suffered at the site. Finally, the location's sheer number of identities obviously brought hundreds of people into the building over the years, any one of whom may have revisited the Sise home after death.

To find the ghosts of the Sise Inn, book a night's stay and request suite 214. At night, spend at least an hour or two observing the nearest ice machine, rocking chair, and the elevator for any unexplained movements. Be sure to prop open the door to the suite whenever you leave the room, as the ghosts may decide to playfully lock the room when you leave. If this should happen, you can be certain that your key will not work and you will be trapped outside the suite for upwards of two hours until the spirits tire of the game. Female ghost hunters should be alert for any ghostly activity when studying the closet or reclining on the bed.

THE STAGECOACH INN

VITAL STATISTICS

LOCATION: Stagecoach Inn Museum, Ventu Park Road, Newbury Park, California 91320. Call (805) 498-9441 for hours of operation

NUMBER OF GHOSTLY RESIDENTS: Three

IDENTITIES OF GHOSTLY RESIDENTS: Mountaineer Pierre Devon, an unidentified female ghost, and an unnamed child who disappeared in the hills near the inn in the 1890s

TYPE OF ACTIVITY: Phantoms, bizarre smells, cold spots, and a disembodied voice

DEMEANOR OF GHOSTLY RESIDENTS: Lonely and melancholic. The ghosts have never harmed, attacked, or intentionally harassed anyone.

ENCOUNTERING THE GHOSTS OF THE STAGECOACH INN: RIP RIP RIP

Inns, hotels, motels, and hostels are all prone to hauntings because they often host a number of deaths while in operation. This is especially true for such buildings constructed during the 1800s, when life was harsh and disease, bandits, or angry Native Americans could unexpectedly sweep through an establishment, claiming the lives of all within. California's Stagecoach Inn, built in 1876, is just such a site, attracting tragedy and sorrow during its time as a hotel. The inn is now a museum, but during its heyday it experienced several mysterious deaths, resulting in the modern hauntings.

The Stagecoach Inn is home to several ghosts, but the most well known is the spirit of Pierre Devon (or Duvon), a burly, bearded mountain man who died in the hotel. According to psychics, Devon was brutally murdered while he slept in one of the upstairs bedrooms in 1885. Now, Devon causes small poltergeist disturbances in the room, as well as unnerving cold spots on the staircase. At one point, medium Sybil Leek actually conversed with Devon, who identified himself and admitted that he had passed away at the Inn; a month later, a holster and a pair of chaps allegedly belonging to the mountaineer were mysteriously donated to the museum.

Another prominent ghost living within the Stagecoach Inn museum is the spirit of a tall, elegant woman. She is most often glimpsed out of the corner of the eye before she suddenly vanishes. After the ghost disappears, however, a heavy perfume can be detected drifting through the building. This particular phantom was encountered numerous times between 1952 and 1965, during a period when the building was being restored to its former glory. Often, construction on a house can summon ghosts attached to the building; these spirits may be unhappy about the changes or may simply be attracted by new signs of life. In this case, the phantom woman may have been lured back to the inn once it began to take on its original appearance again.

The Stagecoach Inn is also home to a wayward child, whose chilling voice can be heard calling throughout the house. Legends hold that the child's family was staying at the house in the 1890s, but the young boy wandered away from the inn one day and became hopelessly lost in the nearby hills. He was never found and it is assumed that he died in the wilderness. As with many similar ghosts, the little boy is probably unaware that he is dead and has returned to the inn in search of his family.

The Stagecoach Inn is less than fifteen miles west of Thousand Oaks and only an hour and a half from Los Angeles. It can be reached via the Ventura Freeway and is open to all visitors. When exploring the house, be sure to visit all nineteen rooms, where you may discover new supernatural phenomena. Pay close attention to anything you sense or see in the small upstairs room to the left of the stairwell. When wandering the house, be cognizant of any fleeting shadows or shapes you glimpse out of the corner of your eye—these may be "sightings" of the mysterious phantom lady.

THE SPY HOUSE

VITAL STATISTICS

LOCATION: 119 Port Monmouth Road, Port Monmouth, New Jersey 07758. The house has been converted into a museum on the Sandy Hook Bay.

NUMBER OF GHOSTLY RESIDENTS: Unknown, but in excess of twenty-four!

IDENTITIES OF GHOSTLY RESIDENTS: Several children, including eleven-year-old Peter, a deaf mute named Walter, a girl named Katy, a group of young spirits who play tag in back of the house, and an unidentified girl killed in the road in front of the building. The house also hosts a male spirit named Tom; a dead cleric; an invisible imp who pinches people; a ghostly widow named Abigail; at least one Puritan specter; a few Native American braves; the ghost of Thomas Whitlock; the drunken spirit of Lord Charles Cornwallis; the phantom of Penelope, a woman who died childless; Lydia Longstreet Seabrook, a ghost found staring out windows; the cryptic Lady in White; a guilt-ridden Mr. Samuels, who may have been a British spy; a frightening bearded apparition; a foulmouthed pirate named Captain Morgan, his first mate, and at least one of his victims; and an assortment of other unidentified spectral guests.

TYPE OF ACTIVITY: Virtually every known ghostly manifestation, including a number of phantoms, strange noises, moving objects, and eerie sensations

DEMEANOR OF GHOSTLY RESIDENTS: Varies widely, ranging from grief-stricken to belligerent. The ghosts of Captain Morgan and Lord Cornwallis may be capable of physical confrontations. Occasionally, a few of the other ghosts have been known to trail the staff home, and the spirits of the children are often observed at play. At least one of the specters playfully pinches or pulls the hair of visitors, but malice seems to be absent from these gestures.

ENCOUNTERING THE SPY HOUSE GHOSTS:

Veteran ghost hunter Arthur Myers once claimed that the Spy House "is one of the most haunted places I have ever visited or heard about." And indeed, when the number of ghosts and reports of unexplained activity are observed as a whole, this bold statement certainly appears to be true.

The Spy House is home to no less than two dozen ghosts, representing several centuries of tumultuous American history. Throughout its lifespan, the house has been home to Colonial patriots and bloodthirsty pirates, as well as being a tavern, bordello, pirate lair, settler refuge, and inn.

The site was first developed in 1648 by Thomas Whitlock, who constructed what many believe to be the oldest building in all of New Jersey. His home and three other buildings were combined and enlarged throughout the 1600s. During this time, the area was often besieged by Native Americans, whose spirits are sometimes still seen peering into windows in search of their victims. Thomas Whitlock strides through his former home on occasion; he is described as having a deep voice and a tendency to play with women's hair. He may also be the invisible entity accused of pinching portly visitors. A silent Puritan woman and a male ghost with a long nose, black mustache, and buckled shoes (who is known as Tom) appear to have died during this time as well but still linger in the house.

Another family who contributed to the construction of the current Spy House were the Seabrooks. Daniel Seabrook bought the property from Whitlock, his father-in-law, in 1696. At the time, few specters were encountered, but the Seabrooks owned and occupied the land for generations and many still inhabit the site today as ghosts. The so-called Lady in White is believed to be Daniel Seabrook's wife. She floats from the attic and enters the Blue-and-White Room, located on the second floor. There, she lovingly tends an invisible crib, seemingly oblivious to any observers, and then vanishes from sight. Another phantom has been identified as Lydia Longstreet Seabrook, who was married to Thomas Seabrook, one of Daniel's descendants. Lydia frequently spends long afternoons staring from a window at the water, and she can be spotted from both inside and outside the house.

When the Revolutionary War began, the Seabrooks converted the house into an inn and tavern that catered to British soldiers. Allegedly, the building also hid a cadre of Colonial spies during this period, which is how the house earned its current moniker. According to lore, these spies hid in the upstairs rooms listening to the ranting, drunken sailors below. When they learned which British ships were unmanned, they would slip into the harbor and sabotage the vessels. The British eventually began to suspect the Spy House's true nature and attempted to burn the building to the ground, but they were routed by the house's women, who doused the fire with their wash buckets.

A legion of Revolution-era ghosts continue to wander the house. The most well-known is the British Lord Charles Cornwallis, who frequented the tavern. He has entered history books as the man who offered Britain's formal surrender to Colonial forces at Yorktown, Virginia. However, he is important to supernaturalists because he has returned to New Jersey long after his death. His ghost is often spotted wandering the hallways in a drunken stupor and is said to be quite boorish when encountered.

Another Revolutionary War ghost is a man known only as Mr. Samuels, who may have been a traitor. According to some reports, he was caught selling secrets to the British and was publicly hanged. Overcome with remorse, he has returned to the Spy House seeking forgiveness. A more sinister figure from the 1700s is the Bearded Man, a tall, imposing phantom who wears a tall black hat and billowing trousers. He often appears in mirrors and on the staircase, and is sometimes surrounded by a strange glow.

During a brief period in the early 1800s, the

Spy House was commandeered by a cutthroat known as Captain Morgan (not to be confused with Captain Henry Morgan of the 1600s). A bellicose, obscene pirate, Morgan reportedly used the house to imprison a wealthy French family whom he captured out at sea. He held the family for three months while awaiting a ransom payment, during which time the women were repeatedly raped. The ransom never arrived, and Morgan ordered the family killed; the women were raped one last time and then strangled, while the men were beaten to death. At least one of his victims, a woman who will reluctantly recount her death when confronted, still haunts the house.

Captain Morgan later died when his ship sank in the Caribbean, but his ghost has found a permanent home at the Spy House, where he can be heard spewing foul rants. Oddly enough, his first mate is also trapped at the site. However, the first mate is said to be wracked by guilt for having participated in Morgan's vile acts and seeks forgiveness from visitors.

Among the Spy House's other prominent ghosts is Abigail, the widow of a sea captain. The forlorn spirit is often observed watching the horizon for any signs of her husband's ship. She wears the black garb of a mourner, and her hair is held back by a single ribbon. Like Morgan's first mate, she is also overcome by guilt: She succumbed to the advances of an amorous relative months after her husband failed to return for his last journey out to sea.

The Spy House is probably most notable for its large assortment of child ghosts. A group of spectral children have been observed playing tag and other games behind the house, while a number of identifiable young spirits wander within the building's walls. There is Peter, a boy of about eleven, who may have died in the 1700s. Like the adult ghost known as Tom, Peter sometimes follows visitors and staff members home for the night, although he always returns to the Spy House eventually. Another known child spirit is Walter, who is both deaf and mute. Walter spends most of his time in the attic, only descending to search for his mother. A playful, spirited little girl ghost named Katy often enters the house from outside when called. Another little girl, who has yet to be identified, haunts the road in front of the Spy House. She is often "hit" by passing motorists as she races toward the building, but will gladly stop to talk. If asked about her death, she will reveal that she once lived nearby and, while on her way to play with children living at the Spy House, was struck dead by a horse and wagon. Finally, a dead boy and girl are often encountered in the company of a spectral clergyman, all of whom have yet to be identified.

This abundance of young ghosts may have attracted Penelope, the sad spirit of a woman who died childless in the house. She almost always manifests before visitors carrying infants. She has even been known to lift babies from the arms of their parents.

When visiting the Spy House, be sure to contact the museum's chief curator, Gertrude Neidlinger, who should be able to answer all of your questions. She, like many of the staff, have been known to sense the presence of ghosts, which are commonly accepted as part of the house. Visit the Blue-and-White Room, the attic staircase, and the attic itself. If possible, also descend into the cellar. Many sensitives report feeling a profound aura of fear in this location, and rightfully so: During the past three centuries, the cellar space has served as a makeshift slaughterhouse, prison, torture room, and hideout. There is also a strong suspicion that Captain Morgan hid his stolen loot in secret tunnels connected to the cellar. Be warned, however, that the cellar often interferes with recording devices, making it impossible to preserve any ghostly encounters on audio, video, or film.

A great many of the Spy House's ghosts can be observed as they go about their business. Pay special attention to the windows and staircases. You might also summon a ghost using a Ouija board, a tactic that has worked in the past. If all else fails, simply holler. In addition, the spectral children have been known to appear shortly after a group of living children has been entertained at the site by a puppet show or story reading.

With the possible exception of Captain Morgan, none of the Spy House ghosts should be considered particularly dangerous. They mostly keep to themselves or participate in small, harmless poltergeist activity. Although known to rustle papers, use sewing machines and typewriters, and playfully pinch or touch visitors, none have directly attacked or molested the living.

THE WHALEY HOUSE

VITAL STATISTICS

LOCATION: 2482 San Diego Avenue, San Diego, California 92110. The house, now a museum on the corner of San Diego Avenue and Harney Street, is maintained by Mrs. June Reading. Contact the museum at (619) 298-2482.

NUMBER OF GHOSTLY RESIDENTS: About eight

IDENTITIES OF GHOSTLY RESIDENTS: Most of the Whaley family, including Thomas Whaley; his wife, Anna Eloise Lannay; one of their daughters; a son who died at only eighteen months; and even the family dog. Other ghosts are a neighbor child named Annabelle Washburn, "Yankee Jim" Robinson, and a few nameless phantoms.

TYPE OF ACTIVITY: Minor poltergeist activity (such as windows that open of their own accord and alarms that sound for no good reason), cold spots, phantoms, disembodied footsteps and voices, and ghost lights

DEMEANOR OF GHOSTLY RESIDENTS: Restless, but not necessarily unhappy. Annabelle's ghost runs wild through the house, but the others limit their activities to mild annoyances.

ENCOUNTERING THE WHALEY HOUSE GHOSTS: RIP RIP RIP RIP

The Whaley House was built in 1857 by Thomas Whaley in a section of San Diego known as Old Town. Although the mansion was gorgeous, Whaley's experiences in the house were far from pleasant. Early on, he rented a portion of the house to the county to serve as a courtroom and records rooms. Unfortunately, San Diego residents attempting to establish a "New Town" section of the city were upset that the county seat was perceived as residing in Old Town. While Whaley was out of town one night, several members of the New Town faction stormed his house, stole hundreds of documents, and threatened the lives of his wife and daughter. Whaley entered an emotionally trying time and made an ultimately vain effort to receive monetary compensation for the attack, but died without winning his case.

Sadness also found its way into the Whaley home in other forms. Thomas and Anna Whaley's son passed on at only eighteen months, leaving both despondent. A young neighbor named Annabelle Washburn was running through the Whaley property when she collided with a clothesline. The impact crushed the girl's trachea and she later died in the Whaley kitchen. The most horrific death involved "Yankee Jim" Robinson, a thief who was sentenced to death after stealing a boat in 1852. At the time, the Whaleys did not yet own the property, but a set of gallows had been erected at the site. However, on the day that Yankee Jim was led to the hangman's noose for the public execution, Thomas Whaley was in the audience. He watched, perhaps as horrified as many others in the crowd, as the trap door on the gallows sprung open. Unfortunately, the rope did not snap Yankee Jim's neck and he was left dangling, slowly strangling to death as he kicked and swung helplessly. It took Yankee Jim a full forty-five minutes to die.

These tragedies have resulted in one of the most haunted houses in the United States. Organ music emanates from empty rooms, a black rocking chair moves on its own, and bolted windows are opened by unseen hands. Thomas Whaley and his wife pace the upstairs rooms, while their dead son can be heard wailing from beyond. Annabelle still races through the house, and a spectral dog believed to have once belonged to the Whaleys can sometimes be spotted romping through the property. Most disturbing is the ghost of Yankee Jim, who appears dangling from the house's main doorway.

Other ghosts at the Whaley site remain unidentified. These include a woman wearing a green plaid gingham dress who frequents an upstairs bedroom and a well-dressed gentleman standing on the staircase.

The Whaley House is still considered an incredibly active site. The most-often sighted ghost is Annabelle, who can usually be found in the kitchen where she died. Yankee Jim is only observed as one enters the mansion, while Mr. and Mrs. Whaley spend most of their time upstairs. All areas of the house should be considered ripe for exploration.

THE WHITE HOUSE

VITAL STATISTICS

LOCATION: 1600 Pennsylvania Avenue N.W., Washington, D.C. 20500. The White House Visitors Center, which provides information on tours, can be reached at 1450 Pennsylvania Avenue N.W., Washington, D.C. 20004, or call (202) 208-1631. For recorded tour information, call (202) 456-7041. General information on the White House can be obtained from the National Capitol Region at 1100 Ohio Drive S.W., Washington, D.C. 20242.

NUMBER OF GHOSTLY RESIDENTS: At least 14

IDENTITIES OF GHOSTLY RESIDENTS: Dolley Madison, Anne Surratt, Abigail Adams, Abraham Lincoln, Daniel Webster, Thomas and Willie Lincoln, Andrew Jackson, Mrs. Grover Cleveland, an unnamed British soldier, Thomas Jefferson, John Tyler, William Henry Harrison, former White House owner David Burns, and perhaps several other ghosts, mostly ex-presidents or their relatives

TYPE OF ACTIVITY: Phantoms, disembodied cackles and other weird noises, cold spots, and unsettling auras

DEMEANOR OF GHOSTLY RESIDENTS: Perfectly lifelike for the most part. The younger ghosts, such as Lincoln's sons, periodically run down the hallways as if they were mortal boys. The others simply wander around, conducting their own mysterious business.

ENCOUNTERING THE GHOSTS OF THE WHITE HOUSE: RIP RIP RIP RIP

Aside from being the seat of the nation's government, the White House is also one of America's most famous haunted houses. Boasting an active population of past presidents and their relatives, the White House has been recording ghostly visitations since it was built. There are so many ghosts here, in fact, that the most expedient way to mention them all is to discuss each haunted area, beginning on the ground floor.

As visitors to the White House discover, the site is graced by a beautiful rose garden, where many press conferences are held today. The picturesque garden, planted by Dolley Madison, was almost destroyed during Woodrow Wilson's term by Mrs. Wilson's orders. An enraged Dolley Madison returned from the grave to stop the workmen from fulfilling this terrible task, and their description of this terrifying encounter has protected the gardens ever since.

The ground-floor front entrance to the White House is commonly known as the North Portico. The ghost of Anne Surratt appears at this spot on the seventh of July each year to mourn the death of her mother, Mary, who was hanged on that date in 1865 after being convicted in the plot to assassinate President Lincoln. When she manifests, the grief-stricken Anne wildly pounds on the White House door for a few moments, and then vanishes for another year.

The White House Rose Garden.

Eisenhower, and many, many others. One of Franklin Roosevelt's servants, Mary Eben, observed Lincoln as he put on his boots, and others have encountered the tall spirit resting on the nine-foot-long bed in the room.

Although most often associated with the Lincoln Bedroom, Abraham Lincoln's ghost was first reported in the Yellow Oval Room, where he was originally encountered by Grace Coolidge. Since then, Lincoln's spirit has been observed staring longingly from the windows in this room, where he was known to read and meditate. The Yellow Oval Room is also home to Thomas Jefferson and John Tyler, both of whom were spied by Mary Todd Lincoln.

Even before Lincoln's death, the room now designated as the Lincoln Bedroom was charged with supernatural energy. In fact, Abraham Lincoln was an amateur spiritualist and held numerous séances in the room. Dur-

The East Room, also on the ground floor, is haunted as well. There, the ghostly resident is commonly identified as Abigail Adams, whose phantom goes about hanging laundry. She often passes through walls, astonishes staffers, and leaves behind the scent of soap and wet clothing.

On the second floor, the most haunted room is undoubtedly the Lincoln Bedroom. Originally serving as President Lincoln's Cabinet Room, the room now hosts a record number of sightings of the murdered president. Witnesses include Theodore Roosevelt, Eleanor Roosevelt, Winston Churchill, Harry Truman, Lady Bird Johnson, Jacqueline Kennedy, Maureen Reagan, Susan Ford, Grace Coolidge, Dwight

The White House at night .

The Lincoln Bedroom.

ing these, he contacted spirits such as Daniel Webster. The séances also led to premonitions of his own death.

President Lincoln encountered other ghosts in the White House as well, including his own sons Thomas and Willie, the latter of whom died in the building at the age of twelve. Willie's ghost is still spotted wandering the hallways at night, and today Lincoln's own

footsteps can be heard in these corridors. Since the Taft administration, Abigail Adams has been observed silently floating through closed doors and wandering the hallways as well, perhaps on her way to the first-floor East Room.

The Rose Bedroom, or Queen's Suite, is the personal abode of Andrew Jackson, who first manifested for Mary Todd Lincoln in 1865. Since then, White House personnel have repeatedly encountered Jackson's laughter, and his presence causes an inexplicable cold spot near the bed. People working in the room have felt the president's presence lurking nearby, and in 1964 one of Lyndon Johnson's aides heard the ghost cursing and shouting. The spirit of Lincoln also visited the room on at least one occasion: During the Second World War, Queen Wilhelmina of the Netherlands was staying in the room when, upon answering a knock at her door, she discovered Lincoln standing in the hallway.

Almost all of the other bedrooms on the upper floor are haunted by ghosts as well. Willie Lincoln has appeared in one of the rooms many times and even held conversations with members of Ulysses S. Grant's family. The torch-wielding ghost of a British soldier suspected of trying to burn down the White House in 1814 appears in another room; while the anguished labor screams of Grover Cleveland's wife, the first woman to give birth in the White House, haunt yet another room in this section of the building.

Even the White House's attic is haunted. From this uppermost room drifts the disembodied voice of David Burns, the man who owned the White House property in 1790. William Henry Harrison is also heard in the attic as he moves about in search of some unknown object.

With the number of ghosts said to inhabit

> "I sit here in this old house, all the while listening to the ghosts walk up and down the hallway. At 4 o'clock I was awakened by three distinct knocks on my bedroom door. No one there. Damned place is haunted. . . ."
>
> —Harry Truman, in a letter to his wife written from the White House

the White House, the building is clearly a ghost hunter's dream. Unfortunately, many ghost hunters have had difficulty gaining entrance to portions of the White House deemed haunted. Although the building is technically "owned" by the people, it is still considered the private residence of the president and his family. A standard tour can be arranged, but only the first floor (including the East Room, the Rose Gardens, and the North Portico) is open to the public. The most interesting rooms, such as the Lincoln Bedroom, are off limits to visitors.

The East Room.

White House Collection, © White House Historical Association

THE WINCHESTER MYSTERY HOUSE

VITAL STATISTICS

LOCATION: 525 S. Winchester Boulevard, San Jose, California 95129. The house is open to the public for guided tours; call (408) 247-2101.

NUMBER OF GHOSTLY RESIDENTS: Innumerable

IDENTITIES OF GHOSTLY RESIDENTS: Sarah Winchester and everyone ever killed by a Winchester firearm

TYPE OF ACTIVITY: Ghost lights, phantoms, strange noises such as unexplained organ music, and eerie auras

DEMEANOR OF GHOSTLY RESIDENTS: Impossible to determine. The sheer number of ghosts and the fact that most come and go frequently makes it impractical to predict the personalities or actions of the spirits.

ENCOUNTERING THE WINCHESTER MYSTERY HOUSE GHOSTS: RIP RIP

The Winchester Mystery House in California is unique among haunted houses because it seems to be open to a great many ghosts who can visit the home freely whenever they wish. These spirits do not actually reside within the building, as is the case with many other haunted abodes. Rather, they come and go as they please.

The Winchester House was built by Sarah Pardee Winchester, who formerly lived in Connecticut with her husband, Oliver Winchester, founder of the Winchester Repeating Arms Company. When Oliver and the couple's only daughter died within months of one another, Sarah was grief-stricken. Seeking to speak with her loved ones one last time, she met with a Boston sensitive named Adam Coons, who summoned Oliver's spirit. According to Coons, Oliver was tormented in death by the spirits of those slain by his weapons. In order to appease these ghosts, Oliver begged Sarah to build a home for these phantoms.

Driven by this message, Sarah relocated to San Jose, California, where she purchased a forty-acre farm. Over the next thirty-eight years, she continually expanded the original property, ultimately building a house that contained no fewer than seven hundred rooms, nine hundred fifty doors, forty staircases, ten thousand windows, and forty-seven fireplaces. The house was also a warren of secret passages and hidden hallways.

While she lived in the house, Sarah invited a host of spirits to share the home with her. Most nights, she held large banquets for up to twelve phantoms. She also forbade mortals to interfere with the spirits and allowed only Harry Houdini, who was known for his love of ghosts, into the building. Unfortunately, the home also attracted several evil spirits who tormented Sarah. She was forced to sleep in a different room each night to confuse these malicious ghosts. To further confound the

The caption on the photograph reads: *Winchester Mystery House Near San Jose Before the Earthquake*

Winchester Mystery House just before the earthquake.

phantoms, she built dead-end hallways, empty rooms, and stairs that led nowhere.

Sarah finally died in 1922, leaving her niece the estate and the responsibility of caring for the house's many ghostly visitors. Less than a year later, Sarah's niece opened the house for public tours, which have continued into the present.

Today, the ghosts still visit the Winchester Mystery House. Ghost lights, unexplained noises, and the voices of phantoms are often reported. Numerous psychics have used the site to contact a wide variety of ghosts as well. Most important, many visitors have glimpsed a silent, gray-haired phantom on the grounds, who may be the spirit of Sarah Winchester. If this is so, Sarah may be the house's only "full-time" spectral resident. Even visitors who do not actually encounter ghostly phenomena report that the house possesses a strong and chilling aura.

The guided tour is the best (and only) method for ghost hunters to explore this particular house. While it is true that many of the rooms are boarded up and the tour only covers a small portion of the estate, a substantial number of ghost encounters have occurred within the area set aside for the tour. In addition, the house maintains a detailed file recording of each and every strange happening at the Mystery House.

UPI/Corbis-Bettmann

Photo of the staircase leading down one floor and continuing up to the same floor level at the Winchester Mystery House, planned and built by the late Sarah Winchester.

Other Haunted Houses

The list of North America's haunted houses is truly massive, with each state and Canadian province recording dozens of suspected ghostly abodes. Below are simply a fraction of the innumerable haunted houses reported.

- **Rocky Hill Castle, Rocky Hill, Alabama:** This mansion in Lawrence County is plagued by phantom hammering, a mysterious Lady in Blue and a surly male phantom. Built in the 1840s, the house's chief ghost is said to be James Saunders, who built the Castle.

- **Gakona Lodge and Trading Post, Gakona, Alaska:** One ghost known to open doors, jump on beds, and pull mischievous pranks on visitors inhabits this site. The specter also causes the smell of smoke to fill the rooms it visits.

- **San Carlos Hotel, Phoenix, Arizona:** The ghost of Leone Jensen, who leapt to her death from the hotel's roof in 1928, appears as a misty cloud in rooms of this hotel.

- **Grant-Humphreys Mansion, Denver, Colorado:** Home to at least five ghosts, the mansion is the abode of A. E. Humphreys, killed in a suspicious gun accident in 1927.

- **Governor's Mansion/Woodburn, Dover, Delaware:** At least four ghosts linger here, including a ghost who enjoys stealing expensive wine from residents and a little girl phantom who sometimes plays with guests. A tree outside is surrounded by chilling moans, said to belong to a slaver who died near the spot.

- **Artist House, Key West, Florida:** This bed-and-breakfast inn owns a life-size doll rumored to possess an evil personality. The doll is a likeness of the artist Gene Otto as he appeared at five. The doll moves on its own and sometimes whispers or laughs wickedly. Two benign ghosts also haunt the inn.

- **MacKay's Trading House, Augusta, Georgia:** Ranked as one of the most haunted houses in all of America, this is home to at least a dozen ghosts. Many are the spirits of American patriots tortured and hanged at the site by the British.

- **Hannah House, Indianapolis, Indiana:** One of many haunted houses tormented by foul odors, Hannah House constantly reeks of rotting flesh. Poltergeist activity, cold spots, and phantoms are also recorded here. Television crews studying the house have captured many disturbances on film.

- **Phi Gamma Delta House, Manhattan, Kansas:** A ghost named Duncan, who died of a brain concussion after being accidentally hit on the head by a paddle during a Theta Xi initiation ceremony, wanders this fraternity house. The ghost has a slack face and blank stare, and first appeared in the 1960s after the Phi Gamma Deltas took over the houses and removed a collection of Theta Xi paddles.

- **Liberty Hall, Frankfort, Kentucky:** The "Gray Lady" has made this mansion her home, where she has willingly done chores around the house for the last 150 years. An opera singer, who was kidnapped and murdered by Native Americans while staying at the house in 1805, and a slain soldier are also encountered.

- **Captain Fairfield Inn, Kennebunkport, Maine:** Captain James Fairfield has haunted this quaint inn since he died of pneumonia in the house in 1820. He often appears in the basement and has also been known to hover near guests in their rooms.

- **Poe House, Baltimore, Maryland:** The attic of Edgar Allan Poe's former home is now the habitat of a heavyset female specter. Poe himself also appears at the site, if only to frighten away would-be vandals. Local gang members refer to the author's spirit as "Mr. Eddie" and reportedly give the house a wide berth.

- **Coffin House, Nantucket, Massachusetts:** Although now a restaurant, this site was once home to banker William Coffin. Wrongfully accused of embezzlement, Coffin has returned from the grave to haunt the premises. He was once encountered by author Peter Benchley (*Jaws* and *The Beast*), who lived in the house in the 1960s.

- **Saint Mary's College, Winona, Minnesota:** Numerous mysterious deaths reported here have been blamed on the phantom of a dead Catholic priest. In life,

Father Laurence Lesches was sent to an insane asylum after he killed another priest; in death, he has returned to the college to haunt the third floor of the building.

- **Bee Hive Whorehouse, Carson City, Nevada:** Several former prostitutes, at least one of whom was brutally murdered at the site, now wander the building.

- **Hoyle's Castle, White Oaks, New Mexico:** This site is an abandoned residence building haunted by Andy Hoyle, who disappeared in the 1880s after he lost his true love. Witnesses report his heartbroken ghost has returned.

- **Andrew Johnson Home, Raleigh, North Carolina:** The childhood home of Andrew Johnson, seventeenth president of the United States, is haunted by a ghostly candle that appears in the downstairs window at night.

- **Tiedeman Castle, Cleveland, Ohio:** Overrun by strange noises, poltergeist activity, psychic disturbances, and apparitions, this home has been through a series of owners due to its haunted nature. It is currently open for weekend tours, during which a mysterious woman in black can be glimpsed staring from one of the tower windows.

- **Hot Lake Hotel, La Grande, Oregon:** Former residents of this hotel often hold raucous parties on the third floor. When they are not reveling, they can be heard pacing the hallways or unexpectedly screaming.

- **General Wayne Inn, Philadelphia, Pennsylvania:** A surprising number of ghosts haunt this home, which dates back to 1704, including eight Hessian soldiers. Edgar Allan Poe also visits the site from time to time. The basement is the most active area in the house, but spirits have appeared in the bedrooms, as well.

- **Farr House, St. Johnsbury, Vermont:** This abandoned house exhibits an extreme form of ghostly activity by shaking violently at night. The house may tremble because it is possessed by the ghost of Jake Farr, who was murdered by his wife in 1880 after she discovered that he had been molesting their teenage daughter. Jake's wife, Sally, is sometimes spotted in a nearby orchard.

- **The Mansion, Bellingham, Washington:** A family of ghosts regularly reenact their personal tragedy at this site. Long ago, a husband lost his wife during childbirth. Today, he can still be heard pacing the hallways while his wife screams in anguish. Their unborn infant also appears, clutching at the fingers of sleeping guests.

2. HAUNTED VESSELS AND PHANTOM CRAFT

THIS CHAPTER COVERS a variety of hauntings connected in some way with vehicular travel.

In practice, the term "haunted vessel" is often used to refer to two distinct entities. First, it denotes a vehicle that happens to serve as the *location* of a haunting. Like the true haunted houses described in the previous chapter, these sites are usually inhabited by the spirits of those who died tragically aboard the vessel. Generally, the ghosts aboard follow many of the same rules of their haunted house cousins, although they usually haunt much smaller venues and must restrict their activities considerably. In addition, the ghosts of haunted vehicles seem to possess a uniform sadness. Some may have been headed toward a new life or career, while others were journeying to meet loved ones. In any case, the ghosts might feel cheated or depressed by what they perceive as a truly great loss, or they may regret that they did not die in the comfort of their homes. Thus, they have returned to the land of the living in order to complete their journeys.

The term "haunted vessel" is also frequently applied to apparitions that take the form of a vehicle, such as a translucent ghost ship or an eerie phantom train. These "phantom craft," as they will be referred to here, may have ghostly passengers aboard (making them locations of hauntings as well), but they are still considered ghosts in their own right.

Phantom craft are perhaps the most complex of all supernatural phenomena and deserve special attention. They are usually the apparitions of vessels that were destroyed violently: a ship that was set ablaze by pirates, for example, may rise from the water again to make ghostly voyages. Phantom craft are largely nocturnal spirits, and a majority appear in conjunction with a full moon. They move silently and many reenact their final moments again and again, seemingly oblivious to the real world around them. When passengers are observed aboard phantom craft (which is uncommon), they are easily identified as ghosts and are likely to have skeletal or decomposing features. Like their transports,

these phantoms are also mute and rarely interact with humans.

Phantom craft come in every variety of vessel known to humankind, including trains, planes, automobiles, trucks, buses, steamboats, carriages, and canoes; but by far the most prevalent phantom craft are ghost ships. Almost all ghost ships are believed to be sailing vessels lost at sea. Violent storms and pirates are often blamed for these disappearances, but a great many simply vanished without a trace. In almost all cases, the entire crew and all the passengers aboard were presumably killed. Like many other forms of phantom craft, ghost ships are generally silent, have few discernible passengers, and appear largely at night. In addition, a surprising number of ghost ships are surrounded by flames or, at the very least, a glowing aura of some sort.

Despite the wealth of information about their appearance and behavior, phantom craft remain puzzling simply because it is difficult to understand how these apparitions come to be. Phantoms of dead mortals are easily identified as the souls or spirits of those who refuse to pass on for a variety of reasons. Ships and other vessels, however, are not commonly believed to have souls or spirits. Certainly, vehicles have personality, but this is usually a result of their manufacture, upkeep, and use. How then, could a ship, train or other vessel possibly manifest as a ghost?

Perhaps phantom vessels are a form of

"collective spirit," an apparition composed of several different dead souls. The ghosts involved in creating a collective spirit trade their autonomy for the ability to survive well past death, and together they take the form of something with which they all identify, most often the vessel upon which they died. In the case of a phantom ship, the craft could very well be made up of the sailors who perished aboard the boat. They all lived similar lives, suffered identical deaths, and were unable or unwilling to leave this realm for the next. Rather than appear as a series of individual ghosts, these poor souls join together and take the form of the one thing that they have in common: the ship upon which they died.

THE USS CONSTELLATION

VITAL STATISTICS

LOCATION: Fort McHenry Shipyard, Dry Dock #5, Baltimore, Maryland, where the ship is undergoing restoration.

NUMBER OF GHOSTLY PASSENGERS: Three

IDENTITIES OF GHOSTLY PASSENGERS: Neil Harvey, a sailor murdered on the ship in 1799; Captain Thomas Truxtun, the man responsible for Harvey's death; and Carl Hansen, the ship's twentieth-century watchman

TYPE OF ACTIVITY: Phantoms, ghost lights, and unexplained noises

DEMEANOR OF THE *CONSTELLATION* AND ITS PASSENGERS: Generally forlorn, but still deeply attached to the ship and all it represents. The ghosts are capable of conveying their emotions to those around them, but this does not cause any lasting damage.

ENCOUNTERING THE GHOSTS OF THE USS CONSTELLATION: RIP RIP RIP RIP

The history of the vessel currently known as the USS *Constellation* actually involves two separate ships. The first ship, a frigate called the USF *Constellation*, was constructed in Baltimore in 1797. By all accounts, it had a bloody history. Numerous hands died in battles or of disease, and life aboard the ship proved very harsh. In 1799, a sailor named Neil Harvey was found asleep on his watch. For this failure, the ship's captain, Thomas Truxtun, ordered the young man executed in a most gruesome fashion: Harvey was tied to one of the ship's thirty-eight guns and blown to bits.

The original *Constellation*'s fate remains unknown, but another ship bearing the same name, the USS *Constellation*, was launched in Norfolk, Virginia, in 1854. Over the course of the following century, the 176-foot vessel sailed into battle against the French, a host of pirates, slave

Constellation Foundation, Inc.

The USS *Constellation*

traders, and the Barbary corsairs. It served in no less than five wars, including the Civil War and World War II. During its tenure, numerous sailors died aboard the vessel, leaving a lasting imprint on the ship.

Finally, in 1955, the USS *Constellation* was retired and permanently docked in Baltimore. The ship was donated to a local nonprofit foundation created specifically to care for the aging vessel. However, as the group set about restoring the ship, they rebuilt the vessel to resemble the original 1797 frigate *Constellation*, constructed in Baltimore. About a decade later, the reborn *Constellation* finally received its first visitors. In the years since, over a million people have explored the ship.

The USF *Constellation*'s bloody history, as

well as the past of the younger USS *Constellation*, has left an indelible mark on the surviving ship, and the vessel is now haunted by at least three ghosts. The first supernatural phenomena—ghost lights and strange noises—were reported in 1955, almost immediately after the *Constellation* was decommissioned. Sailors aboard the submarine *Pike*, which was moored near the *Constellation*, observed the spectral activity and caught sight of phantoms walking the ship's decks. Lieutenant Commander Allen Ross Brougham even managed to photograph one of the apparitions, which appeared as a "bluish-white radiancy" wearing an outdated uniform and a sword.

Since 1955, at least three separate ghosts have been identified aboard the *Constellation*. The first is Neil Harvey, the sailor brutally executed in 1799, who now wanders the orlop deck located below the main deck. Because his body was totally obliterated, he only appears as a formless apparition. His presence is very strong, filling those who encounter the ghost with his sorrow and fear.

Harvey's superior, Captain Truxtun, can also be found on the *Constellation*, perhaps trapped on the vessel as punishment for his heinous crime against the junior sailor. This may have been the ghost photographed by Commander Brougham in 1955. It is not known how these two ghosts, spawned by the original frigate, arrived on the USS *Constellation*, but it is likely that they were drawn to the ship because of its resemblance to the vessel they recognized.

A third ghost aboard the *Constellation* appears to be Carl Hansen, who served as a night watchman on the boat until an electric alarm was installed in 1963. He can be found playing cards in the lower decks and has manifested before various guests, including a Catholic priest. He is the only spirit on the boat believed to be truly happy aboard the ship.

Other ghosts are also suspected. One may be the spirit of a young boy, who apparently served as a surgeon's assistant aboard the USF *Constellation* in the 1820s. It is believed that he was stabbed to death by two other sailors, for reasons unknown, in 1822. A fifth ghost has been detected by psychics as well. They feel that he was once a sailor on one of the vessels who became overwhelmed by the terrible conditions on board and hanged himself. Now, he is a sad spirit who floats quietly across the gun and forecastle decks.

As proven by Commander Brougham, the *Constellation*'s ghosts are best observed around midnight on the nights between Christmas (December 25) and New Year's Day. The ghosts are often accompanied by the smell of gunsmoke, which can usually be detected shortly before the apparitions appear. At least one of the ghosts can be photographed, and you would do well to set up cameras on the gun deck, as well as the orlop deck and the forecastle deck.

Should you encounter Neil Harvey, be kind and sympathetic. This is not an evil spirit, but a man forced to endure many horrors aboard the boat until his young life was tragically cut short. However, if you are confronted by Captain Truxtun, flee immediately. Although he has yet to harm anyone, the repugnant murderer could harbor a hatred of the living and may lash out if given the chance.

HMS DEBRAAK

VITAL STATISTICS

LOCATION: The HMS *deBraak* appears off the point of Cape Henlopen, at the entrance of Delaware Bay in Delaware.

NUMBER OF GHOSTS INVOLVED: Unknown

IDENTITIES OF GHOSTS: Presumably, all aboard the HMS *deBraak*

TYPE OF ACTIVITY: Collective spirit and disembodied screams

DEMEANOR OF THE HMS *DEBRAAK* AND ITS PASSENGERS: Cryptic. The phantom ship's agenda is completely unknown, but those aboard appear to be in terrible agony. Regardless, the ship hasn't had an ill effect on witnesses.

ENCOUNTERING THE HMS *DEBRAAK*:

On the night of May 25, 1798, the HMS *deBraak,* a 125-foot British sloop, was dashed against the Delaware coastline. The ship was tossed about by gale winds until it collided with the rocks and cracked apart, spilling all aboard into the sea. The *deBraak* sank, seemingly never to be seen again.

For the past two hundred years, the phantom form of the *deBraak* has repeatedly risen from the waves. The ship, which appears under a full moon, drifts through the fog and reenacts its final voyage again and again. The *deBraak* moves silently through the water, and even its collision with the shore is soundless. However, witnesses report hearing the agonized screams of those who died aboard the vessel drifting through the darkness. The wreckage of the *deBraak* was raised this century, but its phantom voyages still continue.

Cape Henlopen, the site where the *deBraak* is encountered, is replete with its own supernatural energy and occurrences. The "Corpse Light," a luminescent aura that lights up the area, has often been mistaken for a lighthouse. Researchers maintain that the Corpse Light is a manifestation of the so-called Bad Weather Witch, an entity capable of causing intense storms in a limited area. The Witch has been blamed for the 1655 sinking of the *Devonshireman,* which followed the Corpse Light's path until it ran aground. The Bad Weather Witch is also suspected of causing the *deBraak*'s sinking and may have claimed the USS *Poet,* a grain carrier that vanished in 1980.

Today, sightings of the *deBraak* are still reported. It only manifests beneath the full moon, and usually when the weather is particularly poor. Its spectral voyages are brief but dramatic and can best be observed from shores in the Cape Henlopen State Park area.

THE GRIFFIN

VITAL STATISTICS

LOCATION: Green Bay Harbor and Washington Island, Lake Huron, Wisconsin

NUMBER OF GHOSTS INVOLVED: Unknown

IDENTITIES OF GHOSTS: Presumably the entire crew of the *Griffin*

TYPE OF ACTIVITY: Collective spirit

DEMEANOR OF THE *GRIFFIN* AND ITS PASSENGERS: Unknown

ENCOUNTERING THE *GRIFFIN*:

In the annals of damned vessels, few are as infamous as the *Griffin.* Built in the late 1670s at Niagara Falls in New York, the ship was viewed by Native Americans as an insult to the Great Spirit because its construction marred the natural beauty of the Niagara Falls area. To avenge the offended entity, an Iroquois prophet named Metiomek levied a powerful curse on the sixty-foot-long ship. Heedless of this bad omen, French explorer Robert Cavelier de La Salle, who owned the *Griffin,* sailed to Washington Island in

Green Bay Harbor. There, the vessel was loaded with furs. In September of 1679 La Salle decided to explore the St. Joseph River by canoe while his ship returned to Niagara Falls.

By remaining behind, La Salle avoided certain death, for during its return voyage, the *Griffin* mysteriously disappeared. According to lore, the ship may have sailed through "a crack in the lake" or a "crack in the ice," swallowed by the elements forever as a result of the Iroquois curse. But like so many ships that have suffered similar fates, the *Griffin* has not truly vanished forever. On foggy nights, the craft's outline can still be seen sailing through Green Bay Harbor and around Washington Island.

In 1900, a sunken ship was discovered in the waters off Bruce Peninsula in Lake Huron. Many researchers believe that the wreck was all that remained of the *Griffin*. In fact, the ship was officially identified as the cursed *Griffin* in 1955, but this assertion has been challenged by skeptics on many occasions. Whatever the case, the ghostly vision of the *Griffin* is still spotted, suggesting that the vessel has not yet been put to rest.

The *Griffin* is difficult to pinpoint, as it is constantly on the move and remains deep in the fog. Its last known course took it from Washington Island, near Door Peninsula in northeastern Wisconsin, toward Niagara Falls. The phantom vessel may be encountered anywhere along this path, although it is most often sighted within Green Bay Harbor. Bruce Peninsula, where the alleged remnants of the *Griffin* were recovered, may also be a viable ghost hunting site.

THE GHOSTS OF FLIGHT 401

VITAL STATISTICS

LOCATION: The so-called ghosts of Flight 401 have appeared across the country on Eastern Airlines jets. Flight 401 crashed in the Florida Everglades just miles from the Miami International Airport.

NUMBER OF GHOSTS INVOLVED: Two

IDENTITIES OF GHOSTS: Captain Robert Loft and Second Officer Don Repo

TYPE OF ACTIVITY: Phantoms that issue frighteningly accurate predictions

DEMEANOR OF GHOSTS OF FLIGHT 401: Helpful and driven to protect those in danger. The spirits involved in this case seem possessed by the need to prevent another airline crash.

ENCOUNTERING THE GHOSTS OF FLIGHT 401:

The case of Flight 401 has advanced the research of ghosts far more than almost any other confirmed haunting because the spirits involved have been spotted by more than twenty witnesses between 1972 and 1974. The ghosts have openly interacted with the living and have displayed keen intelligence and the ability to communicate effectively. Most important, it has proved increasingly easy to locate the ghosts, as will become evident from the information below.

The saga of the ghosts of Flight 401 begins with the tragic crash of an Eastern Airlines L-1011 Tristar jumbo jet. On December 29, 1972, the jet plunged into the Florida Everglades when a landing gear warning light distracted the pilot, Captain Robert Loft. While seventy people escaped the wreckage alive, 101 passengers were killed. Loft was trapped in the cockpit, where he died an hour after the accident. Second Officer Don Repo was rescued from the smoldering plane, but passed away thirty hours later at a nearby hospital.

After it was determined that Flight 401's fall from the sky was caused by minor design faults, the entire plane was salvaged and many of its working parts were integrated into other Eastern Airlines L-1011 jets. Evidently, these components carried with them the ghosts of Loft and Repo. The ghosts were encountered more than twenty times, always by reputable witnesses. One of the most dramatic incidents involved an Eastern Airlines vice president who, while sitting in first class, began talking to a uniformed pilot sitting near him. Soon it dawned on the executive that the pilot bore an uncanny resemblance to Captain Loft, at which point the man simply vanished into thin air.

Don Repo's ghost pulled similar disappearing acts as well. On one flight, a woman sitting next to an Eastern Airlines flight officer became concerned when the man suddenly took on a pale, sickly hue. She called a stewardess for help and then the man faded away before the eyes of several witnesses. The woman later identified Repo from a series of photographs of Eastern Airlines employees.

Other, more pressing appearances were also recorded. Captain Loft manifested aboard a plane awaiting takeoff at JFK International Airport and spoke briefly with the pilot and two flight attendants. The pilot took the visit as an ill omen and canceled the flight. Later encounters have shown that this was the wisest course of action. In February of 1974, Don Repo's ghostly visage appeared reflected in the window of an oven used to warm in-flight meals. He warned a flight engineer, "Watch out for fire on this airplane." Soon after, as the plane was leaving Mexico City, one of the engines suddenly caught fire and had to be extinguished in flight.

During one incident, Repo took it upon himself to announce the preflight safety instructions over the PA system, much to the confusion of the flight attendants, who had yet to switch on the system. On that same flight, an engineer conducting the final flight checks found Repo at a control panel and spoke to the ghost. Repo told the engineer that he had already conducted the flight checks. During another flight, Repo told the captain, "There will never be another crash. . . . We will not let it happen." From this statement, as well as the actions of the two ghosts, it became apparent that they were desperately trying to prevent another tragedy from claiming more innocent lives.

Unfortunately, after receiving numerous reports, Eastern Airlines tried to end the hauntings by stripping their planes of any parts salvaged from Flight 401. Evidently, this tactic worked, as the ghosts of Repo and Loft have not been reliably reported since. If you do encounter *any* ghosts aboard *any* plane, it is usually best to disembark as soon as possible, for the appearance of specters in this situation is undoubtedly a very, very bad omen.

THE *HALF MOON*

VITAL STATISTICS

LOCATION: The Hudson River, New York

NUMBER OF GHOSTS INVOLVED: Unknown

IDENTITIES OF GHOSTS: Presumably Henry Hudson and his entire crew

TYPE OF ACTIVITY: Collective spirit

DEMEANOR OF THE *HALF MOON* AND ITS PASSENGERS: No outwardly hostile or malign intentions have been detected. It is likely that Henry Hudson has returned in the *Half Moon* to ensure the safety of the area that bears his name. The ship's appearance is often an omen of bad weather, although it is improbable that the *Half Moon* actually causes such a phenomenon; rather, the ship probably manifests to warn the local populace of a coming storm.

ENCOUNTERING THE *HALF MOON*:

The *Half Moon* is perhaps the oldest ghost ship plying the waters surrounding North America. With sightings reported in the early 1660s, the vessel has logged hundreds of miles sailing through the Hudson Bay and into the mouth of the Hudson River.

The *Half Moon* was first spotted by Dutch settlers at the colony of New Amsterdam (which later became New York), who observed the ship sailing around the southern tip of Manhattan Island just shortly after a dreadful storm had lifted. Initially, the settlers believed the vessel to be a harbinger of hope delivering relatives and supplies to the struggling community. The entire settlement gathered at the harbor and hailed the ship as it approached, but they received no response. The boat merely sailed past silently, moving against both the wind and the tide to travel up the Hudson River. The colonists at New Amsterdam were completely confused and waited in vain for the ship to return.

Over the course of the next few months, New Amsterdam received numerous reports of a mysterious ship sailing the Hudson River. In some cases, the vessel drifted close to shore and witnesses could hear a deep voice shouting orders from the boat, although no one was ever observed on deck manning the sails or the wheel. The ship soon became known as an omen of bad weather, because it almost always manifested when a storm was on the rise.

Finally, those living along the Hudson River identified the phantom boat as the *Half Moon*, Henry Hudson's personal ship. Hudson, who discovered the Hudson River in

Haunted Henry Hudson

Henry Hudson, one of North America's earliest and most successful explorers, has left an indelible mark on the continent. His discoveries helped to shape the nation, but his name is also attached to some of the most supernatural sites in North America.

The Hudson Valley is one of the continent's most active UFO windows, recording over six thousand sightings. Alien abductions, ghost lights, disembodied voices, and phantoms are also reported in the area. Caves throughout the Kent Cliffs in the Hudson Valley are home to the spirits of dead Vikings, several ghosts wearing long cloaks, and a glowing red apparition. The fabled Ichabod Crane fled from the Headless Horseman in the Hudson Valley, and Rip Van Winkle fell into his legendary slumber in the same area.

Along with the *Half Moon*, the Hudson River hosts the spirit of "Mad" Anthony Wayne. He roams the shores on a horse named Nag, whose hooves are surrounded by blue and orange sparks. Like the *Half Moon*, Wayne's appearance often foretells an approaching storm.

The ghost of Henry Hudson has also been reported in many areas of the East Coast and eastern Canada, especially at sites he allegedly discovered. He is often said to be friendly and outgoing, although he does not like to tarry long and is always driven toward some new, unknown discovery just beyond the horizon.

1609, died in 1611 after spending many years in search of the Northwest Passage. Some supernaturalists theorize that he returned from the dead to continue his quest. Today, it is widely accepted that Hudson has probably returned to protect the area from all threats, supernatural or otherwise.

The *Half Moon* appears only on moonlit nights during storm season. Its topsails are observed first, glowing a ghostly white as the ship glides down the river. Although it does not emerge from the netherworld often, its appearances are usually long-lived affairs. The ship rarely vanishes suddenly, preferring instead to sail the river slowly until it rounds a bend, at which point it disappears from sight.

Ghost hunters seeking the *Half Moon* must set up observation posts along the Hudson River directly before or during a storm. Watch the horizon for any sign of the vessel and photograph the craft when it finally appears, as this has never been attempted. However, be warned that the *Half Moon* is viewed as a bad omen. In the past, its arrival was almost always followed by horrible storms, which often resulted in the loss of lives, homes, crops, and livestock. The *Half Moon* has also been blamed for the personal tragedies endured by those who witness the phantom ship. The death of a loved one, poverty, loneliness, disease, and injury could afflict anyone who is exposed to the shroud of bad luck and disaster that surrounds the *Half Moon*. Ghost hunters should proceed with caution.

HANGAR 43

VITAL STATISTICS

LOCATION: Johnson County Industrial Airport, along I-35 eight miles southwest of Olathe, Kansas

NUMBER OF GHOSTLY RESIDENTS: One

IDENTITY OF GHOSTLY RESIDENT: Unconfirmed, but presumably a young navy pilot, whom locals know as the Captain

TYPE OF ACTIVITY: Minor poltergeist activity and unexplained noises, including footsteps, knocking, and disembodied whistling

DEMEANOR OF GHOSTLY RESIDENT: Quiet and unassuming. It seems the ghost is simply forced to live silently in the shadows of the hangar.

ENCOUNTERING THE GHOST OF HANGAR 43:

Commissioned in 1942 as a navy flight training base, the U.S. Naval Reserve Air Base in Olathe, Kansas, experienced a fairly unusual number of fatalities along its runways and within its hangars. During World War II, at least forty-five hundred naval cadets trained at the base, and about thirty were killed in crashes or other accidents. The ghost of at least one of these unfortunates still haunts Hangar 43 at the site, which has been incorporated into the Johnson County Industrial Airport.

The hauntings in Hangar 43 consist of one invisible spirit wandering the grounds, making a variety of noises as he travels about. His footsteps and eerie whistling are heard in the catwalks above the hangar. He frequently opens and closes doors, knocks on the walls, turns faucets on and off, and topples small objects. In one instance, the mischievous entity overturned a full cup of coffee in front of several amazed witnesses.

The ghost is locally known as the Captain, and it is believed that he was once a young navy pilot who crashed at the base in the early 1940s. This assumption may be based on the single sighting of a phantom at the hangar. Late one night, a guest staying in the hangar's visitors quarters spotted a man dressed in a white military uniform. When followed, the ghost headed toward the latrines, then vanished.

The Captain's true identity is somewhat suspect, however. First, the oft-cited young pilot had collided with the administration building, some three blocks from Hangar 43. His plane had not been stored in Hangar 43, nor was the pilot stationed at the base. Thirty-four other pilots lost their lives at the base, and any of these could easily be the ghost as well.

It is much more likely that the spirit belongs to one of two men who died in accidents in the hangar itself. Both fell from the catwalks (where footsteps and whistling are now heard) while performing routine maintenance in Hangar 43. One of these men actually collided with the nose of a plane in the hangar before hitting the ground. Given the nature of ghosts and their tendency to lurk near the site of their deaths, either of these falling victims are clearly prime candidates for the haunting, which continues today.

The spirit of Hangar 43 manifests at all hours of the day and night, but he can only be encountered within the structure. Observe the catwalks and monitor all doors for spectral activity. If you manage to encounter the ghost, especially in his phantom form, be sure to ask him his name. Depending on the ghost's demeanor, you may be able to discuss the circumstances around his death as well. The Captain, or whoever the ghost may be, has shown no hostility and has been only a minor irritant to those visiting the hangar, so you may explore the site without fear.

THE PALATINE LIGHT

VITAL STATISTICS

LOCATION: Waters off Block Island, Rhode Island. For information on the island, contact the Block Island Chamber of Commerce, Drawer D, Block Island, Rhode Island 02807; (401) 466-2982.

NUMBER OF GHOSTS INVOLVED: Unknown

IDENTITIES OF GHOSTS: Unknown, but believed to be the spirits of those who died aboard either the *Palatine* or the *Princess Augusta*

TYPE OF ACTIVITY: Ghost lights, apparitions, and disembodied screams

DEMEANOR OF THE PALATINE LIGHT AND ITS PASSENGERS: Tragic and lost. The Palatine Light has never intentionally hurt anyone, and it is probable that the apparition appears merely as a reminder of the terrible fate that befell the *Palatine* or the *Princess Augusta*.

ENCOUNTERING THE PALATINE LIGHT:

The Palatine Light is the spectral remnant of a ship alternately identified as the *Palatine* or the *Princess Augusta*, both of which were said to have suffered a terrible fate during the mid-1700s. Today, this lost vessel appears as a fiery light moving silently through the dark waters off the coast of Block Island.

The Palatine Light has been explained through several tragic tales. The first story claims that the Light was once the *Palatine*, a Dutch ship transporting immigrants to Philadelphia in 1752. When the ship was badly damaged by storms off the coast of New England, the crew panicked and mutinied. They murdered the *Palatine*'s captain and robbed the passengers before abandoning the ship in the lifeboats. Left to fend for themselves, the immigrants ran the boat aground on Block Island, where they were met by pirates. The pirates unexpectedly saved the passengers, but one insane woman refused to leave the ship. Unwilling to let the wreck attract unwanted attention to Block Island, the pirates set the *Palatine* ablaze and pushed it out to sea. The single remaining passenger went down with the ship, her crazed screams echoing out across the water.

In another version of the *Palatine* tale, the ship was full of German immigrants when the captain *and* crew conspired to crash the boat and rob the passengers. But upon intentionally running aground Block Island, the *Palatine*'s crew were met by pirates who plundered the ship. The outlaws then trapped everyone onboard, set the *Palatine* on fire, and let the ship drift out to sea, where the crooked captain and his crew, along with all of the unlucky passengers, suffered horrible deaths. The final tale of the *Palatine* claims that the captain became confused during a storm and was lured onto Block Island by decoy lights planted onshore by the pirates. Again, the crew and passengers met a grisly demise.

While it has widely been accepted that the *Palatine* is indeed the ghostly light spotted off the coasts of Block Island, historical records of the ship are curiously absent. However, the tale surrounding the *Palatine* bears a remarkable resemblance to the tragic fate of a similar ship, the *Princess Augusta*. The Dutch ship left Rotterdam, Netherlands, in August of 1738 with fourteen crew members and 350 passengers, most of whom were Protestants bound for Philadelphia. While sailing for the New World, 114 people, including half of the crew and the captain, were poisoned by contaminated drinking water and buried at sea. Andrew Brook, the first mate, took control of the ship, but he proved an unskilled captain. As the *Princess Augusta* neared New England, it was caught in

> "Now low and dim, now clear and higher
> Leaps up the terrible Ghost of Fire
> Then, slowly sinking, the flames expire . . ."
>
> —John Greenleaf Whittier, the "Palatine Light"

a massive storm that blew the vessel in all directions. Conditions on the ship descended into anarchy as people attacked one another for food and water. Finally, Brook and his crew banded together and held the remaining provisions for ransom.

On December 27, the *Princess Augusta* collided with a hummock near Block Island and the boat's hull ruptured. As the ship began to sink, Brook took a lifeboat and sailed to shore, where he persuaded some local residents to help him rescue the ship. Those aboard the *Princess Augusta* were subsequently rescued, save for one deranged woman named Mary Vanderline. She would not leave the boat and could not be overpowered or persuaded. The helpful locals also removed about twenty trunks belonging to the passengers, but the *Princess* eventually broke loose from its saviors, impacted against a large rock, and sank. Vanderline drowned.

A year after the *Princess Augusta* was lost, people living near Block Island began reporting the burning phantom light. The first confirmed sighting occurred in 1739, nearly twenty years *before* the *Palatine* allegedly sank, when the crew of the *Somerset* spotted the ghost light while sailing past the isle. According to the *Somerset*'s captain, they "followed the burning ship to its watery grave, but failed to find any survivors."

Regardless of the veracity of any of the legends recounted above, the Palatine Light is a very real ghostly phenomenon still reported regularly. Witnesses testify that the light can change size and intensity, and always appears at night. Some claim to hear the terrified screams of the woman left onboard as well.

When searching for the Palatine Light, concentrate your efforts on Settler's Rock Grove or State Beach, two locations from which the glowing apparition has been sighted most often. Do not chase the Palatine Light or follow it out to sea, as many oceanic ghost lights have a tendency to lead the curious to their deaths.

THE PHANTOM TRAIN OF WELLINGTON

VITAL STATISTICS

LOCATION: Wellington, Prince Edward Island, Ontario, Canada

NUMBER OF GHOST PASSENGERS: Unknown

IDENTITIES OF GHOSTLY PASSENGERS: Unknown

TYPE OF ACTIVITY: Phantoms

DEMEANOR OF THE PHANTOM TRAIN AND ITS PASSENGERS: Completely aloof. The phantom train merely moves past without indicating any substantial personality. The train's passengers simply want to board and disappear.

ENCOUNTERING THE PHANTOM TRAIN OF WELLINGTON: RIP RIP

The Phantom Train of Wellington is one of the most unusual ghostly manifestations yet reported, because it seems to transcend both space and time, totally ignoring the "real world" as it goes about its spectral journey.

Very little is known about the Phantom Train, aside from minimal facts regarding its appearance and behavior. The train consists of an engine and three cars and only manifests in the world of the living at night. It enters Wellington, on Ontario's Prince Edward Island, via a bridge just outside of town, and travels to the town's train station, where it is met by a group of ghostly passengers! These apparitions slowly board the train, as if they are living travelers, and the phantom locomotive continues on its journey, disappearing into the darkness. The phantom train was first spotted in 1885 and has continued to make frequent appearances, most often in December.

Supernaturalists have few explanations for Wellington's phantom train. There are no records of a similar vehicle meeting a terrible end on the island, nor were there any unusual deaths or murders on the trains that ran through the town prior to 1885. Prince Edward Island has no other reported hauntings and is not considered a gateway to the Spirit World, Hell, the land of the dead, or any other dimension reputed to house the spirits of the deceased. Still, the most appealing theory about the Phantom Train of Wellington suggests that it is a transport for the dead, arriving to carry away the souls of those who have recently passed on. Why Wellington would be chosen as the "station" for the train is not known, nor has there been any indication that the locomotive travels to other portions of the continent (a smattering of phantom trains have been reported throughout North America, but none match the description of Wellington's train).

Because so little is known about the Wellington phantom train, ghost hunters should collect as much data as possible. Observe the train as it enters town during cold December nights (remember to pack for the weather!). Pay special attention to the faces of the passengers and search through local obituaries for any likeness that you might recognize. If a link between the recently deceased and the phantom train can be established, we might finally understand the vehicle's purpose.

THE *QUEEN MARY*

VITAL STATISTICS

LOCATION: The *Queen Mary* Hotel, Pier J, Port of Long Beach, 1126 Queens Highway, Long Beach, California 90802-6390. Reservations can be made at (800) 437-2934, while (562) 435-3511 is a general information number. A wide range of rooms and locations are haunted, but cabin B340 is perhaps the most active spot.

NUMBER OF GHOSTLY RESIDENTS: At least a dozen, but probably many more

IDENTITIES OF GHOSTLY RESIDENTS: John Pedder, Senior Second Officer William Stark, and several other unidentified persons who died aboard the ocean liner

TYPE OF ACTIVITY: Poltergeists, ghost lights, disembodied voices, mysterious footprints and footsteps, phantoms, unsettling auras, bizarre knockings, and virtually all other forms of ghostly manifestation

DEMEANOR OF GHOSTLY RESIDENTS: Varies. Some of the ghosts are lonely and tired, but others seem to enjoy pretending that they are still alive. A few are tormented by death and continually experience their last moments, hauntings that profoundly rattle those who encounter the spirits responsible.

ENCOUNTERING THE GHOSTS OF THE *QUEEN MARY*: RIP RIP RIP RIP

O ften touted as the most haunted vessel in the world, and perhaps the most haunted site in western North America, the *Queen Mary* in Long Beach, California, is home to an amazing diversity of spirits.

Commissioned in 1936, the *Queen Mary* made over one thousand Atlantic crossings before being dry-docked in Long Beach harbor in 1967. During its thirty years of active use, it served as a general passenger liner and

One of the *Queen Mary*'s haunted pools.

unmanned hydraulic hatchway. After the ship was permanently moored in 1967, it was converted into a hotel, and during this construction Pedder reappeared. The first witness was a security guard patrolling D deck. He began to sense the ghost's presence when his faithful German shepherd grew agitated as the pair neared hatchway 13. Ultimately, the dog refused to pass through the portal and attempted to bolt from his master's side. Shortly after, the guard heard a loud noise, as if something huge and metal were rolling toward him. Overcome with fear, he bolted from D deck.

Although the infamous watertight door has been removed and the area now contains an escalator leading from the engine room, Pedder's spirit persists. He appears as a morose young man wearing dark clothes. Although he disappears as soon as he is spotted, his face is clearly recognizable and can be easily matched to his photograph.

Another frequent spectral visitor is Senior Second Officer William Stark. In 1949, Stark was searching for booze when he stumbled across an old gin bottle kept by the staff captain. Unfortunately, the staff captain stored tetrachloride in the bottle, and Stark was poisoned when he downed the caustic liquid. Now, his phantom wanders the ship looking for a more suitable last drink.

The most haunted areas of the *Queen Mary* include the first-class and tourist-class swimming pools. The former is haunted by two women who drowned in the pool in the 1930s

inevitably experienced many tragic and terrible deaths. In all, it is estimated that thirty-one passengers, sixteen crew members, and at least two soldiers died while aboard the ship. A large number of these fatalities have returned to the vessel as restless spirits.

The most well-known ghost is that of eighteen-year-old John Pedder, who appears near an escalator and engine room on D deck. Originally, the area contained a watertight door, ironically designated as hatchway 13. During a routine drill simulating a sinking, Pedder was caught in the door as it began to automatically seal. He was painfully crushed to death in the and 1960s, respectively. Both wear the styles of their day. A young boy playing near the first-class pool once fell overboard and was lost at sea; today, his sad ghost wanders a passageway connected to the pool room. The other pool, in the tourist-class section, was the site of at least one drowning death as well, and now that female victim remains in the water. Disembodied voices, the sounds of people playing in the water, and other noises have been reported near both pools. In addition, many witnesses have described seeing wet footprints appearing before their eyes.

Although most of the deaths aboard the *Queen Mary* were purely accidental, the vessel was no stranger to murder. One of the most persistent ghosts is the spirit of a purser who was murdered in cabin B340 on the third level. The circumstances of his death are unclear, but it appears to have been a robbery attempt, and the murderer eluded justice. The purser has returned in the form of a restless poltergeist that hurls objects, shakes the bed, rattles drawers, knocks on the walls, and even grabs visitors. The unexplained disturbances are so severe, in fact, that the hotel has closed the room to guests.

The kitchen is also victimized by an unruly poltergeist, said to be the angry specter of a cook who served on the ship during World War II. At that time, the ocean liner was carrying troops to Europe, and it was the cook's duty to prepare all the meals for the soldiers. Unfortunately, his cooking was terrible, and the troops began to riot. As the violence escalated, the cook was shoved into a hot oven, where he perished. His horrendous, tortured screams still fill the kitchen, and he has been known to hurl small objects on occasion.

The worst tragedy involving the *Queen Mary* also occurred during World War II.

While transporting troops, the ocean liner collided with the *Curacoa*, a British light cruiser. The crash severed the *Curacoa* in two, spilling its crew into the water. Unfortunately, the *Queen Mary* was under strict orders and could not stop to rescue the *Curacoa*'s survivors: 338 men drowned as a result. Today, visitors report hearing frantic knocking near the bosun's locker, the very portion of the hull that ruptured the *Curacoa*.

Among the other apparitions appearing on the *Queen Mary* is the spirit of an alluring woman wearing a long white gown. This unidentified beauty haunts the Queen's Salon, which was once the first-class lounge. In the nearby first-class suite area, a dark-haired man wearing a suit from the 1930s and several ghost lights have been encountered by tour guides. The sounds of children laughing and playing fill the forward storage area, where the archives are currently stored. Finally, the ghost of a bearded man dressed in blue-gray overalls has been reported in the shaft alley, which provides access to the propeller shafts. Like many of the *Queen Mary*'s other ghosts, his identity and the circumstances of his death remain unknown.

Clearly, the *Queen Mary* is a ripe training ground for the novice ghost hunter. Begin by arranging a guided tour of the boat, which includes many of the most haunted areas of the ship, such as the kitchen and swimming pools. Attempt to visit each of the areas described above and watch for the variety of spectral incursions. Next, spend a few nights in one of the hotel's many rooms. If you are truly courageous, plead with the hotel staff for the privilege of a night in cabin B340. None of the ghosts on the *Queen Mary* are considered dangerous, although their sudden manifestation can be disconcerting.

THE SHIP OF DEATH

VITAL STATISTICS

LOCATION: Platte River, Wyoming. Most sightings occur near Bessemer Bend and the small town of Guernsey

NUMBER OF GHOSTLY PASSENGERS: Unknown

IDENTITIES OF GHOSTLY PASSENGERS: Varies

TYPE OF ACTIVITY: Phantoms

DEMEANOR OF THE SHIP OF DEATH AND ITS PASSENGERS: Ambiguous. The Ship of Death has but one purpose: to announce impending doom. Its appearance is always followed by tragedy.

ENCOUNTERING THE SHIP OF DEATH:

In many cases, the appearance of specific types of ghosts can foretell death. In Ireland, for example, any who hear the scream of the wailing banshee are sure to die within days. Native American lore tells of ghostly canoes, spirit animals, and other spectral beings that carry the curse of imminent death whenever they manifest. Such is the case with Wyoming's Ship of Death, a phantom ship that cruises the Platte River in order to deliver messages of doom.

The Ship of Death is an outdated craft that always sails from a mysterious, unnatural fog bank. Its cracked masts, rotten decks, and tattered sails are covered in a strange frost. Most startling are the ship's passengers, a motley collection of phantoms observed crowded onto the deck. They are always gathered around a pale corpse spread out on a canvas sheet. Like the rest of the boat, the Ship of Death's passengers and the dead body are coated in a visible layer of white frost.

When the Ship of Death sails close to lone witnesses, the phantom passengers spread away from the dead body, revealing the identity of the corpse. In every case, the corpse bears the likeness of someone the witness knows extremely well. As foretold by the appearance of the Ship of Death, that person will always die within the day.

The three most dramatic encounters with the Ship of Death occurred in the late 1800s and early 1900s. Leon Weber, a trapper engaged to his true love, caught a glimpse of her aboard the Ship of Death in 1862. She mysteriously died within twenty-four hours. In 1887, Gene Wilson saw his own beloved on the ship's deck, and the cattleman's wife passed away soon after; while Victor Heibe, who lived on the river, lost his best friend after the Ship of Death passed his house in 1903. Since Heibe's sighting, the Cheyenne Bureau of Psychological Research has recorded numerous encounters with the Ship of Death.

Seeking the Ship of Death is not recommended. In fact, if the vessel does appear for you, it is likely to deliver a dark message: The one you see aboard the ship will die within days, despite your best efforts to save the victim. If you positively must see the boat, ignoring the danger inherent in such folly, you will be most successful if you visit the Platte River

during the late autumn, the only time of year the ship has ever been sighted.

The Fetch: A Portent of Death

Among the myriad types of specters and phantoms known to mortals, the most disturbing may be the fetch, an apparition of a person who is soon to die. A fetch's appearance is always a perfect replica of the ill-fated individual and may not be recognized as a spirit until it passes through a wall or performs some other supernatural feat. Fetches are usually encountered by the victim's family members or loved ones, who can identify the specter. They may also manifest before the person whose death they foretell. Sometimes fetches appear near the site of the victim's impending demise, but they may also visit the graveyard plot where the cursed soul will soon find eternal rest. Although usually solitary, some fetches do travel with ghosts, phantom ships (such as Wyoming's **Ship of Death**), demons, or even a cloaked spirit identified as the incarnation of Death.

THE TEAZER LIGHT

VITAL STATISTICS

LOCATION: Mahone Bay, Nova Scotia, Canada

NUMBER OF GHOSTS INVOLVED: Unknown

IDENTITIES OF GHOSTS: Presumably the spirits of all the pirates aboard the *Young Teazer*

TYPE OF ACTIVITY: Collective spirits and ghost lights

DEMEANOR OF THE TEAZER LIGHT: Unknown. Although the passengers were once terrible pirates, the Teazer Light itself has never exhibited any violent behavior.

ENCOUNTERING THE TEAZER LIGHT:

Pirates are notorious for returning from the dead (see chapter 4), often in forms that inspire fear and terror. This is clearly evident in the return of the *Young Teazer*, a pirate vessel lost in the Mahone Bay in the 1800s.

Before its final hours, the *Young Teazer*'s history was fairly hideous. The pirates aboard the ship were brutal killers who had made plunder a profession, and they used the craft to terrorize the Atlantic. The *Young Teazer* was undoubtedly the site of many murders, and may have been the stage for rapes, tortures, and other crimes as well.

Eventually, however, the *Young Teazer* fell under attack. British warships assigned to track down and destroy the vessel cornered the pirate ship in Mahone Bay on June 26, 1813. The pirates attempted to fight back, but when they realized they were doomed, they initiated a suicidal contingency plan. Rather than allow themselves to be captured and their loot confiscated, the pirates set the *Young Teazer* ablaze. The British, unable to board the flaming ship, backed away and watched the vessel sink. It is unknown how many of the pirates actually escaped the conflict, although folklore holds that all perished when the *Young Teazer*'s smoking remains disappeared beneath the water.

Shortly after the *Young Teazer*'s final voyage, the craft rose from the waves as a fiery phantom ship. It continues to appear in modern times, often emerging from the fog off the coast of Borgals Point on Mahone Bay. Like other ghost ships, it frequently precedes a terrible storm, and it is often reported within three days of a full moon. All of these criteria should be remembered when seeking the Teazer Light.

Despite the brutal history of those who died aboard the *Young Teazer,* the vessel poses little threat to the living. It is most often sighted a mile or two offshore, only rarely manifesting near other ships. However, in these circumstances, many witnesses report that they felt as if the ship was about to ram theirs. Fortunately, this has never occurred, but ghost hunters on the Mahone Bay would do well to keep their distance.

Other Haunted Vessels and Phantom Craft

Haunted vessels and phantom craft appear throughout North America. The Atlantic coastline is especially active with phantom craft activity, recording hundreds of ghost ship sightings throughout the past two hundred years. The highways of North America are also home to phantom semis, ghostly trains, and spectral cars. Below is a small sampling of phantom craft and haunted vessels that may also be of interest.

- **The Phantom Train of Dragoon, Dragoon Mountains, Arizona:** A ghostly locomotive travels the area around the Dragoon Mountains, although tracks have never been constructed in this portion of the alkali flats. The train's single, glowing light and eerie whistle can be discerned when the train manifests. Some witnesses have observed an engineer, covered in soot, yanking on the train's whistle as it barrels across the flats.

- **Grand Junction, Colorado:** Home to the phantom train Locomotive Number 107, which derailed several times in this area and claimed dozens of lives. The ghost train, nicknamed Dread 107, was retired in 1909, but today witnesses often hear its eerie whistle or sight the spectral vehicle as it travels along the horizon.

- **Port Mahon, Delaware:** An unnamed ship once owned by Joshua McCowan sails into this port, with the corpse of its former master hanging from a rope on the ship's bowsprit. McCowan had romanced the governor of Delaware and was strung up by a crewman jealous of the affair.

- **Bachelor's Grove Cemetery and the Midlothian Turnpike, Chicago, Illinois:** Although primarily the home of restless spirits and ghost lights, phantom cars have been spotted around the cemetery. Most notably, ghostly automobiles appear directly in front of motorists traveling the Midlothian Turnpike, which passes the cemetery. Collisions between the spectral vehicles and normal cars occur frequently, although the crashes leave no tangible damage. Phantom trucks have been reported in the area as well.

- **The *Edmund Fitzgerald*, Lake Superior, Michigan:** This 730-foot freighter was overcome by a storm in 1975 while trying to reach Detroit, Michigan. Unfortunately, it was bogged down by its cargo of iron pellets and sank near Whitefish Bay, killing all aboard. It still attempts to cross Lake Superior on occasion.

- **The *W. H. Gilcher*, Straits of Mackinac, Michigan:** This ancient steamer went down in fog near the shores of Mackinac Island in 1892. Now its ghostly horn can be heard echoing over the water on foggy nights. Another ghost ship, said to belong to a French explorer, also appears in this same area every seven years.

- **The Phantom Steamboat, Jefferson City, Missouri River, Missouri:** About twenty ghostly passengers cruise the river nightly aboard a silent paddle-wheel steamboat. It is usually observed by fishemen, who claim that the boat floats above the water's surface.

- **The *Adventure*, Ocracoke Island, North Carolina:** The *Adventure* was the ship of the infamous pirate Blackbeard and, since his death in 1718, it has continually reappeared in the water of the Pamlico Sound. It is often covered in lights. See chapter 4 for more information on Blackbeard.

- **Galveston Bay, Texas:** Another pirate, Jean Laffite, is said to sail this bay at night. He is allegedly searching for someone worthy to receive his vast treasure, which has never been recovered and may be hidden in Central America or Louisiana.

- **Utah State Historical Society, Denver and Rio Grande Railroad Depot, Salt Lake City, Utah:** The ghost of a woman with long black hair and a purple dress roams this site. Long ago, she was abandoned at the train station by her fiancé, who flung the woman's engagement ring onto the train tracks. When she attempted to retrieve the ring, she was struck dead by an oncoming train.

- **Big Bend Tunnel, Talcott, West Virginia:** Big John Henry, who died in the tunnel, still roams this site. In 1870, the huge man entered a contest with a Burleigh steam-powered drill to see who could drill the most holes within a specified amount of time. Henry won the day, but suffered a fatal stroke within moments after claiming victory. Today, his hammering can still be heard in the tunnel, and many visitors report seeing the tall, well-built black man roaming the area.

- **Devil's Lake, Wisconsin:** Along with lake monsters and shadowy apparitions, Devil's Lake is home to a phantom canoe.

- **Northumberland Strait, Cape John, Nova Scotia, Canada:** A flaming phantom ship sails these waters, most often at dusk and midnight. It is visible for a full thirty minutes, sitting motionless as it continues to burn. The boat's identity is unknown, but it may be a pleasure ship set ablaze by careless drunks.

- **Merigomish, Nova Scotia, Canada:** Yet another unidentified ship appears near Prince Edward Island and the eastern end of the Northumberland Strait. It is usually observed at dusk shortly before or after the autumnal equinox. During the course of its manifestation, it collides with an invisible shoal, bursts into flames, and rapidly sinks. Sometimes, phantom people are seen leaping overboard as the ship vanishes beneath the waters.

- **Pleasant Bay, Nova Scotia, Canada:** Home to a phantom ship seeking lost treasure, Pleasant Bay has experienced a rash of sightings of a ghostly vessel that lands near the village of Tangier and unloads a phantom crew. The crew speak an unidentified language and are often seen drinking heavily as they trudge into the woods where treasure is said to be buried. As soon as they enter the forest, the crew members vanish. The boat, which only appears on clear nights when the moon is bright, disappears soon after.

- **Lost Seven Shore, Prince Edward Island, Canada:** A huge phantom ship fully engulfed in flames sails past the southern shores of Prince Edward Island at speeds that boggle the mind. The ship is said to foretell coming storms.

- **The *Bannockburn*, Lake Superior, Ontario, Canada:** A grain transport attempting to deliver its load to Caribou Island in 1902 has returned as a phantom vessel. When the boat arrived at the island, the lighthouse was in disrepair and the blind *Bannockburn* crashed into a reef. The hull was torn open, the ship sank, and the entire crew drowned. The ghost ship appears only at night and during storms, perhaps searching for the lighthouse.

- **Qu'Appelle River, Saskatchewan, Canada:** This river is often sailed by a ghostly canoe paddled by a phantom who continually cries "Who calls? Who calls?" The ghost is that of a brave who once traveled the river to meet his bride. He was overcome by an eerie fog and heard his lover's voice through the mist. He shouted out "Who calls?" repeatedly, but received no answer. When he reached her village, he found that she had passed away the night before, his name on her lips. The river is named for his phantom cries.

3. HAUNTED CEMETERIES AND BURIAL SITES

FILMS, NOVELS, CAMPFIRE tales, and our own imaginations often portray cemeteries, graveyards, and other similar sites as overrun by the restless spirits of those buried within.

However, this fantasy is a great exaggeration. In reality, although certainly places strongly associated with death, relatively few burial grounds are actually inhabited by ghosts.

The reason for this seemingly impossible dearth of spectral activity within graveyards is actually quite simple: a ghost will usually only manifest in a locale that held profound emotional significance for him in life. The ghost's chosen haunt could be a childhood home, a favorite park where many fond memories were created, or the site of the ghost's death. As we move through life, we all form bonds with various locations where we have lived happily or suffered great loss. However, few of us visit our own cemetery plots or become attached to the local graveyard in any way.

When ghosts do appear in graveyard and cemeteries, it is often because the spirit did spend some time in the area before death. For example, a mother who visits her dead child's grave on a regular basis is sure to develop some emotional connection to the cemetery and may very well be drawn to the place after death. Those murdered in graveyards are also likely to begin haunting their own graves. Finally, lonely or lost ghosts who simply have no place to go may also linger by their headstones.

Although the number of haunted graveyards and cemeteries in North America is relatively small, these sites all share a surprising number of similarities. To begin with, most haunted burial sites are extremely old and hold several generations of corpses. Because they are filled to capacity, these cemeteries no longer receive new bodies, and are thus less likely to see living visitors. Such places become overwhelmed by a sense of loneliness, prompting frustrated ghosts to rise. In addition, many cemeteries eventually close for good and begin to fall into serious disrepair, further disheart-

ening any spirits. A cemetery or graveyard that is completely closed to the public is especially likely to suffer a rash of hauntings.

Because haunted cemeteries seldom boast security guards or caretakers, they attract another type of ghoul: the vandal. Graffiti, empty beer bottles, syringes, trash, condoms, and other distasteful items litter the graves. The supernatural energy within a haunted graveyard also draws cultists and satanists, who may burn candles or sacrifice animals within the graveyard during their rituals. The presence of such diabolic forces may cause angry ghosts to appear.

Haunted burial sites are frequently located near bodies of water, usually a small lake or stream. This often causes the cemetery's soil to become wet and unstable. It is not uncommon for the dead to literally rise from their graves as their coffins are shifted by erosion.

Finally, almost all haunted cemeteries have visible boundaries that the ghosts cannot cross. Such borders can be marked by iron gates, stone walls, creeks, lonely roads, statues, trees, rocks, bridges, and a host of other manmade structures and natural formations. Before entering a haunted cemetery, you should always be aware of the site's perimeter markers: If you are pursued by a dangerous ghost, you must leave the graveyard's grounds at once. After you have left the graveyard, you will be safe from any phantoms, as ghosts tend to dissipate whenever they try to stray too far from their new homes.

BACHELOR'S GROVE CEMETERY

VITAL STATISTICS

LOCATION: Bachelor's Grove Cemetery, Rubio Woods Forest Preserve, Midlothian, Illinois. The cemetery is about three-quarters of a mile off of I-294.

NUMBER OF GHOSTLY RESIDENTS: At least five, but probably many, many more

IDENTITIES OF GHOSTLY RESIDENTS: The White Lady (also known as Mrs. Rogers or the Madonna of Bachelor's Grove) and her infant, a nameless farmer and his spectral steed, and an unidentified two-headed spirit, as well as countless ghost lights

TYPE OF ACTIVITY: Ghost lights, apparitions, spectral automobiles, and at least one "phantom house"

DEMEANOR OF GHOSTLY RESIDENTS: Lonely and generally unable to accept death. The spirits are so varied and active that it is difficult to predict their reactions, which may range from harmless curiosity to blatant murder.

ENCOUNTERING THE BACHELOR'S GROVE GHOSTS: RIP RIP RIP RIP

Bachelor's Grove is believed by many to be the most haunted cemetery in North America, if not the world. It has yielded over one hundred reports of ghostly manifestations ranging from simple ghost lights to complex apparitions. This is hardly surprising, as the graveyard exhibits almost all of the characteristics common to haunted burial sites. First, the cemetery is a particularly lonely site: It is named for the fact that it is predominately occupied by young bachelors, many of whom died in their prime or alone. A new tenant has not been introduced to the Bachelor's Grove since 1965, and living visitors are therefore infrequent. The graveyard has also been plagued by vandals, Voodoo practitioners, and cultists who perform animal sacrifices. The cemetery is near water (a lagoon rests at one end of the graveyard) and has been the site of at least one accidental death. Finally, the bodies of those murdered by the Mob were often hidden in the area. All of these factors have conspired to transform the Bachelor's Grove Cemetery into a desolate place where the dead do not rest in peace.

The most haunted sections of the cemetery include the shores of the lagoon, which are said to attract ghosts in huge numbers. In the 1870s, a farmer who once plowed the land near the cemetery was dragged into the water by his skittish horse, where both drowned. Today, the spectral farmer and his horse and plow can be seen working the land at night. Other spirits, which appear as humanoid phantoms or amorphous globes of blue light, are probably the ghosts of those murdered for crossing the Mob; a great many of these unfortunates were dumped into the lagoon during the 1920s.

The most frightening of the Bachelor's Grove Cemetery ghosts is a two-headed phantom. The grotesque creature wanders between the headstones, often accompanied by a legion of small, dancing blue lights. His identity is unknown, but he may be the spirit of a deformed man who was kept hidden from society by his parents and secretly buried at the site upon his death.

While the Bachelor's Grove specters are predominately male, the one spirit reported most often is the White Lady. Alternately known as the Madonna or Mrs. Rogers, the White Lady wears a flowing ivory gown. Sometimes, she appears to be holding a phantom infant who wails soundlessly. Unlike the other ghosts of Bachelor's Grove, the White Lady manifests only beneath the full moon. While her identity has never been confirmed ("Mrs. Rogers" is simply a quaint nickname applied by locals), it is widely believed that she was a woman whose son died young; when she passed on many years later, she was buried next to his corpse.

Bachelor's Grove Cemetery is also home to some of the most unusual ghostly phenomena ever reported. The weirdest reports involve a phantom farmhouse surrounded by a white picket fence. The farmhouse, which has been encountered on several occasions since the 1950s, rises from the mist and wavers for several minutes before fading away again. Phantom cars and trucks race around the cemetery as well, running other motorists from the road, and some of the ghosts in the area have been known to approach and touch visitors.

Because it has attracted such widespread attention among supernaturalists, Bachelor's Grove has been a target for a small group of skeptics who do not believe in the spirit world. In 1984, one such cynic visited the cemetery and, within minutes, witnessed the graveyard's many ghost lights. One of these floating orbs took the shape of a yellow phantom. Seconds later, the ghost dissipated in an explosion of shooting red lights.

The Bachelor's Grove Cemetery is a choice site for novice ghost hunters to begin their careers. However, there are many dangers that you should keep in mind as you wander the cemetery. First, as you approach the cemetery, be watchful of phantom cars. These automobiles may try to run you off the road, and if you lose control of your own vehicle while trying to avoid the oncoming apparitions, you may be seriously injured. If you see a phantom car or truck coming your way, it is best to run headlong into the spectral craft: They have often passed through real cars with no ill effect.

Second, while in the cemetery, be wary of vagrants, gang members, cultists, or other unsavory characters who may be attracted to the area. Because the cemetery must be traveled at night, always go with several other ghost hunters.

Finally, should you be approached by a ghost, keep your distance. Most of these spirits may be extremely lonely and frustrated. They may attack simply because they have been driven insane in death. It is best to watch the spirits from afar, save for the White Lady, who may be approached safely.

CHEESMAN PARK AND CITY CEMETERY

VITAL STATISTICS

LOCATION: Cheesman Park, between Eighth and Thirteenth Avenues, Denver, Colorado. The most haunted area is the section between Congress Park and the Botanical Gardens.

NUMBER OF GHOSTLY RESIDENTS: Inestimable

IDENTITIES OF GHOSTLY RESIDENTS: Presumably the bulk of the people once buried in the "city" section of the former cemetery

TYPE OF ACTIVITY: Disembodied moans and voices, phantoms, and an aura of profound sadness

DEMEANOR OF GHOSTLY RESIDENTS: Extremely active and reluctant to stay buried. The ghosts of Cheesman Park openly walk abroad, enter homes, and chase humans. It is widely believed that the spirits are retaliating for the mistreatment of their corpses, so they should not be considered evil, but they are definitely somewhat malicious.

ENCOUNTERING THE GHOSTS OF CHEESMAN PARK:
RIP RIP RIP

I n 1893, the modern site of Cheesman Park became the setting for one of the largest mass uprisings the dead have ever staged. The 320-acre park was originally zoned as the Mount Prospect Graveyard in 1858. The burial ground, known locally as Boot Hill, was divided into three sections: a Catholic sector, a Jewish zone, and a general "city section."

When the City of Denver took control of the cemetery in 1873, the city section quickly became a planting ground for dead transients, criminals, orphans, paupers, and victims of disease or epidemic who could not afford to pay for plots. This portion of the cemetery quickly fell into disrepair, with the rest of the graveyard following suit within a few years. By 1893, the city's mismanagement of the land forced the closure of what was now called City Cemetery. City officials notified the local populace that they had but ninety days to claim and remove the bodies of their loved ones before the land was torn asunder and the corpses were relocated by city workers.

The local Catholic and Jewish churches organized quickly and had their respective sections cleared well within the city's time frame. The vast majority of the bodies in the city section, however, remained unclaimed. When the ninety-day grace period ended, city workers set about moving the bodies from City Cemetery. The process was gruesome. Most reports estimate that approximately 10,000 bodies were yanked from the ground, each to be delivered to nearby Riverside Cemetery for reburial. In order to facilitate shipping the corpses, the bodies were shoved into ludicrous pine caskets one foot wide and three and a half feet long. Needless to say, most of the bodies had to be broken, folded, or otherwise mangled to fit within their new homes.

Throughout this horrific relocation process, City Cemetery was littered with body parts, which were mixed up and shoved into the nearest available casket. The stench of death filled the surrounding neighborhoods, as the workers became more callous with each passing day. Eventually, the hired laborers began looting the graves, stealing whatever jewelry or personal belongings they could find.

Psychics living in the area had warned the city workers to say a prayer for each body exhumed, lest the dead become angry. These words were ignored, but the prophecy proved all too true. As the workers continued stealing from the corpses, they began to feel a sinister presence growing around them. Finally, a grave robber was actually attacked as he attempted to remove brass from one of the coffins: The spectral assailant leaped on the worker's back, beating him around the face and head until the hapless man ran from the cemetery and vowed never to return. This first manifestation opened a floodgate of spectral activity the likes of which has seldom been reported in all history.

The ghosts rose from their graves in such massive numbers that almost all the men digging up the cemetery reported at least one sighting. Although hardened by years of grueling labor, many of the workers were frightened away from the site for good. Soon, the ghosts spread into the surrounding neighborhoods as well. The spirits were first seen roaming the streets aimlessly, and then local authorities received innumerable calls from frantic citizens who claimed that confused ghosts had wandered out of the cemetery and into their homes. Others sighted the phantoms in mirrors or hovering over their shoulders.

Finally, public outcry transformed the transgressions against the dead of City Cemetery into a major scandal. This, combined with a genuine concern for the public health, prompted Mayor Platt Rogers to halt the relocation process. The workers abandoned the site, leaving behind a mess of bodies and body parts. Investigators could not clean up the mess, and the entire area was furrowed under. In a halfhearted attempt to correct the mistake, grass and trees were planted and the cemetery was converted into Cheesman Park.

However, the ghosts of the past have not left. While phantoms are rarely reported, many people have heard unearthly moaning from beneath the ground. The ghosts frequently whisper, mumble, and scream as well. In addition, psychics who visit the place feel a profound sense of sorrow and bewilderment, as if the dead have yet to fully comprehend the horror that they have been forced to endure.

Finding the ghosts of Cheesman Park is best reserved for sensitives who have a proven ability to detect emotional auras. If you feel strong auras of fear, loathing, sadness, depression, or other overwhelming emotions while visiting any of the haunted sites described in this book, you may have psychic gifts and should consider exploring Cheesman Park. The Botanical Gardens and the area of the park known as Congress Park can be ignored, for these were once the cemetery's Catholic and Jewish sections respectively; the dead in these sections were removed long ago and have not returned as ghosts. All other areas of Cheesman Park should be investigated. Spend time with your ear pressed to the ground, listening for the sounds of the spirits trapped below. It is also wise to carry a small mirror at all times. As you gaze into this device, watch for phantoms that may appear over your shoulder.

If you encounter a spirit while in Cheesman Park, try to gently explain that the tragedy which occurred at the site so long ago was the result of ignorance, inept politicians, and base human greed. If at all possible, try to convince the ghost to leave behind the mortal world, despite the injustice it may have suffered. If the specter can lead you to its remains, uncover whatever is left of the body and have it properly interred in consecrated ground. Any of these steps could finally release the spirit from this plane and allow it peace at last.

INTERSTATE 65 AND THE SACRED CREEK BURIAL GROUND

VITAL STATISTICS

LOCATION: The portion of I-65 considered haunted is the forty-mile stretch of road in south central Alabama running from Greenville to Evergreen.

NUMBER OF GHOSTLY RESIDENTS: Unknown

IDENTITIES OF GHOSTLY RESIDENTS: Presumably the spirits of dead Creek Indians and the ghosts of highway fatalities

TYPE OF ACTIVITY: An aura of misfortune

DEMEANOR OF GHOSTLY RESIDENTS: Angry and vengeful. The aura of misfortune surrounding I-65 is believed to emanate from the remains of Native Americans buried near the site. These ghosts are furious over their suffering at the hands of colonists and settlers.

ENCOUNTERING THE GHOSTS OF I-65:

Of all the vengeful dead, few are as tenacious as the spirits of Native Americans wrongfully persecuted and murdered by whites. Such specters appear throughout the country, where they are blamed for a host of misfortunes ranging from bad crops to sudden deaths. When the sacred values of these Native American spirits are trampled, their rage grows even more intense. Such forces are evidently at work along a stretch of I-65 in south central Alabama, a section of road considered to be among the most dangerous in the nation.

The forty miles of highway running between Evergreen and Greenville was, quite unfortunately, built upon a Creek burial site. The area was used by the Creek Indians to house and honor their dead long before the arrival of whites. In the 1830s, however, the Creek were forced to leave the land and relocate to Oklahoma. The move was emotionally devastating, as the Creek were deeply devoted to their homelands, but it also proved deadly as well: Of the 15,000 Creek who were driven from Alabama, more than 3,500 perished during the arduous journey.

The sad fate of the Creek peoples was not lost upon their dead ancestors. As early as the 1840s, reports of strange happenings at various burial sites throughout the former Creek territory were being reported. Thus, when whites extended I-65 between Greenville and Evergreen, they defiled a sacred site and engendered the wrath of spirits already hateful toward the non-Natives.

This rage has manifested clearly. From 1984 to 1990, the stretch of I-65 atop the Creek burial grounds claimed over twenty-three lives; 519 accidents and at least 208 injuries were also recorded in this six-year time period. Authorities have been unable to explain the highway's unusually high accident rate, as I-65 is a straight, even roadway, impeccably maintained and patrolled. Most supernaturalists believe that the spirits of the dead have come back to haunt I-65.

When traveling I-65, watch for ghost lights, flaming apparitions, or other sudden ghostly manifestations that might cause a driver to lose control and crash. Also be cognizant of your ability to operate your motor vehicle. Should you begin to feel drowsy, confused, or panicked, pull over until you regain your composure. Other effects of the highway's spectral community may include sudden blindness, loss of depth perception, and unexplained mechanical failures ranging from an unexpected blowout to a spontaneous engine fire. Ghost hunters trekking this portion of Alabama should carry flares, a first aid kit, at least one spare tire, extra spark plugs and fuses, a fire extinguisher, a working flashlight, a fully charged car battery, and a wide array of tools.

MCCONNICO CEMETERY

VITAL STATISTICS

LOCATION: McConnico Cemetery, Monroe County, Alabama, near I-84 and the Alabama River. Mount Pleasant Road runs near the cemetery and is the most actively haunted area.

NUMBER OF GHOSTLY RESIDENTS: Twelve (twenty-four counting the horses ridden by the human phantoms)

IDENTITIES OF GHOSTLY RESIDENTS: All the ghosts are dead Union soldiers on horseback.

TYPE OF ACTIVITY: Phantoms

DEMEANOR OF GHOSTLY RESIDENTS: Orderly, disciplined, and dignified. While generally considered passive, these ghosts may be searching for new ears to replace those they have lost and could, conceivably, attack humans in this pursuit.

ENCOUNTERING THE GHOSTS OF MCCONNICO CEMETERY:

One of the most prevalent types of ghosts are the spirits of those who have lost body parts just prior to, during, or immediately after their deaths. Often, the mere fact that one dies missing a major limb or feature prevents the ghost from resting peacefully. In fact, the spirit may be motivated to return to the land of the living in search of the lost body part. Native American folklore confirms this behavior: Among many tribes, there are tales claiming that one who dies with an incomplete body will never be able to find peace in the afterlife. Headless phantoms are the best known of these apparitions, but ghosts without legs, arms, eyes, noses, and other glaring absences have also been widely reported both in North America and around the globe.

The ghosts of McConnico Cemetery typify the "physical mutilation" ghost. Numbering twelve in all, these phantoms are spotted wandering the borders of the cemetery on horseback. They wear the garb of Union soldiers and travel in an orderly procession formed of two columns, each consisting of six horsemen. Along with their stained and tattered uniforms, they wear white gloves and have white bandages wound about their bowed heads.

According to lore, these twelve soldiers were unfortunate victims of Lafayette Seigler, a Confederate officer known for ambushing Union troops at every possible opportunity. Seigler always killed his captives, but not until he had cut away their ears with his knife. The Confederate had an expansive collection of ears by the time the Civil War ended, twenty-four of which belong to the phantom horsemen of McConnico Cemetery.

The wounded cavalrymen of McConnico were first spotted in 1865 by Captain and Mrs. Charles Locklin, both considered upstanding and honest citizens. The Locklins testified to the identity of the phantom horsemen, who have been reported dozens of times in the past 130 years.

The only mystery surrounding the Union phantoms is their attachment to McConnico Cemetery and the surrounding area. It is unknown whether they were actually murdered at the site or were buried in the vicinity after their deaths. Regardless, the McConnico Cemetery ghosts are observed in all corners of the cemetery, but most often they travel down Mount Pleasant Road near the site. They are completely silent, never attempt conversation, and move very slowly. On rare occasions, they look up from their mounts, but usually they keep their heads down as their horses plod forward.

When they manifest, the Union soldiers are easy to spot, for they remain in the area for several minutes and do not try to vanish or run away. However, they should be observed from a distance: Like many ghosts of this nature, they may be searching for new ears to replace those lost so long ago. If this is the case, they could attack anyone whose ears look suitable for the taking.

MISSION SAN ANTONIO DE PADUA

VITAL STATISTICS

LOCATION: Fort Hunter Liggett, Mission Creek Road, Monterey County, California. The mission is situated near U.S. Highway 101, about twenty miles south of King City. Call (408) 385-4478 for hours of operation and complete directions.

NUMBER OF GHOSTLY RESIDENTS: At least three

IDENTITIES OF GHOSTLY RESIDENTS: A headless horsewoman, numerous friars, and Gigi Giardino, a little girl buried at the mission

TYPE OF ACTIVITY: Ghost lights, phantoms, disembodied footsteps, strange auras, and flowers that appear mysteriously

DEMEANOR OF GHOSTLY RESIDENTS: Serene and peaceful. Only the headless horsewoman is in the least bit frightening, but even she has never shown any aggressive tendencies.

ENCOUNTERING THE MISSION SAN ANTONIO GHOSTS: RIP RIP RIP

Churches, cathedrals, and any other locations where funeral rites are routinely held often suffer hauntings. Missions, in particular, are prone to ghostly manifestations because they are usually the homes of monks, friars, and other religious individuals who return to the sites after death, perhaps seeking to visit the one place they were truly at peace. The vast majority of the missions throughout the southwestern United States suffer some form of supernatural phenomena, but few are as active as the Mission San Antonio in California.

Like many other haunted missions, Mission San Antonio is inhabited by at least one ghostly friar, who wanders the hallways at night. He wears a long robe and carries a candle. Usually, he moves into the chapel and prays for a moment before vanishing. Other, formless apparitions believed to be the spirits of the dead Franciscan monks who built the mission have also been observed floating through the courtyard, and their footsteps have been heard in the attic.

Along with phantom friars, the mission is visited by numerous ghost lights of every hue and size. More frightening, however, is the headless horsewoman found roaming the edges of the mission atop a spectral steed. The woman wears a white petticoat, but is bare-breasted. Most reports indicate that she is the angry ghost of a murdered Native American woman.

The most common tale surrounding the headless horsewoman claims that she married a gold miner (or a Spaniard), who later caught her in a tryst with another man. In a rage, the jilted husband butchered his wife, her lover, and her favorite horse with an ax. To prevent her from achieving peace in the afterlife, the husband decapitated the woman and buried her head and body in separate holes. Now, the woman rises each night and, with the aid of her faithful steed, searches for her lost head.

The headless horsewoman has been sighted almost two dozen times. Officers and soldiers stationed at the nearby Fort Hunter Liggett have also reported encounters with the mutilated woman. In one case, four MPs spotted the specter and chased her in their Jeep. Although they pursued her for several miles, she eventually outdistanced them and vanished.

The most surprising supernatural development surrounds the death of a young girl named Gigi Giardino, who was struck down by cancer at the age of seven. Her request to be buried at the mission was honored by the Franciscan monks. Miraculously, a short time after she was interred, the friars found that a beautiful patch of violets had appeared on her grave. Normally, violets would not survive in the hundred-degree heat that bombards the mission during the summer, and yet these delicate flowers have thrived at the site. Moreover, when Gigi's mother passed away, one of the brothers living at the mission noted that a single white violet appeared amid the purple flowers.

The Mission San Antonio is so overrun by supernatural forces that it prompted writer Richard Senate to become an avid ghost hunter after he encountered a phantom monk at the site. Archaeologists, psychics, and countless visitors, as well as current brothers living in the mission, have sensed the unseen spirits, proving that this is one of the most active haunted sites in the country.

The Mission San Antonio is not a routine tourist stop, although it is open to visitors. This makes it a quaint research site for ghost hunters who wish to avoid crowds and morbid curiosity seekers. Be sure to call in advance to arrange your visit, and remember that the ghosts appear both day and night, allowing one to enter the mission during normal hours of operation and still encounter a spirit.

Throughout your exploration of this haunted site, treat the mission and its inhabitants with unfaltering respect. Any show of irreverence could enrage the local spirits, resulting in a healthy dose of bad luck or some other fate far worse. As in the case of the McConnico Union soldiers described previously, avoid the headless horsewoman if at all possible. She may, of course, be harmless; but if she is searching for a new head to replace the one that was taken from her, you may find yourself hounded by the apparition until you too are decapitated.

RESURRECTION CEMETERY AND RESURRECTION MARY

VITAL STATISTICS

LOCATION: 7600 S. Archer Avenue, Justice, Illinois 60458. Directions can be obtained at (312) 767-4644.

NUMBER OF GHOSTLY RESIDENTS: One

IDENTITY OF GHOSTLY RESIDENT: Mary Bregavy, or Resurrection Mary, killed in a car crash in 1934 (or 1931, depending on the source)

TYPE OF ACTIVITY: Phantom

DEMEANOR OF GHOSTLY RESIDENT: Wayward and uneasy. Resurrection Mary has difficulty remaining in her grave and enjoys wandering abroad in pursuit of some unknown goal. In her travels, she has never harmed anyone, but her manifestations are usually unsettling.

ENCOUNTERING RESURRECTION MARY:

V anishing hitchhikers are a well-known breed of ghost, so named because they are often spotted alongside lonely roads at night. They almost always appear as young women, usually wearing flimsy dresses despite the cold weather. When they are picked up by sympathetic motorists, they seem completely alive and normal. Many engage in animated conversations while giving detailed directions "home."

However, as the motorist transporting a vanishing hitchhiker nears the house designated by the ghost, he (for the drivers are frequently male) turns to find that the lovely girl has disappeared. Hoping that the girl has somehow silently slipped from the car, the confused Samaritan knocks on the front door. He is invariably met by the hitchhiker's mother, who confides that the girl in question has been dead for many years.

The tale related above is typical of vanishing hitchhiker cases, but for every rule there is an exception, and the exception here proves to be Resurrection Mary. Mary is different from the vast majority of vanishing hitchhikers because she actually directs motorists to her *new* home: the Resurrection Cemetery.

Resurrection Mary was once known as Mary Bregavy, a young Polish girl with striking blue eyes and beautiful blond hair. In the early 1930s, Mary was returning from a dance at the O'Henry Ballroom (which has since been renamed the Willowbrook Ballroom) when her escort lost control of his vehicle along Archer Avenue. Mary was killed in the crash, and she was buried in Resurrection Cemetery wearing her white evening gown and dancing shoes.

About five years after Mary's death, motorists began spying a female apparition along Archer Avenue. Described as a young woman wearing an outdated white dress, Mary is often seen wandering the shoulder of the road or hitchhiking. If a car stops, she readily accepts a ride. Other times, she suddenly leaps into vehicles, often passing right through the closed passenger door. In a smattering of reports, she appeared at the ballroom, where she danced with a few men before requesting a ride home.

Regardless of the method by which she gains entrance to a car, Mary always asks to be taken home to Resurrection Cemetery. When the bewildered driver (who may or may not have realized that his passenger is a ghost) opens the door for the girl, she politely says goodnight, walks to the bars surrounding the graveyard, and simply passes through the iron gates.

In the 1970s, the Resurrection Cemetery underwent a series of renovations, during which time Mary made a record number of appearances, as if the turmoil from the remodeling drove her from her grave. The most sensational of the decade's sightings occurred in 1979, when a motorist passing the cemetery spotted a young girl clutching the iron gates. Believing that the girl was trapped in the graveyard, the driver called the police. By the time the authorities arrived, the young woman had vanished. Yet investigators discovered two small handprints etched into the iron bars, which were visibly bent apart.

Since 1979, Resurrection Mary has continued to manifest repeatedly along Archer Avenue. Frequently she is observed by taxi drivers, who often take pity on the girl and offer her a free ride. In 1989, one cabbie encountered a pretty young girl in white at the Old Willow Shopping Center. He offered her a lift, but when they passed the Resurrection Cemetery, she disappeared from his side.

Resurrection Mary remains one of the most reliable and oft-reported vanishing hitchhikers in the world today. Her legend has spread to all parts of the country, and her name has been applied to several unidentified copycat roadside phantoms. For these reasons, she is often a compelling subject for ghost hunters, who should be encouraged to search for the girl.

In order to find Resurrection Mary, travel Archer Avenue alone on particularly cold, stormy, or dark nights. Drive slowly and keep your eyes fixed on the side of the road. Male ghost hunters have a much better chance of interacting with Mary, but any diligent researcher should be able to catch a glimpse of the phantom. If you are approached by Mary, kindly offer her a ride. She is completely harmless and has never caused anyone an ounce of bad luck, but be prepared for her sudden departure when you reach the cemetery. Many drivers are emotionally or mentally scarred simply because they cannot cope with the impossibility of Resurrection Mary's existence and abilities. Do not be lulled by her seeming normalcy, and do not be shocked when she glides from your car and effortlessly passes through the cemetery gates.

SAINT MARK'S EPISCOPAL CHURCH

VITAL STATISTICS

LOCATION: Nineteenth Street and Central Avenue, Cheyenne, Wyoming 82001. The church can be reached at (307) 634-7709. The haunted room is located below the carillon bells and can be identified by the fact that it is surrounded by Gothic windows.

NUMBER OF GHOSTLY RESIDENTS: One

IDENTITIES OF GHOSTLY RESIDENTS: A Swedish stonemason buried in the church's foundation

TYPE OF ACTIVITY: Poltergeists, mysterious footsteps, a disembodied voice, and a phantom

DEMEANOR OF GHOSTLY RESIDENT: Content. In the past, this spirit was restless and prone to creating disturbances, but he has since found a way to peacefully coexist with his living neighbors.

ENCOUNTERING THE GHOST OF SAINT MARK'S EPISCOPAL CHURCH: RIP RIP

Few ghosts enjoy full acceptance by the living, and those spirits who haunt churches and cathedrals are even less likely to find understanding mortals living nearby. Given these sad facts, it is apparent that the specter inhabiting Saint Mark's Episcopal Church in Cheyenne, Wyoming, is extremely fortunate, for not only has he been embraced by the church, the institution has even constructed a private room for the phantom.

Like most hauntings, the Saint Mark's spirit was conceived from tragedy. The church was originally constructed in 1868, but in 1886 the congregation elected to add a bell tower to the house of worship. Unfortunately, work on the tower stalled when two Swedish stonemasons hired to perform the job mysteriously vanished. The church elders were so disturbed by the sudden disappearance that they delayed the tower's completion for another forty years. During these intervening years, the rector repeatedly heard the sound of hammering and whispering in the attic, which was directly above his own room, although no one could be found in the area.

Finally, construction was resumed on the bell tower in 1926. However, the workers began experiencing strange poltergeist disturbances and repeatedly threatened to quit the site. The project was continually halted, and almost fell apart completely when the laborers were chased from the site by a phantom. Finally, it was decided that the construction crew would build the ghost its own private room. The workers complied and crafted an ornate, hidden room in the church that can only be reached by climbing an eighty-five-foot spiral staircase originating in a concealed compartment in the basement.

The ghost took up residence in the secret room and stopped harassing the construction crew. The bell tower was finally completed, and the church seemed to return to normal. However, several years later, the phantom reappeared. Many witnesses encountered the ghost wandering the church, whispering strange secrets involving a body entombed somewhere in the building's walls.

In 1966, the spirit's eerie claim was proven to be true. One of the Swedish stonemasons who had seemingly vanished in 1886 came forward, miraculously still alive after eighty years. He confessed that his partner had plummeted from the bell tower and been killed. Fearing that he would be suspected of foul play, the surviving stonemason shoved the corpse into a four-foot-wide opening in the church's foundation. He sealed the hole and quickly fled the region.

Now that the circumstances of his death have been revealed, the dead stonemason seems to have become somewhat inactive. But because his body has never been discovered or provided with a proper burial, his ghost will likely remain at the site for quite some time. Fortunately, he seems content to remain in his hidden room and seldom ventures forth to frighten visitors.

The only reliable method for contacting the ghost of Saint Mark's is by gaining access to the secret room. This can only be done from the basement, where the spiral staircase begins, and only with the permission of the church staff. Please consult with the church's rector if you plan to visit the site. Also, keep in mind that the church has every right to refuse your request to see the ghost's room, as it has always been reserved as the phantom's own personal quarters.

SILVER CLIFF CEMETERY

VITAL STATISTICS

LOCATION: Silver Cliff, Colorado, at the junction of Highway 69 and Highway 96, about sixty miles southwest of Colorado Springs and located near Rosita in the Wet Mountains

NUMBER OF GHOSTLY RESIDENTS: Unknown

IDENTITIES OF GHOSTLY RESIDENTS: Possibly dead pioneers or Native American spirits

TYPE OF ACTIVITY: Ghost lights

DEMEANOR OF GHOSTLY RESIDENTS: Puzzling and detached. The Sliver Cliff ghost lights have never interacted with humans in any way, so they cannot be considered dangerous.

ENCOUNTERING THE SILVER CLIFF GHOSTS:

RIP RIP RIP RIP

The most active ghost lights in North America may very well be the Silver Cliff Cemetery spooks. These apparitions, believed by many to be the spirits of dead pioneers and prospectors, manifest as twinkling blue lights that float above the headstones throughout the graveyard.

The community of Silver Cliff is just over one hundred years old. The town sprang up in the 1880s, when a cache of silver was unearthed in the Wet Mountain Valley, attracting hordes of miners. Within a few months, Silver Cliff boasted over five thousand citizens. Life was harsh in the mining town, and the first deaths were recorded within a year after the town's foundation. These unfortunates were buried in the new Silver Cliff Cemetery, and soon after a group of prospectors observed a series of glowing lights in the graveyard. Because these early witnesses were drunk at the time of the sighting, their report was largely ignored until other citizens came forward with similar tales. The ghost lights rapidly became well known to Silver Cliff's residents, who felt that the lights were the ghostly lanterns of dead miners searching for precious metals.

A few years after the settlers arrived in Silver Cliff, the nearby silver lode was depleted. The town began to shrink as miners left in search of more prosperous regions. Within fifty years, only about a hundred people remained in the town. Despite this mass exodus, the ghost lights lingered in the Silver Cliff Cemetery and continued to appear to the small handful of local residents.

In 1956, the ghost lights of this small ex–mining town began to attract even greater attention. That year, an article about the spirits was published in the *Wet Mountain Tribune*, a local newspaper. By 1967, the story of the floating balls of light had reached the *New York Times*. After that venerable paper published news of the ghost lights, tourists and investigators flocked to Silver Cliff.

Finally, the Silver Cliff spirits received full recognition when Edward J. Linehan, *National Geographic*'s assistant editor, visited the site in 1969. He recorded his encounter with one of the lights in vivid detail, describing how he and another man chased one of the "dim, round spots of blue-white light" for over twenty-five minutes. Several of the lights appeared before Linehan, then disappeared again as he approached them, during the course of investigation.

Since Linehan's sightings, numerous scientists, researchers, skeptics, and psychics have tried to explain the phenomenon. Some claim that the ghosts are little more than reflected lights from nearby towns or passing automobiles, although this theory has been continually disproved on countless occasions. Radiation has been suggested as the cause of these and similar ghost lights, but Geiger counters have failed to detect radioactive material at the site. Others hold that the ghost lights are caused by bog gas, released from decaying matter beneath the ground; unfortunately, no one has been buried in the graveyard for decades and all of the cemetery's current residents rotted away long ago.

Although the ghost lights may very well be the spirits of dead prospectors, as many locals still believe, they may also be much older than the town of Silver Cliff. In some Native American traditions, the dead were buried in sacred hills charged with supernatural energy. According to folklorist Dale Ferguson, these "dead men's hills" were often visited by "dancing blue spirits."

The Silver Cliff Cemetery spirits are still quite active. At night they can frequently be observed weaving through the headstones, going about their cryptic business. They do not interact with humans and cannot be summoned through any known means, but they manifest on most nights, especially when the ground fog is thick. If you spot the ghost lights while investigating the site, be sure to keep a respectable distance; although the spirits are completely harmless, they tend to vanish suddenly if approached.

Other Haunted Cemeteries and Burial Sites

Below is a list of graveyards and such believed to be haunted by at least one ghost. Many others exist across the continent, but those described previously and below are among the most prominent and active.

- **Bladon Springs Cemetery, Bladon Springs, Alabama:** The anguished Captain Norman Staples returns from the dead to protect the graves of his four children, all buried at this site.

- **Westwood Memorial Cemetery, Westwood, California:** One of the most famous women in all the world, Marilyn Monroe, is buried in this graveyard. Her apparition is often sighted rising from the ground.

- **Los Angeles Pet Cemetery, Calabasas, California:** Several animal actors and the pets of many famous celebrities have been interred here, but few have found rest in death. The most active ghost is the playful spirit of Rudolph Valentino's Great Dane, Kabar.

- **Union Cemetery, Easton, Connecticut:** Ghosts who enjoy talking to visitors live in this graveyard. They are often encountered by their loved ones.

- **Huguenot Cemetery, Saint Augustine, Florida:** In the 1800s, a corpse buried in this cemetery, one of the oldest in America, was pulled from his grave and beheaded by unknown vandals. Ever since this transgression, a headless phantom has been spotted wandering the graveyard as if searching for its missing noggin.

- **New Enterprise Freewill Baptist Church Cemetery, Bainbridge, Georgia:** Among the strange spirits haunting this site are a fiery ball of light and a huge black demon dog that leaves no footprints as it patrols the graves.

- **Park Cemetery, Fairmount, Indiana:** This cemetery holds the remains of actor James Dean, tragically killed when his Porsche spun out of control on Highway 46 in Los Angeles (an area also believed to be haunted by the sounds of screeching tires). Literally hundreds of people visit Dean's grave each year, and many report feeling the actor's presence nearby. Others claim that they have actually spoken to his invisible spirit.

- **Oak Hill Cemetery, Cedar Rapids, Iowa:** One of the few ghosts known to actually attack mortals resides at this graveyard. Believed to be the spirit of a young Czech girl named Tillie, the specter frequently attempts to grab visitors and drag them into one of the cemetery's mausoleums. When not harassing guests, she strolls through the headstones carrying a candle.

- **Stull Cemetery, Kansas City, Kansas:** One of the most evil haunted sites in all the world, Stull Cemetery is often referred to as the Gates of Hell because of the dark energy that surrounds the place. A "devil child" is allegedly buried here, a fact that has attracted numerous cultists and satanists to the area to perform vile rituals. The spirit of a teenager struck down by typhoid fever also manifests in the trees here, often taking the form of a large black werewolf.

- **Saint Louis Cemetery, New Orleans, Louisiana:** This site is home to the infamous Voodoo queen Marie Laveau, whose grave is marked by graffiti, Voodoo offerings, and a large **X**. The witch's soul often appears as a large black crow or a massive black dog.

The Top Ten Causes of Ghost-Inducing Death

There are certain causes of mortal death that inevitably result in a spectral manifestation of some sort. Below is a list of the tragic fates known to generate ghosts, ordered from least significant to most significant. Note that any of the deaths listed below can be the result of either a murder or suicide—both of which are likely to force a ghost to rise, regardless of the means by which the murder or suicide was accomplished—but this list is more concerned with the exact clinical cause of death.

10. **Poisoning,** which includes, but is not limited to, the intentional consumption of a lethal substance, the accidental ingestion of a caustic substance (such as a cleaning solvent), a drug overdose, an allergic reaction to medicine, and other cases in which a natural or manufactured chemical disagrees violently with the subject's physiology. Most poisonings are incredibly painful affairs, resulting in internal hemorrhaging, massive swelling of the extremities, hysteria, blindness, organ failure, and other symptoms. People who have suffered in this manner are likely to reappear as ghosts. Suicides are especially prone to becoming specters: Many of these individuals believe that an overdose of sleeping pills will deliver them into death peacefully, only to be rudely awakened when their stomachs rupture. After being cheated out of a quiet demise, they may find themselves compelled to rise again as phantoms who wallow in self-pity and loneliness.

9. **Starvation,** which is the simple deprivation of food. Starvation is an agonizing process in which the body slowly digests itself to compensate for a lack of food. Such victims are usually lost and lonely at the time of their deaths, factors that further heighten the likelihood they will return as ghosts.

8. **Disease** or death due to any type of plague, incurable sickness, or physical degeneration. When a disease afflicts a young person, it is especially prone to creating a ghost. Plagues that sweep through entire villages, towns, or colonies can result in a mass uprising of ghosts who feel that they have been cheated by early deaths.

7. **Drowning** beneath the waves of the ocean, a lake, river, or other body of water. Drowning victims are often suicides who have leaped from bluffs or cliffs into the frigid embrace of a churning sea. A great number are also sailors who perished aboard lost ships. If they do not manifest as phantom vessels, the ghosts of the drowned may appear as pale specters wandering the shores near the site of their demise.

6. **Immolation** or any other death resulting from exposure to intense heat or flames. When someone burns alive, they actually suffocate after the flames surrounding

the victim consume all nearby oxygen. The torturous demise can take minutes, time spent writhing in agony as skin bubbles and blackens. Some people who are burned alive survive long enough to feel their eyeballs rupture. Most ghosts who died due to immolation appear as fiery spirits still ensconced in glowing, flickering flames.

5. **Strangulation,** either through hanging, being choked to death by another, autoerotic asphyxiation, or other means in which the windpipe is crushed and the brain is deprived of oxygen. Like almost every other method of death described here, strangulation can be a slow and torturous process before one finally loses consciousness. While a hanging is meant to break the victim's neck and kill instantly, the procedure is often botched and the subject can be left dangling for up to an hour before death occurs. Clearly, such trauma is suitable for generating a ghost.

4. **Severe body or head trauma,** usually the result of being crushed, trampled, mauled, or bludgeoned. Most ghosts who have died in this manner perished from internal injuries of some sort. Victims of car accidents form the bulk of these spirits, but those who have fallen from great heights or who have suffered similar accidents also appear frequently. A small percentage of the ghosts in this category exhibit signs of their injuries (such as bruises or broken limbs) in their phantom forms.

3. **Shooting,** including those who are killed instantly by a single bullet and those who bleed to death after being shot several times. In either case, death is incredibly violent and often unexpected. Ghostly gunfighters, gangsters, and police officers often fall into this category.

2. **Stabbing** or any other death attributed to wounds caused by a sharp object. Most victims bleed to death after being punctured in the gut or chest by a long, vicious knife. Others may receive several blows from an ax or have their brains punctured by a screwdriver or awl, resulting in instant death. In any case, these deaths are usually very personal, incredibly violent, and cause a great deal of bloodshed. The ghosts that result may wear bloodstained garments or display the murder weapon still embedded in their bodies.

1. **Decapitation or dismemberment.** As evidenced by the hundreds of reports of headless ghosts, those individuals who lose their heads in battle, murder, or even suicide (as a result of a mishap during a hanging attempt), are likely to return in search of their lost heads. This compulsion may be a result of a desire to be recognized in the afterlife. Headless ghosts are almost always violent and willing to kill to achieve their goals.

Corbis-Bettmann

- **Old York Cemetery, York Village, Maine:** The kindly ghost of a white witch named Mary Miller Jason receives visitors at her grave here. She has appeared frequently since her death in 1774, and often plays with children in a park across the street.

- **Loon Lake Cemetery, Lakefield, Minnesota:** Yet more witches haunt this graveyard, where three women murdered for practicing the black arts rise up from their faded headstones at night. The most active of the witches is "Witch Mary Jane," who was decapitated by a mob in October of 1881.

- **Laurel Grove Cemetery, Totowa, New Jersey:** This graveyard is haunted by a woman in white, who is often noticed by passing motorists as she wanders the roads around the cemetery.

- **Camp Chase Confederate Cemetery, Columbus, Ohio:** During a Civil War memorial ceremony held at this site in 1988, ghostly weeping was heard by several witnesses. The sobs may have belonged to the Lady in Gray, a mourning ghost who frequently appears near the grave of Ben-

jamin Allen. She is also known to pass through trees, gates, and headstones as she circles the grave of the Unknown Soldier.

- **Apache Cemetery, Lawton, Oklahoma:** Home to the fallen Geronimo, who died imprisoned at Fort Sill, Apache Cemetery is infused with the dead warrior's proud and noble spirit.

- **Chestnut Hill Cemetery, Exeter, Rhode Island:** This cemetery has been haunted since 1892 by the spirit of Mercy Brown, who was pulled from her grave and mutilated by her own father. George Brown believed that his daughter had risen as a vampire and killed her mother and older sister (who both really died of tuberculosis). To prevent her from continuing the murders, he had Mercy exhumed and ordered her heart and liver burned. Mercy now appears as a ghostly ball of blue light.

- **All Saints Waccamaw Cemetery, Myrtle Beach, South Carolina:** Alice Flagg, buried beneath a marker that reads simply "Alice," can be summoned to this site by walking backwards around her grave thirteen times. When she does appear, she places flowers near her headstone, then vanishes.

- **Old Berkeley Cemetery, Charles City, Virginia:** Among the many ghosts at this site is a forlorn little boy with red hair and a drum. The sad spirit stands on a hilltop, beating his drum and staring out at the James River.

4. NATURAL HAUNTS

MORTALS HAVE *ALWAYS* encountered ghosts.

Long before the rise of modern civilization, lonely caves, overgrown riverbanks, windswept beaches, twisted forests, and endless plains were home to spirits of every kind. Even boulders, toadstool rings, and individual trees could serve as a specter's lair. These locations, often known as power points or sacred sites, overflow with supernatural energies and are viewed by ghost hunters as the original "haunted houses." In fact, in recent years it has been revealed that a great many of North America's haunted buildings were originally constructed atop sites that Native Americans believed to be haunted, sacred, or otherwise saturated with energies beyond mortal comprehension. While it is unknown whether or not such power points actually create ghosts or merely attract them, natural sites continue to be among the most active haunted locales on the continent.

Almost all natural haunted sites share a number of traits that are, quite logically, ex-hibited by most other haunted locations as well. For instance, a large percentage of natural haunts are near a body of water, a trend also found in haunted cemeteries and other burial sites (see chapter 3).

The most obvious attribute used to identify a natural haunt is the somber atmosphere that clings to such places. Although often located in the heart of pristine nature (such as in the center of a forest or along an isolated stretch of coastline), natural haunts are devoid of any signs of life and are likely to be surrounded by an eerie stillness. Foliage may have difficulty growing within a few feet of the haunt, and the sounds of birds or other animals will be strangely absent. The climate around a natural haunt operates by its own rules: For example, ghost hunters who approach one of these locations will find that the breeze they may have enjoyed earlier in the day has suddenly been replaced by a chilling wind.

Because of the overriding supernatural presence, numerous natural haunts are considered cursed. Misfortune, ranging from injury to death, afflicts a staggering number of people who visit such haunted locales. In many cases, those who are slain by a natural site's "curse" rise again to join the ranks of those haunting the area, further intensifying the spectral manifestations.

However, lest one assume that all natural haunts are evil or malign, it must be noted that a great many are also places of great serenity and beauty. In some cases, the supernatural energies present actually enhance the natural surroundings to an amazing degree. Water blessed by paranormal forces is often pure and capable of cleansing the body and mind; while a forest "haunted" by benevolent spirits can actually be welcoming and pleasant. For this reason, many people are drawn to such sites for meditation and reflection. In fact, many mortals become extremely attached to these retreats and refuse to leave, even after death. Thus, nature's most divine creations often become haunted by kindly ghosts who simply wish to enjoy the beauty of the natural world for all eternity.

BOSTON PUBLIC GARDENS

VITAL STATISTICS

LOCATION: Central Boston, Massachusetts, near the Boston Common

NUMBER OF GHOSTLY RESIDENTS: Two

IDENTITIES OF GHOSTLY RESIDENTS: Unknown, but believed to be guests of the Ritz-Carlton during the 1930s

TYPE OF ACTIVITY: Phantoms

DEMEANOR OF GHOSTLY RESIDENTS: Kind and polite. These ghosts are simply enjoying a day out in the park and have little desire to molest the living.

ENCOUNTERING THE GHOSTS OF THE BOSTON PUBLIC GARDENS: RIP

Tranquil public gardens and parks are often scenes of hauntings because the dead find these places comforting in death, much as they did in life. One who visits a particular park, garden, campsite, or other location celebrating the beauty of nature may be prone to return to the site to escape the monotony of death. In such cases, the ghosts who visit these locales are happy and pose no threat to the living unless they are prevented from enjoying their brief outing.

The peaceful environs of the Boston Public Gardens, which allow the living to escape the hectic city, seems to invite ghosts as well as tourists and nature lovers. Situated in central

Boston, along the Boston Common, the gardens have hosted visits by a pair of kindly female ghosts who do nothing more than wander the area, enjoying the pastoral surroundings and fresh air. Although seemingly elderly, the women move gracefully, usually with their arms entwined. They are dressed in bright white dresses cut in the style of the 1930s and appear to belong to the social elite. Their faces are visibly pink, perhaps even flushed, but otherwise they are surrounded by a pale halo. At least one witness felt that the ghosts had emerged from the Ritz-Carlton, which looks onto the gardens, suggesting that the women may have been guests at the hotel at one time.

The spirits of the Boston Public Gardens are pleasant and gentle. They smile sweetly at those around them, are not averse to making eye contact with the living, and give no sign that they do not belong in this realm. They have been known to spend their time sitting on one of the park's benches, simply observing the world around them.

Encountering the Boston Public Gardens ghosts may be difficult, as they are rarely sighted. However, novice ghost hunters or those easily frightened by more active and aggressive spirits should begin their search for ghosts with this pair of friendly spirits. Begin by simply wandering the gardens, preferably on warm, sunny days. Spend some time observing the benches in view of the Ritz-Carlton and watch the hotel for any sign of the phantoms exiting the building. While visiting the gardens, wearing clothes in the style of the 1930s may be useful for attracting the ghosts.

When the spirits do appear, quietly observe them for a few moments. Glance about to discern if other people have also spotted the ghostly women, but be aware that the spirits usually appear before one witness at a time. Do not look away from the ghosts for more than a few seconds, as they will undoubtedly and inexplicably vanish.

After you have memorized their appearance, slowly make contact with the phantoms. Begin by establishing eye contact. Do not forget to smile broadly, as they seem to enjoy the happiness of others. If they return your gesture of friendship, wander over and attempt to converse with the ghosts. Any discussion should include gentle questions about the identities of the ghosts. Remember to be extremely polite and observe the social conventions of the 1930s: Speak formally, do not sit too close or attempt physical contact (unless invited to do so), and carry yourself in a genteel fashion.

Boston Public Garden.

DEVIL'S HOLE

VITAL STATISTICS

LOCATION: Niagara Falls, New York, near U.S. Highway 62, along the Niagara River Gorge. The spot is located between the Whirlpool Rapids and Lewiston.

NUMBER OF GHOSTLY RESIDENTS: Unknown, but presumably at least a dozen and probably many, many more

IDENTITIES OF GHOSTLY RESIDENTS: Unknown, but suspected to be the ghosts of those who were murdered or died in accidents near the site. The Seneca also believed that the Hole was home to the Evil One, a powerful entity who oversees all malignant spirits.

TYPE OF ACTIVITY: Incredible aura of misfortune, apparitions, and strange noises

DEMEANOR OF GHOSTLY RESIDENTS: Extremely tormented. Most of these ghosts died in accidents or were horribly murdered, and now suffer eternally in the cursed pit of Devil's Hole. They are not particularly dangerous, but the aura that surrounds the site can be lethal.

ENCOUNTERING THE GHOSTS OF DEVIL'S HOLE:

RIP RIP

Of all the sites across the continent cursed with an aura of sheer bad luck, few have caused as many tragedies as the Devil's Hole in Niagara Falls, New York. Known as a place of disaster long before white settlers arrived, the site earned its current name when the Seneca Indians told explorers that the twenty-foot-deep cave was the home of a malevolent entity known as the Evil One.

Charged with commanding legions of dark demons and vile spirits, the Evil One was said to rise up and murder any who disturbed its rest. Unfortunately, most who heard this tale dismissed it as ignorant superstition, and thus began a long series of calamities involving the Hole.

One of the earliest documented tragedies caused by Devil's Hole afflicted the famed French explorer Robert La Salle, who ignored the Seneca's persistent warnings and entered the site in the 1680s. His expedition was forever after plagued by accidents, unexplained deaths, and rampant illness. Unable to escape the curse of Devil's Hole, La Salle was butchered in 1687 by mutineers.

Throughout the three centuries since LaSalle's murder, Devil's Hole has continued to extinguish mortal life. In 1763, a group of British troops passing the cave were slaughtered by Native Americans. The bodies of the British were dumped into the rushing waters near the Hole and into the cave itself. In the years that followed, countless wagon trains carrying settlers into the West were similarly ambushed. In many cases, screaming women and children were violently pushed into Devil's Hole, where they fell to their deaths.

The Seneca themselves were also frequent victims of the Evil One lurking in Devil's Hole. Many one-sided battles pitting the

Seneca against well-armed British soldiers were waged close to the Hole, and numerous braves lost their lives within sight of the sinister cave. In most cases, the bodies of these warriors were unceremoniously dumped into the raging waters beneath the Hole. Later, when the Seneca were forced to wage war against American settlers throughout this region, the area surrounding Devil's Hole saw the deaths of an untold number of Indians *and* whites.

Devil's Hole has also caused at least two tragedies that affected the entire nation. Despite the Hole's notorious history, the builders of the Great Gorge Route Trolley allowed their carefully constructed line to pass extremely close to the cave of misfortune. After the trolley line was completed, hundreds of people were exposed to the terrible aura of Devil's Hole on a daily basis. This disastrous arrangement culminated in death in September of 1901, when President McKinley visited the Hole via the Great Gorge Route Trolley. Just hours later, he was assassinated.

The Hole's worst disaster occurred on July 1, 1917, when the Great Gorge Route Trolley derailed. One of the cars actually flew from the tracks, sending at least fifty screaming passengers into the gorge. There were no survivors.

In modern times, the body count at Devil's Hole continues to climb. Since 1850, the site has still averaged about one death a year, and today the bodies of those who plummet into Niagara Falls from Devil's Hole are recovered with frightening regularity. Most of these unfortunates slip and fall to their deaths or are

Devil's Hole.

killed in freak accidents, although murders and suicides in the area are also recorded.

The sheer number of untimely deaths connected to Devil's Hole has undoubtedly led to at least a few unhappy and irritated ghosts who are trapped at the site. Not surprisingly, visitors have reported many strange noises, including shrieks and moans, from within the cave. Phantoms of those who have died nearby have also been observed on rare occasion, usually replaying their deaths by leaping into the Falls or the cave itself.

Those ghost hunters who wish to explore Devil's Hole must do so at tremendous personal risk. Only those blessed with extremely good luck or who feel that they have nothing left to lose should even attempt to study this site. The forces at work in this area are so strong and unpredictable that even experienced ghost hunters with extraordinary climbing, survival, and caving skills are likely to fall victim to the cave's intense aura.

With the above warning in mind, if you do enter Devil's Hole, be very cognizant of every step you take and employ state-of-the-art climbing gear, as death can be just a slip away. Also be wary of those around you, including trusted partners or companions, as Devil's Hole seems to encourage betrayal and murder.

Although lonely and in pain, most of the ghosts within Devil's Hole are probably harm-less (but keep your distance all the same). How-ever, there is the possibility that the Evil One still resides within the cave. Unfortunately, there are no physical descriptions of the fiend. It could be a huge, amorphous cloud with red eyes and a booming voice, or it could be an in-visible poltergeist. Regardless, if you encounter anything that instills within you a sense of dread or even remotely resembles your interpre-tation of the "Evil One," flee immediately.

DEVIL'S TOWER

VITAL STATISTICS

LOCATION: Devil's Tower National Monument, Crook County, Wyoming. For directions and additional information, contact Devil's Tower National Monument, Devil's Tower, WY 82714; (307) 467-5370.

NUMBER OF GHOSTLY RESIDENTS: Unknown, but at least one powerful spirit and probably many of its minions

IDENTITIES OF GHOSTLY RESIDENTS: Unknown, but some of the phenomena reported atop the mountain have been alternately attributed to the spirit of the Great Bear or the mythical Thunderbird

TYPE OF ACTIVITY: Ghost lights and phantom animals

DEMEANOR OF GHOSTLY RESIDENTS: Beyond mortal comprehension. The ghosts atop Devil's Tower have their own, supernatural agendas. Fortunately, none seem intent on injuring humans.

ENCOUNTERING THE GHOSTS OF DEVIL'S TOWER:

Wyoming's Devil's Tower is among the most recogniz-able natural formations in the world and one of the most pow-erful supernatural sites on the continent. The Tower is a rock formation standing some 1,280 feet tall, and it is unique be-cause its peak is almost com-pletely flat. The geological oddity was named in 1875, and in 1906 it became the first American national monument at Teddy Roosevelt's request. Many readers will remember that the Tower was also the site of an alien landing in Steven Spielberg's 1977 film *Close En-counters of the Third Kind.*

Although whites know the rock column as Devil's Tower, some Native Americans called it "God's Tower" because of the proliferation of benevolent spir-its said to reside at the peak. The Sioux referred to it as *Mato Tipila* (or *Mateo Tipi*), which can be translated as "Bear

Copyright 19**11**
Perkins, Lead, S.D.

Library of Congress

The Devil's Tower.

Lodge." Regardless of its name, all local tribes believed Devil's Tower was an excellent site for vision quests and sacred ceremonies because it radiated supernatural power. Sitting Bull even visited the formation in an attempt to gain the mystical insight needed to defeat the white invaders.

The host of spirits said to occupy Devil's Tower is varied and vast. The most commonly cited is a phantom Thunderbird, a giant eagle or falcon with a wingspan capable of blocking out the sun. The bird is said to roost atop Devil's Tower, watching over the Sioux and the rest of the Native American tribes.

Another commonly sighted spirit, which has been observed well into modern times, is the Great Bear. Described as a giant animal surrounded by a blue aura, the Great Bear is often seen scaling the side of the Tower. Its might and wisdom are legendary, and it is said to be able to command numerous spirit animals throughout the region.

Finally, Devil's Tower is also haunted by a strange legend of abduction. According to Kiowa tales, once long ago seven young girls scaled the Tower and were taken up into the heavens by beings of vast power. There, the girls were transformed into the seven stars that make up the Pleiades cluster. From earth, the naked eye can only discern *six* of the Pleiades stars, although seven can be spied through a telescope, lending support to the Kiowa tale.

Today, Devil's Tower is most appropriate for ghost hunters seeking Native American spirits or supernatural manifestations. The site offers a comfortable change of pace for those tired of pursuing headless phantoms or pesky poltergeists, as the brand of haunting at this location is much more subdued. Anyone intent on excitement and danger may be bored by the restrained ghosts of Devil's Tower, but ghost hunters attuned to powerful auras, nature's beauty, and Native American influences should find the site extremely rewarding.

Aside from simply detecting the overwhelming supernatural energy at Devil's Tower, patient ghost hunters may encounter the Great Bear. As with most phantom animals, it is wise to keep your distance from this entity. Although its level of intelligence probably rivals most human intellects, the Great Bear is also unpredictable and vastly powerful. It may not take kindly to trespassers, especially non-Native ghost hunters unable to perform the proper rituals of respect or deference. If you are confronted by the creature, make sure to remember that the mountain belongs to the Great Bear and back away quickly. Unless the Great Bear invites contact, do not attempt any communication. Once you have reached a safe distance, observe the phantom until it disappears, but do not impede its progress in any way.

Other less understood phantoms and spirits may also be encountered on Devil's Tower. These could range from simple phantom animals serving the Great Bear to omnipotent animal totems, such as the Thunderbird. Use common sense when dealing with anything out of the ordinary in this area, and flee immediately if you feel at all threatened. Finally, there may be a possibility that Devil's Tower is indeed an alien landing site. While trekking through the area at night, be aware of any unusually bright lights, especially emanating from above. Such radiance could signal the arrival of a flying saucer or other alien craft. Depending upon your inclination to contact alien life forms, stand your ground or seek shelter.

Other Devilish Haunts

Across the continent, there are numerous sites named after the Devil, and almost all of these have exhibited some form of supernatural phenomena. Below is a truncated list of such locales.

- **Diablo (Devil) Valley, California:** The Diablo Valley region includes geological formations such as Mount Diablo and Devil's Hole, where mysterious black panthers, including the Black Mountain Lion of Devil's Hole, and at least one phantom alligator, have been reported.

- **Devil's Footprint, Connecticut:** An oddly shaped depression on a rock at this site is said to have been created when the Devil stepped on the stone as he was attempting to leap across the ocean.

- **Devil's Bake Oven, Illinois:** Located near the towns of Grand Tower and Little Egypt, this oddly named site is the home of a scary female ghost who screams constantly. Not far from the Bake Oven is the town of Cairo, which boasts appearances by a train of spectral wagons pulled by ghost horses and is also a hot spot of phantom animal activity.

- **Devil's Kitchen, Illinois:** This is the site of an abnormally high number of UFO sightings as well as numerous reports of mystery animals and phantom felines.

- **Hockomock (Devil) Swamp, Massachusetts:** One of the most haunted areas in the country, this swamp hosts demons, ghosts, devils, fairies, imps, goblins, specters, and phantom animals.

- **Devil's Promenade, Missouri:** Since 1866, this gravel road located near the town of Hornet has been visited nightly by a ghostly ball of light known as the Devil's Jack-o'-Lantern, the Neosho Spook Light, or the Hornet Ghost Light. On at least one occasion, it chased a bus full of children. The glowing light may be the lantern of a wandering ghost or the spirits of two illicit Native American lovers who committed suicide together.

- **Devil's Hole, Nevada:** Charles Manson, the disturbed mastermind behind the horrible Tate-LaBianca murders of 1969, allegedly believed this formation in the Death Valley National Monument would allow him access to Hell. He planned to lead his twisted Family through Devil's Hole in order to escape the race war he hoped the Tate-LaBianca murders would spark.

- **Devil's Den, New Hampshire:** Near the town of Chester, the Den is afflicted by numerous evil spirits, inexplicable temperature changes, demonic visions, and a host of ghost lights.

(continued on next page)

- **Devil's Stairs, North Carolina:** Ghosts have been reported here since 1910. Such apparitions include the spirit of a miner who was killed in an explosion, the phantom form of an infant left here to die, and a ghostly man who is seeking a new horse to ride.

- **Devil's Tramping Ground, North Carolina:** Several hundred years ago, a mysterious dirt circle suddenly appeared on the ground here. Vegetation refuses to grow in this large circle, which is some forty feet in diameter. Legends hold that the Devil created the weird formation by pacing in a circle.

- **Devil's Lake State Park, Wisconsin:** Aside from the mysterious effigy mounds located here, nearby areas are haunted by ghostly elephants, and the lake itself is home to phantoms, strange shadows, a spectral canoe, and a lake monster.

- **Devil's Head Mountain, Alberta:** The grave of White Eagle, a Stony Indian leader, rests in these hills. Today, his spirit still manifests regularly.

- **Devil's Garden, Rigaud Mountain, Quebec:** According to folklore from the region, this desolate field of stones was created when farmer Baptiste Laronde attempted to plow a potato field on a Sunday, despite repeated warnings from a local pastor. As retribution for his blasphemy, Laronde sank into the earth as he worked, eventually disappearing forever. The potatoes he planted sprouted as rocks, and today, most often on Sunday mornings, mysterious wisps of smoke appear and eerie noises can be heard echoing between the stones.

FRANKLIN'S HAUNTED ORCHARD

VITAL STATISTICS

LOCATION: Orchards throughout Franklin (formerly Norwich) in eastern Connecticut, especially on the land that once belonged to the Rood family

NUMBER OF GHOSTLY RESIDENTS: One

IDENTITY OF GHOSTLY RESIDENT: An unnamed traveling salesman

TYPE OF ACTIVITY: See below

DEMEANOR OF GHOSTLY RESIDENT: Just and pure. The activities of the haunted orchard ghost are designed to prove that a murder occurred at the site many years ago.

ENCOUNTERING THE HAUNTED ORCHARD PHENOMENON: RIP RIP RIP RIP

Sometimes, a ghost makes itself known in strange and unpredictable ways that defy any classification and can only be viewed with wonder. Ghost hunters are familiar with phantoms and disembodied screams, poltergeist activity and cold spots; but when ghosts shun these phenomena for more creative avenues of self-expression, ghost hunters are often left staggered.

Take, for example, the eerie case of Connecticut's Haunted Orchard, a tale involving a brutal murder and a chilling message from beyond the grave. The story begins in 1759, when a cultured peddler arrived in the small town of Norwich, Connecticut. Hawking vital goods, exotic wares, and news of the outside world, the peddler was visited by most of the town's residents throughout the day. Many commented on his strange accent, which sounded almost French, and were impressed by his polite manner and fair prices.

The welcome peddler earned a hefty sum as he sold most of his merchandise, but as night fell he suddenly realized that he had tarried in Norwich too long. Fearing bandits, the peddler was unwilling to travel or sleep outside at night. Thus, he inquired about nearby inns or boardinghouses that might take him in for the night. Unfortunately, Norwich was a tiny community far removed from other settlements, and therefore lacked any such accommodations. Still, the peddler was persistent and was eventually directed toward the home of Micah Rood, an ill-tempered farmer living on the outskirts of town with his widowed mother.

The peddler did indeed visit the Rood farm, where he met his end. According to local suspicion, Micah Rood met the peddler in his apple orchard as the stranger approached. Initially, Rood may have been friendly, but when he heard the peddler's thick accent, his demeanor changed. Rood harbored a deep hatred for the French because his father had been slain in the French and Indian War. Within moments, Rood silently convinced himself that the stranger was a French spy, and then he lost control and attacked the man with a hatchet or similar weapon. With a single blow, Rood cleaved through the peddler's head, killing his visitor instantly.

Rood left the peddler's body beneath one of the apple trees, but rooted through the dead man's belongings and stole his heavy purse to convince authorities that the murder had been the work of thieves. Of course, suspicion fell squarely on Rood, who was known for his incredible temper and violent streak. But authorities could not link Rood to the murder, and the killing remained unsolved.

Although Rood was never convicted in a court of law, a powerful message visited Norwich in the months following the murder, an omen that convinced many of Rood's guilt. When the trees in Micah Rood's apple orchard began to bloom, witnesses noticed that the blossoms throughout the grove were stained with bright, bloody streaks. Soon after, Rood's orchard bore fruit, but the apples were unlike any seen by mortal eyes: The pulp within each was laced with crimson stains. More horrifying, on the tree where the peddler's battered corpse had been discovered, the blossoms were entirely red, and the innards of the apples were marked with red patches resembling drops of blood.

The mere existence of these remarkable apples convinced most residents that Micah Rood had indeed killed the peddler. Despite the overwhelming supernatural evidence, he again eluded trial and went on to live a prosperous life. In the years since Rood's own death, Norwich has been renamed Franklin

and, as remarkable as it may seem, the orchards in this area continue to produce the bloody apples.

Ghost hunters are encouraged to seek out these special, tainted apples in order to witness the many wondrous ways in which ghosts can manifest. In early spring, travel eastern Connecticut in search of any tree bearing reddish blossoms, then return to these when fruit begins to appear on the boughs. Remember to ask permission from the land's owner before you pick any apples. Be sure to make note of the trees from which you have taken fruit in the event you wish to return to the site. When the collected apples are ripe, split them down the middle to reveal the rich, crimson streaks. It is very important that you study these stains to determine if any resemble tear-shaped drops of blood; if you find an apple marked in this manner, return to the tree that bore the fruit for further study, as this is very likely the site where the peddler's body was discarded.

In the event you do discover the exact location of the "murder tree," be sure to explore the area at night. Aside from the bloody apples, there has yet to be a sighting of a phantom or other ghostly phenomena connected to this case. However, it is possible that the haunting could intensify given the magnitude of the murder. At the very least, the continued existence of the bloody apples proves that the supernatural force originally responsible for the strange fruit is still present in the orchard, lending support to the theory that the site might yield other ghostly happenings as well.

GRAND MANAN ISLAND

VITAL STATISTICS

LOCATION: Bay of Fundy, New Brunswick, Canada. The most haunted spots are Little Dark Harbour, Indian Beach, and Ghost Hollow.

NUMBER OF GHOSTLY RESIDENTS: At least five

IDENTITIES OF GHOSTLY RESIDENTS: Edmond Chatfield and Desilda St. Clair, who were murdered by pirates; Lemushahindu, a Passmaquoddy maiden known today as the Flaming Indian Woman; the enigmatic Rowing Man; and another phantom known as the Little Man

TYPE OF ACTIVITY: Phantoms and ghost lights

DEMEANOR OF GHOSTLY RESIDENTS: Varies. The Rowing Man has no known purpose and avoids humans. The Flaming Indian Woman simply allows herself to burn, while the Little Man frequently darts out in front of cars. Desilda is quite insane, while Edmond spends his time searching for his lost head; both could be prone to murder.

ENCOUNTERING THE GRAND MANAN ISLAND GHOSTS: RIP RIP RIP RIP

P ossibly the most haunted site in all of Canada, and certainly one of the most active ghostly abodes along the eastern seaboard, Grand Manan Island is home to no fewer than five separate phantoms. Each of these spirits has been well documented and sighted on numerous occasions throughout the past several centuries.

Of the five ghosts inhabiting Grand Manan Island, the most reliably reported is the Rowing Man, who surfaces in Little Dark Harbour in a spectral canoe. This phantom appears only at night when the moon is full, usually in late November. He is completely silent, making no sound save for gentle splashes as his oars hit the water. The Rowing Man's identity is unknown, but it is believed that he is a drowning victim who perished in the harbor long ago.

Just a few miles from the Rowing Man's haunt, ghost hunters can find the spirits of Edmond Chatfield and Desilda St. Clair. The couple once lived in Maine, presumably in the late 1800s, but found themselves shipwrecked on Grand Manan Island during a fateful sailing trip. When they realized that the island was being used by pirates as a hideout, they attempted to stay out of sight. One evening, they watched from the brush as a group of the scoundrels buried a gigantic treasure chest. Unfortunately, the pirates discovered the couple and began pursuing them across the island.

The pair was ultimately captured and Edmond was brutally hanged from a tree before Desilda's horrified eyes. The malicious pirates then raped and beat Desilda before releasing her into the woods, where she was eventually transformed into a half-starved wild woman and began plotting to kill her tormentors. One by one, she lured the pirates into the forest, where she crushed their skulls with rocks.

Today, both Desilda and Edmond still wander the island. Edmond appears as a headless phantom who roams the shores in search of all he has lost. Desilda, who died alone and insane on the island, manifests as a lunatic with wild hair and eyes. She hysterically shrieks Edmond's name, even as she races past the headless specter who was once her true love.

Another tragic spirit is the ghost of a Passmaquoddy maiden named Lemushahindu, who is now known as the Flaming Indian Woman. This phantom appears with surprising regularity, manifesting exactly every seven years on the shores of Indian Beach. There, she stands in the surf as bright flames erupt from her body. She remains motionless for several moments as the fire consumes her body, eventually reducing the silent specter to ashes, which are then swallowed by the ocean. As with the Rowing Man, the circumstances surrounding the Flaming Indian Woman's demise are unknown, but given the nature of the haunting it is likely that she was set afire by some sadistic soul. The murderer may have been a jealous lover, vile pirates, or some brutal explorer.

The fifth and final ghost living on Grand Manan Island is the curious Little Man, who seems to enjoy tormenting motorists. Wearing a strange top hat, the Little Man only manifests on nights when the fog is thick. He lurks alongside lonely roads near Ghost Hollow and leaps from the brush when a car passes by, usually diving toward the windshield. Panicked motorists swerve and try to stop, but the Little Man disappears without colliding against the vehicle.

All of the ghosts on Grand Manan Island may pose a danger to the living. The Little Man's reckless actions could conceivably cause a motorist to lose control and crash, and ghost hunters traveling this area are therefore urged to drive with utmost caution. Both the Rowing Man and the Flaming Indian Woman should be observed from afar, as their motivations are unknown. In the case of the Flaming Indian Woman, it is possible that the fiery aura that surrounds her could inflict pain and injury on anyone who came too close, so avoid contact with the spirit. However, if you can establish verbal contact with either of these spirits, attempt to ascertain their identities and the circumstances surrounding their deaths.

Desilda's spirit is thoroughly psychotic and confused, greatly increasing the chance that she is dangerous and even lethal. Headless phantoms are almost always threatening; Edmond may assault the living in an ill-conceived attempt to gain a new head. Clearly, ghost hunters exploring Grand Manan Island should be extremely wary of all spectral manifestations. However, while potentially dangerous, the island also offers a rare opportunity for ghost hunters because the resident spirits appear with such regularity. Plan to visit the island in the late fall, preferably between the nineteenth and twenty-fifth of November. Search for the ghosts at night, visiting both Indian Beach and the areas surrounding Dark Harbour if the moon is bright and full. If fog descends, try your luck along the roads leading through Ghost Hollow in search of the Little Man.

HAT CREEK BATTLEGROUND

VITAL STATISTICS

LOCATION: Hat Creek (alternately Warbonnet Creek) Monument, a state historic site in northwestern Nebraska

NUMBER OF GHOSTLY RESIDENTS: Unknown

IDENTITIES OF GHOSTLY RESIDENTS: Countless Cheyenne Indians, including Yellow Hand, and members of the Fifth U.S. Cavalry

TYPE OF ACTIVITY: Disembodied voices, green ectoplasmic mist, phantoms, and unexplained noises

DEMEANOR OF GHOSTLY RESIDENTS: Aggressive and warlike. The Hat Creek ghosts, like most battlefield spirits, rise to reenact their war, but they avoid humans.

ENCOUNTERING THE HAT CREEK GHOSTS:
RIP RIP RIP

Almost all battlefields throughout the world are cloaked in a strong aura of pain, sadness, death, and fear. The massive energies generated by men dying in intense anguish seems to seep into the very ground, where it transforms into an almost palpable wall of negative emotions detectable by most mortals who visit the site. Quite often, these energies also give rise to a number of spectral manifestations, ranging from haunting cries to complete reenactments of the battle. Along with the **Little Bighorn Battlefield** (see page 104), Hat Creek in Nebraska exemplifies this phenomenon.

In July of 1876, just one month after General George Custer was defeated at Little Bighorn in Montana, the Fifth U.S. Cavalry clashed with a large contingent of Cheyenne Indians alongside Nebraska's Hat Creek. Although many U.S. soldiers died during the conflict, the Cheyenne were massacred in obscene numbers and left to rot on the shores of the river.

During the conflict, the U.S. troops were joined by a rising hero, William F. Cody, better known to most as Buffalo Bill. The thirty-year-old showman did not hesitate to enter the battle, where he confronted and killed the infamous warrior Yellow Hand. Never one to let an opportunity for profit pass him by, Bill collected Yellow Hand's warbonnet, weapons, and other personal effects, which he then displayed as part of his touring sideshow for the next several years.

As is to be expected, the destruction and desecration of the Cheyenne at Hat Creek have led to an intense haunting with a variety of elements. At its most benign, the site only yields reports of phantom voices, presumably Cheyenne braves, whispering from the brush. On moonless nights around the anniversary of the battle, the haunting intensifies, and a green ectoplasmic mist can be spotted hovering over the battlefield.

Finally, as the ghostly energies coalesce at the site, phantoms begin to emerge from the mist. Both Cheyenne braves and U.S. soldiers appear, prepared to clash once again. Surrounded by the sound of an invisible battle, the warriors attack one another, reenacting the battle that took their lives so many years ago.

Hat Creek is best visited during late June and throughout July, when the spectral activity is at its most intense. The first signs of the haunting will be disembodied whispers which, although unsettling, cannot harm you. When the green mist rises from the ground, however, be on guard. Neither scientists nor supernaturalists have been able to identify the mist and it is possible, although unlikely, that the substance could cause living humans harm. In the worst possible scenario, the mist could transport anyone who enters the ectoplasmic fog to the land of the dead.

The warring phantoms who represent the haunting's most severe manifestation usually fight without acknowledging any living observers. They seem doomed to repeat the same battle over and over again, unwilling or unable to turn on new enemies. Still, if you come too close to the battle, you may unwittingly place yourself in danger. A stray bullet, wildly swung hatchet, or other lethal weapon could find mortal flesh if you place yourself into the thick of the fray. Given the savagery of the conflict, in this instance it is best to keep your distance and observe the phantoms from afar.

LITTLE BIGHORN BATTLE- FIELD NATIONAL MONUMENT

VITAL STATISTICS

LOCATION: Custer Battlefield National Park, Crow Agency, Montana, on I-90 about fifteen miles from Hardin. One of the most haunted sites is Reno Crossing, five miles from the area designated as the central battlefield. The Stone House, where employees once slept, the Battlefield Cemetery, Last Stand Hill, and the Visitors Center are also plagued by spirits.

NUMBER OF GHOSTLY RESIDENTS: Unknown, but the population may be as high as 265—the number of U.S. soldiers slain on the battlefield in 1876.

IDENTITIES OF GHOSTLY RESIDENTS: Numerous combatants killed during the Battle of Little Bighorn, including General Custer, Second Lieutenant Benjamin Hodgson, and several others

TYPE OF ACTIVITY: Ghost lights, phantoms, and an aura of intense sorrow

DEMEANOR OF GHOSTLY RESIDENTS: Hopeless, suffering, and sad. These ghosts lost everything in a terrible conflict, butchered on a lonely battlefield. While they cannot harm mortals, they continue to ferociously attack one another.

ENCOUNTERING THE GHOSTS OF CUSTER BATTLEFIELD NATIONAL PARK:

On June 25, 1876, General George Armstrong Custer led the six hundred soldiers of the Seventh Cavalry Regiment onto a battlefield in Montana to confront Crazy Horse and Sitting Bull, who had united the Sioux Indian nation in an attempt to defend their peoples. In what is often described as one of the most tragic and brutal engagements in the long conflict between whites and Native Americans, Custer and his men were butchered. During the battle, known as the Battle of Little Bighorn or Custer's Last Stand, the Sioux overwhelmed the troops and claimed the lives of 265 U.S. soldiers, including the general. However, according to many witnesses and psychics, the spirits of many of these fallen warriors still linger at the site.

The Little Bighorn Battlefield boasts a number of haunted locations throughout its expanse. A sense of profound sadness and pain pervades the entire site, becoming more pronounced near Last Stand Hill, where Custer allegedly fell, and the Battlefield Cemetery, which houses many of the battle's casualties.

Next to Battlefield Cemetery sits the Stone House, a two-story building once used as quarters for the park's staff. Over the years, numerous employees have reported strange phenomena in and around the edifice, most notably in apartments A and D. In both of these suites, witnesses have stirred from sleep to find radiant phantoms standing near their beds. These spirits quickly disappear, leaving only a lingering glow. Ghost lights have also been spotted on numerous occasions as they circle the Stone House aimlessly or wander through the nearby cemetery.

Although he likely died on Last Stand Hill, Custer has decided to take up residence in the

Custer's Death Foretold

In May of 1876, a month before his defeat at the Battle of Little Bighorn, Custer led his troops from Fort Abraham Lincoln in southeastern Montana. As the soldiers rode from the fort, virtually all of those present to bid the troops farewell watched in awe as about half of the regiment seemed to lift up into the sky and disappear. The assembled witnesses felt that the phenomenon was a telling omen of impending death. And indeed, a month later, about half of the soldiers who had left the fort were lying dead on the Little Bighorn Battlefield.

Battlefield Museum. There, he can be seen roaming the hallways late at night. Many observers feel as if the spirit is checking the building for intruders or other dangers. Whatever his purpose, Custer never interacts with the living and remains eerily silent as he wanders through the building.

The Visitors Center is also haunted, although the identity of this ghost is unknown. He appears as a handsome phantom wearing a soldier's uniform, a brown shirt, and a black cartridge belt slung across his chest. Like Custer, he has been encountered often, but he never speaks or acknowledges those around him.

One of the most tragic deaths that occurred at the site was the murder of Second Lieutenant Benjamin Hodgson, adjutant to Major Marcus Reno. After the major ordered a retreat, Reno, Hodgson, and their men attempted to rescue

Little Big Horn Battlefield National Monument.

their wounded comrades from the battlefield as they fled. During this selfless effort, Hodgson was struck by a bullet that not only shattered his leg but passed through the limb and killed his mount as well. The horse collapsed and Hodgson was thrown free. As the Native American warriors descended, he tried desperately to crawl up a steep hill, but was overtaken and killed. His lifeless body rolled down the embankment and came to a rest near a riverbank.

Today, a marker identifies the spot where Hodgson's body was discovered, and this site is one of the most haunted portions of the battlefield. Hodgson's weary and wounded ghost has been encountered dozens of times by park personnel and visitors as he wanders around the marker bearing his name. He frequently travels the entire length of Reno Crossing as well and has, on occasion, reenacted his own death.

Visiting the Little Bighorn Battlefield National Monument is a rewarding experience

for all ghost hunters. The suffering that occurred on the lonely battlefield was extraordinary and has left a lasting psychic impression on the site. Although you may not actually encounter a ghost, the area is a perfect training ground for those who wish to learn more about the lingering emotional auras found at haunted locales, as almost everyone who treads the battlefield detects the aura of sorrow that enshrouds the place.

Aside from the battlefield's overpowering aura, the ghosts are indeed numerous and oft-encountered. Spend the bulk of your time around Last Stand Hill and Reno Crossing, watching for any wraiths that might rise from the ground. As is the case with many historical tragedies, exploring the site on the anniversary of the battle (June 25) may yield a higher number of ghost sightings.

While the ghosts wandering the Little Bighorn Battlefield have yet to prove dangerous, they may be surly and ill-tempered because of their traumatic defeat and violent deaths. Custer, who is often held responsible for the Seventh Cavalry Regiment's dismal failure, may be especially grumpy. Avoid angering the spirits in any way. If you do manage to establish contact with a ghost at this site, do not discuss the conflict unless prompted to do so. Laud any specters for their heroism and willingness to give their lives for their country.

Finally, while it is tempting to verbally abuse Custer for his long history of murderous actions toward the Native American peoples, avoid doing so if you encounter this particular spirit. It must be remembered that Custer has been forced to suffer in a state of "undeath" for over a century and, while his actions in life cannot be condoned, the living cannot claim to understand the torment he has endured since his death. Many seemingly cruel or barbaric people who have become ghosts eventually become consumed by guilt over their misdeeds and seek to repent in the hopes of finding true peace. If Custer seems to share this drive, encourage him to seek forgiveness for his long war against the Native Americans by making amends with the living descendants of the Sioux. Once this has been done, Custer, along with his fallen troops, may at last enter the afterlife.

MAMMOTH CAVE NATIONAL PARK

VITAL STATISTICS

LOCATION: Mammoth Cave National Park, Kentucky 42259; (502) 758-2328. The park is located in south central Kentucky, along I-65 about twenty miles northeast of Bowling Green. The most haunted areas are the Church, Chief City, Echo River, Purgatory, and nearby Crystal Cave, which is only five miles from Mammoth Cave and today is part of the national park.

NUMBER OF GHOSTLY RESIDENTS: Approximately eight

IDENTITIES OF GHOSTLY RESIDENTS: Melissa, a jilted woman who murdered the man she loved; Mr. Beverleigh, the murder victim; Stephen Bishop, a former guide; Floyd Collins, who died in Crystal Cave; and at least two other unidentified spirits

TYPE OF ACTIVITY: Phantoms, mysterious knockings, disembodied voices, and mild poltergeist activity

DEMEANOR OF GHOSTLY RESIDENTS: Varies. Melissa is seeking the man she wrongly murdered, while Mr. Beverleigh is wandering the cave in search of the exit. Stephen Bishop and several other spirits seem to simply enjoy being in the cave, while Floyd Collins is a bit mischievous. None of the spirits are particularly dangerous, although roaming the cave alone can present certain hazards.

ENCOUNTERING THE GHOSTS OF MAMMOTH CAVE:

Mammoth Cave is the single largest natural cave in the entire world. It consists of at least five known levels and over 330 miles of hallways and corridors. Several of the larger caverns yawn open to heights of two hundred feet, while other sections are barely large enough to allow passage. The entire area is a geological wonder, with numerous secondary caves surrounding Mammoth.

Because of its size and beauty, Mammoth Cave averages about two million visitors each year. To support this great demand, the park hires about two hundred employees, bolstered by volunteers and part-time guides during busy summer months. But it is not the mortal population of Mammoth Cave, or even the natural wonders of the cave itself, with which we are concerned. Rather, it is the large assortment of ghosts residing in the area who will remain the focus.

Among ghost hunters, there is very little doubt that Mammoth Cave is one of the most active haunted sites in the entire world. Since its discovery in 1798, the cave has recorded well over 150 reports of ghostly phenomena, ranging from short-lived poltergeist activity to intricate apparitions. The list of reliable witnesses includes geologists, tour guides, psychics, and a wide variety of tourists with diverse backgrounds.

The most active ghost in Mammoth Cave is the spirit of Stephen Bishop, a black slave whose owner put him to work as a guide at the site beginning in 1838. According to local legend, Bishop quickly became the cave's most skilled explorer, drawing incredibly accurate maps of the area and discovering new chambers and passageways on an astonishingly frequent basis.

Eventually, Bishop's master offered the slave a chance to escape his slavery, on the condition that he leave Kentucky and move north. Bishop declined his freedom, however, claiming that he could never give up his life within the cave. And even after death, Bishop refused to leave Mammoth Cave. His ghost is now a permanent resident.

Today, Bishop most often appears as a fully formed phantom, distinguishable from mortals only by his dress. He frequently wears a dark shirt, white pants, vest, and Panama hat. On occasion, he has been sighted with the ghosts of a woman and two children, whose identities are unknown. While in phantom form, Bishop usually joins a tour for a short time, as if judging the quality of the guide. He never speaks to anyone, but is spotted by several members of the tour group before he silently fades away. Sometimes, Bishop turns off any nearby lights and gently shoves tour guides. He has also been known to blow out the flames of candles and torches used during special excursions known as lantern tours.

Another prominent ghost is the specter of a forlorn woman known only as Melissa. In 1858, a woman calling herself Melissa (who may have been writing under an alias) sent a letter to *The Knickerbocker,* a prominent magazine. In the missive, Melissa revealed that in 1843 she had been a lovely Southern belle infatuated with her tutor, a man she identified only as Mr. Beverleigh. When Beverleigh fell in love with Melissa's neighbor, the jilted girl led her teacher into Mammoth Cave. Once they were deep in the caverns, near a spot along the Echo River known as Purgatory, she slipped away and let the darkness claim him. Beverleigh never escaped the cave: He may have stumbled into a crevice and plummeted to his death, or perhaps he slowly wasted away. Regardless, it is clear that he died alone while waiting for Melissa to return and save him.

Melissa spent the next fifteen years consumed by guilt. Eventually, she was diagnosed with tuberculosis, and her impending death prompted her confessional letter to *The Knickerbocker*. Yet the note did not absolve her of her guilt completely,

> "For fifteen long years I have carried a dark secret buried in my heart, until it has worn away my life; but now that I am tottering on the brink of the grave, I am impelled to make a confession, which tardy as it is, I hope may render more tranquil my last sad hours. . . ."
>
> —Melissa, in her letter published in the February 1858 issue of *The Knickerbocker*

and today it is clear that Melissa is still seeking forgiveness. She wanders the Echo River, mournfully calling out to Beverleigh in the hopes of saving him from his fate. In her anguish, she has also been known to whisper unintelligibly and weep for hours on end.

Due to the circumstances of his death, it is likely that Beverleigh also haunts Mammoth Cave, perhaps searching for a way to escape the caverns. One as-yet unidentified ghost who may in fact be Melissa's murder victim is a stately gentleman who has appeared in an area of the cave known as Chief City. The phantom wears the formal dress of the mid- or late 1800s, commonly described as a black and white suit with a cummerbund. Children and tour guides have spotted the ghost, and at least one psychic detected the spirit's presence.

Other ghosts reported in and around Mammoth Cave include two pairs of strangely disembodied legs. The four legs run side by side down a grassy hill near the Visitors Center and are said to be wearing denim pants and heavy work boots. There are no records of murders or

grisly accidents near the Visitors Center, so the identities of these phantom limbs remain unknown.

Additional spectral manifestations may be caused by ancient spirits of the Native Americans who inhabited the cave prior to its discovery by whites. The former occupants, who left behind mummified remains, bones, pottery, sandals, and other artifacts, may still be reluctant to leave.

In 1842, Dr. John Croghan converted the cave into a hospital for those suffering from tuberculosis (an odd coincidence, considering Melissa's story related previously). He theorized that the cave's steady temperature would benefit his patients, but his experiment was ill conceived, and all of his eleven test subjects were brought to the edge of death while in Croghan's care. Ten months later, shortly before Melissa murdered Beverleigh, the hospital closed. However, the patients, most of whom died shortly after leaving Mammoth Cave, may have been drawn back to the site, as visitors have reported hearing disembodied coughs and moans throughout the caverns.

The most exciting of the Mammoth Cave National Park hauntings revolves around Crystal Cave, a separate series of caverns and tunnels about five miles from Mammoth Cave but still within the park's confines. Like Mammoth, Crystal Cave is plagued by disembodied voices, phantoms, mysterious noises, and poltergeist activity. By all accounts, the spirit of a man named Floyd Collins is responsible for this wide range of ghostly manifestations.

In 1917, Collins, who lived near Mammoth Cave, discovered Crystal Cave. For the next several years, he worked hard to make his find a viable tourist attraction, but Crystal Cave was too far removed and could not compete with Mammoth Cave's size and renown. Although Crystal Cave proved to be an economic disaster, Collins did not forsake the cave industry and continued his explorations. In 1925, he was mapping nearby Sand Cave when he was suddenly trapped beneath a rocky outcropping. Although Collins was stuck some sixty feet below the earth's surface, rescuers could see and hear the panicked man. They lowered Collins food and water, but could not find a way to extract him without causing the cave to completely collapse. For sixteen days, his story dominated the press as the rescue workers searched feverishly for a solution to Collins's plight. Sadly, shortly after Collins spoke with his best friend, Johnny Gerald, a cave-in separated him from his rescuers. He died hours later. The body was eventually retrieved and buried, but the new owners of Crystal Cave realized that Floyd's tragic story had drawn huge crowds to the financially unstable attraction. To increase profits even further, Collins was exhumed, placed in a glass coffin, and put on display in the cave. Instantly, Crystal Cave began generating huge revenues.

However, Floyd Collins would not be allowed to sleep in peace. As they witnessed Crystal Cave's sudden growth, a group of competing cave owners stormed Crystal Cave late one night and absconded with the corpse. Later, they retired to a local tavern and drank themselves silly and admitted to the crime. Unfortunately, during the theft or sometime shortly thereafter, Collins lost his left leg. Despite this disfigurement, when Collins was eventually recovered, he was again put on display in Crystal Cave, where he remained until recently. Today, his corpse resides in a nearby Baptist church cemetery, but his ghost clearly lives in Crystal Cave.

Floyd Collins most often makes himself known by hollering the name of his best friend, Johnny. On other occasions, he throws whiskey bottles about or snatches small objects from geologists exploring the cave. He also wanders the area around his old home, leaving behind large bootprints.

Mammoth Cave National Park has earned its reputation as one of the world's most haunted locations, and ghost hunters would do well to focus much attention and energy on this area. However, it must be noted that while Mammoth Cave is open to the public for tours and study, Crystal Cave is no longer an operating tourist attraction. The Cave Research Foundation spends a great deal of time in Crystal Cave, but all others need special permission from Mammoth Cave National Park before entering these caverns.

While touring Mammoth Cave, be especially alert when you near Echo River, the Church, Chief City, and Purgatory, as all these have been sites of frequent ghostly happenings. Because of the limited light in the caverns, you must rely heavily on your ears. Listen for any strange moans, screams, coughs, whispers, or cries. Also, before you begin the tour, take careful stock of everyone in your tour group; then, after you enter each cavern, look over your fellow tourists once again to see if a new face has joined the group, as the spirits of

Stephen Bishop and the unidentified dapper gentleman (who may be Beverleigh) often tag along with tours.

With the exception of Melissa, none of the ghosts in Mammoth Cave have shown any violent tendencies in life or death. Do not hesitate to approach any phantom you might meet, unless doing so leads you away from the main tour routes or into darkened passages.

Finally, be warned that, although you proba-bly have nothing to fear from the ghosts, the cave itself can be quite treacherous. Mammoth Cave is a dark, expansive labyrinth that should only be explored by the truly skilled. If you are inexperienced at spelunking or have never visited Mammoth Cave before, be sure to remain with your tour guide at all times. Even if you have spent decades wandering caves, independent exploration of Mammoth Cave is strongly discouraged and must be approved by the park.

NIAGARA FALLS

VITAL STATISTICS

LOCATION: The falls are located on the border between New York and Ontario, Canada. Information can be obtained from Niagara County Tourism at (800) 338-7890 or the Niagara Falls Chamber of Commerce, 345 Third Street, Niagara Falls, NY 14303. Haunted areas include the islands known as the Three Sisters near Goat Island and Horseshoe Falls.

NUMBER OF GHOSTLY RESIDENTS: Unknown

IDENTITIES OF GHOSTLY RESIDENTS: The Great Spirit of Thunder Waters; He-No the Thunderer; Lewlawala, the Maiden of the Mist; and numerous suicide victims

TYPE OF ACTIVITY: Phantoms and disembodied voices

DEMEANOR OF GHOSTLY RESIDENTS: Unknown. The ghosts of Niagara Falls are more appropriately viewed as deities or forces of nature. Their motives and goals are their own, but fortunately, they appear unconcerned with human affairs.

ENCOUNTERING THE GHOSTS OF NIAGARA FALLS:

Despite the number of deaths that have occurred near these spectacular waterfalls on the Canadian-U.S. border, the ghosts said to reside in the Niagara Falls are largely ancient Native American spirits displaying vast supernatural powers. The U.S. side of the falls, for example, is rumored to be the home of an entity known as the Great Spirit of Thunder Waters. The being's home is believed to be near the Three Sisters, a trio of islands located off of the western end of Goat Island. Long ago, the Iroquois trav-

Library of Congress

Niagara Falls.

being forced to marry a man she did not love. Known now as the Maiden of the Mist, legends hold that Lewlawala was rescued from her fatal fall by another omnipotent spirit, He-No the Thunderer. He-No granted the woman immortality and took her back to his hidden cave beneath Horseshoe Falls, where the couple resides to this day.

Aside from the Native American ghosts roaming the area, Niagara Falls is home to dozens of suicide victims who threw themselves into the falls during moments of profound sorrow and self-pity. If one listens closely, the collective moan of these unfortunates can be heard rising above the roar of the water.

In modern times, Native American spirits across the continent seem reluctant to appear, especially before non-Natives. Therefore, the majority of ghost hunters will probably have a difficult time encountering the most legendary of the Niagara Falls ghosts. Success can be found, however, by spending days standing near the water with your eyes closed, intently listening to the din of the falls. In time, you may begin to discern the screams of those who have fallen into the tumultuous water. Those with Native American heritage are also advised to watch Horseshoe Falls for any sign of the Maiden of the Mist and to visit the Three Sisters frequently in hopes of encountering any spirits still lingering at these sites. Finally, all visitors to the Niagara Falls area should refer to the previous entry on **Devil's Hole.**

eled to the Three Sisters in order to make sacrifices to the Great Spirit of Thunder Waters, who many claim still lurks near the site. Sensitive visitors often hear whispers and strange voices near the islands, although the identity of those responsible for the disembodied noises has never been confirmed.

Across the Canadian border, Niagara Falls is a much more active haunted site. Numerous witnesses throughout the centuries have reported encounters with a beautiful female apparition rising from the waters near Horseshoe Falls. This phantom has often been identified as a Native American maiden named Lewlawala, who leapt to her death from the falls upon

OAK BAY AND THE VICTORIA GOLF COURSE

VITAL STATISTICS

LOCATION: Victoria, British Columbia. The haunted area of Oak Bay is a rocky outcropping near the eighth tee on the Victoria Golf Course and overlooking the Strait of Georgia.

NUMBER OF GHOSTLY RESIDENTS: At least two, but perhaps as many as twelve

IDENTITIES OF GHOSTLY RESIDENTS: An unidentified husband and wife who died at the site, and possibly others who also perished there

TYPE OF ACTIVITY: Phantoms and disembodied voices

DEMEANOR OF GHOSTLY RESIDENTS: Doomed. These ghosts are trapped in a cycle of violence, forced to repeat their deaths forever. They can be dangerous if they are approached too closely.

ENCOUNTERING THE GHOSTS OF OAK BAY:

RIP RIP RIP

The Oak Bay phantoms are included in this book simply because they are so typical of the types of hauntings that can manifest after a tragic murder. In this case, the victim was a young woman who was married to a drunken lout. In the spring of 1936, the husband discovered that his wife was planning a divorce due to his inability to remain sober. In a murderous rage, perhaps bolstered by alcohol, he dragged her across the Victoria Golf Course and strangled her on the eighth tee.

As is standard in these cases, the husband was overcome with horror and grief when he realized the enormity of his foul actions. In despair, he leapt from the point, plummeting into Oak Bay, where he drowned. The wife's body was found on the green within minutes of the slaying, and shortly afterward, the murderer's body was spotted tangled in the kelp below.

The following spring, a year from the date of the murder-suicide, visitors at the site reported hearing a chorus of strange, invisible voices near the eighth tee. In later years, others witnessed a phantom woman standing near the edge of the point, looking longingly into the waters below. The apparition was identified as the wife murdered in 1936, and it was believed that she was searching the bay for any sign of her lost husband.

As the years passed, the phantom woman was joined by a whole group of ghosts standing together at the site. On calm days, their voices can be heard echoing across the bay, although what they are saying (or possibly singing?) has never been discerned. Most chilling, however, is the sight of the husband and wife reenacting their own deaths, another extremely common occurrence in these types of cases.

The ghosts of Oak Bay are extremely reliable and can be observed by any well-prepared ghost hunters. Plan to visit the area in spring, but you need only visit the golf course's eighth tee on days when the ocean is particularly calm, as the ghosts are reluctant to appear otherwise. If you happen to encounter the husband and wife embroiled in their conflict, use caution when approaching lest you find yourself thrown over the edge during their tussle. Also, when the assembly of anonymous ghosts appears, memorize their faces in the hopes of identifying these spirits later. Should you do so, check local records to see if you recognize photographs of suicides or drowning victims who may have died in the bay.

OLDMAN RIVER

VITAL STATISTICS

LOCATION: Oldman River, Manitoba, near Fort Walsh

NUMBER OF GHOSTLY RESIDENTS: Unknown

IDENTITIES OF GHOSTLY RESIDENTS: The entire populace of a vanished Cree village

TYPE OF ACTIVITY: Phantoms, ghost lights, and disembodied voices

DEMEANOR OF GHOSTLY RESIDENTS: Indistinguishable from humans. These phantoms go about a daily routine as if they were still alive. They cannot approach or be approached by mortals, and thus do not pose a threat.

ENCOUNTERING THE OLDMAN RIVER GHOSTS:

Undoubtedly one of the strangest hauntings is the case of the Oldman River, a site that hosts an entire village of apparitions along its shores. This ghost village is all that remains of a Cree settlement decimated by the Blackfoot Indians, who murdered all of the inhabitants and razed their homes during a vicious raid.

The phantom village was first discovered in 1875 by Sir Cecil Edward Denny, a member of the Northwest Mounted Police. Denny was exploring the area around Fort Walsh via the river when he found himself embroiled in a terrible storm. He escaped to the shore, but began to feel uneasy when he detected the sounds of drumming and chanting in the distance. Nevertheless, Denny steeled himself and investigated the strange sound, only to discover a ghostly village rising out of the rain. Dozens of Cree men and women went about their daily routine, seemingly oblivious to the rain and wind.

Unable to turn back, Denny attempted to enter the village. However, as he neared, he found himself surrounded by a strange blue flame, which flickered around him and took hold of his limbs. Suddenly, he was thrown to the ground, where he found himself paralyzed for several hours. The blue flame did not subside until the storm passed, at which point Denny was finally free to move on again. It is unknown what (or who) the blue flame was, but perhaps it was some sort of spectral guardian assigned to protect the ghostly Cree village from interlopers.

When Denny reached the site of the phantom village, the tipis and inhabitants had completely disappeared. However, he did prove that a village had existed at the site by uncovering some bones and a few rings on the ground marking the spots where tipis had once stood.

The phantom village is likely to be a "place memory" haunting. Place memories are simply "snapshots" of a moment in time which, for one reason or another, manage to linger into the present. They fade in and out of view and can usually be spotted only by psychics or sensitives. Ghosts who exist in place memories do not interact with the present world in any way. They often repeat a single scene again and again, and witnesses of place memory spirits claim to have peered through a window into the past. Clearly, these criteria seem to hold true for the phantom Cree village on Oldman River's shores.

Given that this haunting may be a place memory, there is no predictable manner in which to encounter the phenomena. Certainly, those who feel they have psychic gifts might be able to spy the Cree village, but others could roam the Oldman River for decades and never catch a glimpse of these phantoms.

However, if you do manage to spot the spectral community, do not approach it. As evidenced by Denny's account, trying to enter the village could be dangerous. Denny is very fortunate that his prolonged exposure to the elements did not cause his death, a very likely outcome given the severity of the storm he experienced. Persistent ghost hunters who repeatedly attempt to explore the village may be met with much greater resistance as the mysterious blue flame exerts it power. Such conflict could easily result in death or some fate far worse.

SUPERSTITION MOUNTAINS AND THE LOST DUTCH- MAN GOLD MINE

VITAL STATISTICS

LOCATION: Lost Dutchman State Park, Superstition Mountains, Arizona. The actual gold mine may be near a site known as Weavers Needle in Pinata, at the end of Peralta Road.

NUMBER OF GHOSTLY RESIDENTS: Unknown

IDENTITIES OF GHOSTLY RESIDENTS: Former prospectors, including Enrico Peralta, Dr. Abraham Thorne, Jacob Waltz, and Jacob Weiser, all of whom died in pursuit of the Lost Dutchman gold mine

TYPE OF ACTIVITY: Incredible aura of misfortune, disembodied voices, and phantoms

DEMEANOR OF GHOSTLY RESIDENTS: Lost, cheated, and generally miserable. Most of the spirits died while on a quest for gold, a pursuit they still follow in death. However, the curse that claimed so many lives in these mountains is far more dangerous than the ghosts themselves.

ENCOUNTERING GHOSTS OF THE SUPERSTITION MOUNTAINS: RIP RIP

North America has been the setting for literally hundreds of expeditions for fabled treasures. From the legendary Fountain of Youth to the mysterious Seven Cities of Gold, adventurers and explorers have scoured the continent in search of some metaphorical Holy Grail for centuries. One of the most sought-after treasures is the Lost Dutchman Gold Mine, a cavern allegedly lined with massive gold nuggets. Thousands of people have searched in vain for the Lost Dutchman, which is believed to be hidden in the Superstition Mountains, and an inordinate number of these have lost their lives as a result of the dark forces that surround this fabulous cave.

The earliest reports of the gold mine come from the Apache Indians, who told stories of discovering the Thunder God's home within the Superstitions. According to these tales, the entity's abode is a massive underground labyrinth filled with gold. In later years, Spanish explorers believed that Cibola, the aforementioned Seven Cities of Gold, were in the Superstitions as well.

It was not until 1864, however, that a well-prepared expedition set out to discover whether the tales of hidden gold were true. That year, Enrico Peralta organized a large group of experienced miners to follow him into the mountains, but they were scarcely under way when they were attacked and butchered by Apaches.

Only six years later, Dr. Abraham Thorne befriended the Apaches and persuaded them to take him to the gold mine of which they had often spoken. Although he was blindfolded the entire way, he deduced that he was taken to a deep canyon about a mile from what is now known as Weavers Needle. There, he found a truly spectacular cave filled with gold and was allowed to pluck nuggets from the floor and leave with as much wealth as he could carry. Unfortunately, Thorne became greedy and soon tried to find the mine again, this time with several acquaintances in tow. The betrayed Apaches attacked Thorne and his companions, slaughtering the group as a warning to any who would seek out the gold mine without permission.

The Peralta family entered the search for the mine again in 1871, when they joined forces with German explorers Jacob Waltz (known as "the Dutchman") and Jacob Weiser. This expedition proved highly successful, netting the group over sixty thousand dollars in gold. Word of the gold mine spread quickly, and between 1878 and 1891, over ten thousand people entered the Superstitions in the hopes of uncovering the Lost Dutchman.

In 1879, Waltz and Weiser were drawn back to the mine, where they discovered and killed a group of Mexican prospectors. This barbaric act cursed the pair, and shortly after Weiser was killed by Apaches like so many others before him. The following year, Waltz was found wandering the edge of the Superstitions in a delirium, having struggled to escape the mountains for months. He was taken to a rancher's home, where he wasted away and died within days. Before he passed on, he described the mouth of the gold mine, ensuring that others would follow his misadventures. Soon after, the Apaches covered the mine's entrance to protect the natural treasure forever.

Despite the efforts of the Native Americans, the tragedies continued, although the mine itself was never entered again. In the past century, only a man named Adolph Ruth has come close to finding the Lost Dutchman. In 1931, Ruth uncovered a map that had once belonged to the Peralta family and allegedly led directly to the mine. Thus armed, he headed out toward his fortune, but somewhere along the way, he met his doom. Ruth was decapitated by unknown assailants, his body remaining undiscovered for three weeks.

All told, of the thousands who have embarked to find the Lost Dutchman, almost one hundred have died. According to the Apache, this terrible fate is visited upon the greedy by the Thunder God, who is angry that his land is being defiled. Whether or not a powerful entity such as the Thunder God is involved, there is certainly some supernatural presence at work. The mysterious force, which has caused so much misfortune, has also resurrected some of the prospectors in the form of ghosts, perhaps as a warning to those who would seek the gold mine.

As a result of the proliferation of ghosts in the Superstition Mountains, visitors to the region report hearing disembodied voices whispering in the darkness. Phantom miners, often carrying lanterns, have also been spied wandering mountain passes in the distance.

The strangest spectral manifestation is the so-called Borego Phantom, a specter that only appears to prospectors and miners between Borego, Arizona, and the foot of the Superstitions. A very impressive ghost, the Borego Phantom manifests as a humanoid skeleton standing well over eight feet tall. It usually surfaces at night or in the darkness of a cave or mine. Within its chest cavity a fiery lantern glows brightly, swinging slowly from the rib upon which it hangs. Despite this light, the Borego Phantom gives no warning of its ap-

Selective Ghosts

Much like the Borego Phantom, a small number of phantoms and spirits across the country appear only to a select group of individuals. The ghost of a child might appear only to other children, the spirit of a wild dog might visit only lonely hunters, and the phantom of a schoolteacher might harass only bullies and truants. Usually, the choice of "victims" has some relationship to the manner in which the spirit lived or died. Witnesses are rarely injured and only suffer a momentary fright, with the possibility of some lasting psychological discomfort. In many cases, the selected witnesses are actually aided or rescued by such ghosts.

proach and appears suddenly from the darkness.

In almost all cases, the Borego Phantom does not interact with witnesses. Instead, it merely wanders past the encampment or terrified traveler, seemingly uninterested in human affairs. Its skeletal feet touch the ground, kicking up sand, but the ghost never leaves footprints, nor can it be followed for any length of time. When traveling through cactus stands, over boulders, or into narrow tunnels, the Borego Phantom has also exhibited incredible agility rare among the undead.

Although the Borego Phantom seems to be an aimless wanderer, the fact that all witnesses have been of the same profession clearly shows that the specter does have some agenda. The lantern and the choice of witnesses indicates that the Borego Phantom is the ghost of a prospector who perished, perhaps in pursuit of the Lost Dutchman Gold Mine. The entity may also be a "collective phantom" created and empowered by the ghosts of the numerous men who died while hunting for their fortunes in this area of Arizona.

The most dangerous phantom lurking in the Superstitions is the so-called Monster of Mogollon Rim, who haunts the Mogollon Rim mountain to the north of the Superstition range. Known as Skinwalker by the Navajo, the Monster manifests as a towering creature over seven feet tall and lacking his skin. This grotesque being is believed to be the ghost of an unlucky prospector captured by Native Americans, who hanged the man by his hands as they slowly skinned him alive. Today, he roams the Mogollon Rim in search of victims to murder and has been held responsible for dozens of strange disappearances and deaths.

Finding any of the ghosts of the Superstition Mountains is a daunting task simply because of the bad luck associated with this area. Certainly, traveling the bulk of the range is safe enough, even if one encounters the phantom voices of those who have passed through the area in years past. However, when one nears the Lost Dutchman Gold Mine—where the majority of the ghosts are located—the danger increases exponentially.

Most ghost hunters should be content with exploring the outer edges of Pinata within the Superstitions. Only the truly foolhardy or courageous dare travel the length of Peralta Road to Weavers Needle, which is said to be extremely close to the mine. The completely insane, or those who place no faith in curses or bad luck, can travel another mile or two past Weaver's Needle searching for the legendary gold mine.

Despite the directions given above, it should be remembered that ghost hunters are not treasure hunters and should not be concerned with finding gold. Rather, instructions for finding the mine are given so that one who dares can find the ghosts trapped in this place. When you do encounter any of the ghosts in the Superstitions or the Lost Dutchman itself, be extremely wary of their motives. These ghosts have sought the ultimate prize and failed. They may be extremely jealous of the living, vindictive toward those who succeed in finding the gold, or sworn to guard the secrets of the mine. They could easily attack if they possess any of these motivations. The Borego Phantom, who is as enigmatic as he is frightening, should also be avoided until the spirit's true purpose is discerned.

Finally, if you do succeed in finding the Lost Dutchman and escape with your life, seek out professional supernaturalists for aid in avoiding the bad luck that may follow you from the mine. Experienced witches, druids, Voodoo priests and priestesses, and other practitioners of magic may be able to offer potions, spells, mantras, artifacts, or similar means of thwarting the curse of the Lost Dutchman Gold Mine.

TEACH'S HOLE

VITAL STATISTICS

LOCATION: Near Ocracoke Island in the Ocracoke Inlet, near the Pamlico Sound off the coast of North Carolina

NUMBER OF GHOSTLY RESIDENTS: One

IDENTITY OF GHOSTLY RESIDENT: Edward Teach, also known as Blackbeard the pirate

TYPE OF ACTIVITY: Phantom and ghost light

BLACKBEARD'S DEMEANOR: Wretched, violent, coarse, and disturbed. Blackbeard is more demented in death than he was during his deranged life. He is searching for a new head and will gladly practice murder to accomplish his goal.

ENCOUNTERING THE GHOST OF TEACH'S HOLE:

After Edward Teach was decapitated by officers of the Royal Navy in 1718, his headless ghost returned to ensure that future generations would know the terror of Blackbeard. The ghost, who desperately searches for its lost head, haunts several different locations, including the Ocracoke Inlet (30 miles southwest of Cape Hatteras) where the pirate was slain. The spirit also haunts Blackbeard's favorite lookout point, a cove on Ocracoke Island known as Teach's Hole. Blackbeard's corpse swims through this cove on moonlit nights and occasionally reclines on the surface when the weather is clear.

In addition, Blackbeard occasionally visits Jake's Hole, a

Pirate Ghosts

Numerous pirates have returned from the grave to become monstrous enemies of the living. Most are motivated by greed and a desire to protect their hidden treasures, while others are cursed by their dark deeds to live forever as ghosts. Captain Kidd haunts Screecham's Island near Cape Cod, where much of his treasure remains hidden. The island is also home to a witch who screams whenever anyone approaches the buried chests, alerting Kidd and signaling his appearance. Many pirates were in the habit of killing one of their crew whenever they buried a treasure and throwing the body into the pit with the chests to ensure that a ghost would always be present to protect the loot. Therefore, any site graced by hidden treasure is also likely to be haunted by an insane and vengeful murdered spirit. Jean Laffite is unique among pirate ghosts because he is actually wandering the earth in search of someone worthy of his treasure. When Laffite discovers a person who is without greed or selfishness, he will divulge the secret locations of his many chests of gold. Those who feel worthy should seek Laffite's ghost in the Gulf of Mexico, notably Barataria Bay.

cove on the eastern shores of Maryland. Blackbeard hid his heaviest treasure chests at the bottom of this cove, some fifteen fathoms below the waves. Today, anyone who tries to excavate the treasure is set afire by mysterious green flames or drowned by Blackbeard's spectral hands. The site is marked by a horrendous sulfur smell, which also accompanies Blackbeard when he travels onto land.

Because he is ardently searching for his head, Blackbeard frequently strides onto the beaches of North Carolina. When he travels abroad, he carries a blazing lantern to light his way. Wise travelers know that it is best to flee whenever this bobbing light is seen in the distance.

In order to understand Blackbeard's Ghost, one must first understand the man. Blackbeard, born Edward Teach, enjoyed violence, women, and money. He had no fear of death and even less fear of the Devil or other dark forces.

Teach began his seafaring career as a privateer in Queen Anne's War, but when the conflict ended in 1713, he joined forces with the pirate Captain Benjamin Hornigold. By 1716, Teach had acquired his own ship, the *Queen Anne's Revenge,* and established several hideouts along the coast of North Carolina. At about this time he began calling himself Blackbeard, a name that would soon spread fear throughout the Atlantic.

Teach was a relentless and ruthless opponent. He was far stronger and larger than most men, displayed an innately cruel disposition, and always carried a full complement of weapons, including three loaded pistols, his favorite cutlass, and a wide assortment of knives and daggers. In combat, he was possessed by unequaled fury and would cut down dozens of men before his bloodlust could be quelled. His crew, like their captain, robbed and murdered without compunction.

During robberies, Blackbeard could not be dissuaded from his loot. He tortured, mutilated, and murdered anyone who did not acquiesce to his demands. If a refined gentleman refused to hand over a golden ring, Blackbeard would simply chop off the man's finger to claim the trinket.

Because of his naturally malign disposition, Blackbeard garnered a terrible and fearsome reputation within months of his first crimes. Rumors of a secret pact with the Devil abounded, lore that the pirate himself perpetuated. Blackbeard was a tall and impressive figure, and his beard concealed most of his face, save for his dark and sinister eyes. Teach was in the habit of tying small bones, black ribbons, and various golden trinkets into his thick beard, creating a disturbing and exotic look that his victims would never forget. During battles, he would wear a cap adorned with several burning cannon fuses, and the smoke from these wicks curled around his face and made his appearance even more satanic. When carousing with his companions, Blackbeard secretly mixed minute amounts of gunpowder into his rum; late in the evening, he would light the liquor on fire and drink it down, much to the amazement of his peers.

One evening, Teach was playing cards in his cabin with a few crew members, including his gunner and best friend, Israel Hands. Suddenly, the captain drew his pistols, aimed them at Hands, and doused the room's single candle. For several long moments, the cabin was suspended in silence, and then Blackbeard chuckled and fired both guns. While one pistol misfired, the other shot shattered the gunner's knee and left him crippled. When questioned about the motive behind this attack, Blackbeard merely responded "If I did not now and then kill one of them, they would forget who I am."

On another occasion, Blackbeard led several of his crew into the ship's hold, ordered the hatches closed, and lit a dozen pots filled with brimstone and coal. Thick, suffocating smoke quickly saturated the hold and the men were assaulted by unbearable heat. While the other pirates cried and choked, Blackbeard merely smiled and laughed. After several of the crew passed out and nearly died, Blackbeard finally threw open the hatches. Once again, Teach proved that his resistance to anguish and misery far surpassed that of any other mortal man.

Despite his famed barbarism, Blackbeard could also be merciful and chivalrous. He often spared the lives of his captives for no apparent reason, and he was especially kind toward women. While other pirates were known for raping and pillaging, Blackbeard and his crew merely pillaged. He would not allow his men to treat female captives in any coarse or degrading manner. As amorous as he was violent, Blackbeard fell in love with and married at least thirteen women in five years. He wed many of these maidens aboard his ship and enjoyed several lengthy honeymoons, but he subsequently left each of his wives in her home port and sailed away, never to return. Perhaps he could not bear for his beautiful wives to see his darker, more malevolent side.

It was love that eventually proved Blackbeard's undoing. From the beginning of his career, Blackbeard used a regimen of bribery and intimidation to manipulate North Carolina's governor, Charles Eden. While Eden was well aware of Blackbeard's hideouts, he refused to reveal this information to the Royal Navy. Eden also pardoned Blackbeard and his entire crew on at least two occasions. In exchange, the governor received small caches of looted treasure, sugar, and other important goods. Unfortunately, Blackbeard became obsessed with Eden's young daughter, who was already betrothed to another.

When Eden's daughter rejected Blackbeard's advances, the pirate captured her suitor, lopped off his hand, and drowned the unfortunate gentleman at sea. The severed hand was sent to the young woman in a jeweled box, and when she learned of her lover's demise in this gruesome fashion, the governor's daughter sickened and quickly died.

Enraged at the loss of his daughter, Eden finally betrayed Blackbeard and leaked the location of the pirate's haven to Lieutenant Robert Maynard of the Royal Navy, who had been hired by the governor of Virginia to capture Blackbeard. In 1718, Maynard cornered Teach and his crew in the Ocracoke Inlet. Commanding two sloops and a horde of men, Maynard approached Blackbeard's ship, certain of victory. But the infamous outlaw would not be slain easily.

When Blackbeard recognized Maynard's approaching vessels, he immediately fired his cannons and decimated a great many of Maynard's men. Slyly, Maynard ordered the rest of his troops to hide below decks. When Blackbeard and his crew boarded the ship, Maynard's troops poured from the hold and the pirates suddenly found themselves overwhelmed. Still, Blackbeard fought ferociously. He hacked his way through the fighting men until he confronted Maynard, who shot the pirate in the chest. Yet Teach fought on. The two

dueled, and Blackbeard eventually snapped Maynard's sword at the hilt. As Blackbeard prepared to deliver the killing blow, one of Maynard's men suddenly climbed onto Teach's back and slashed the pirate's throat.

With blood pouring from his mouth and soaking his beard, Blackbeard continued to brawl until he was overwhelmed by Maynard and ten sailors. When he finally collapsed onto the deck, Blackbeard had suffered over twenty cuts and five gunshot wounds. Triumphantly, Maynard decapitated Blackbeard with the infamous pirate's own bloodstained cutlass. Teach's head was hung from the prow of Maynard's ship, and his body was thrown into the water, but Blackbeard miraculously clung to life. With a voice born of fury and rage, Blackbeard screamed at his sinking body. In response, the headless corpse swam around the boat three times before descending to the bottom of the sea. At last, Blackbeard was dead.

Soon after his demise, Blackbeard's Ghost began appearing in several locations along the Eastern seaboard. In the most horrific cases, the headless ghoul tried to kill travelers in an attempt to claim a new head.

Blackbeard's resurrection may be the handiwork of another force of great evil, the Devil. Blackbeard reveled in demonic imagery, and was delighted to learn that many of his crew and most of his victims believed that he was Satan in disguise. Eventually, it is likely that Old Scratch learned of Blackbeard's posturing and visited the man. The pair would have found one another fitting company and may have become good friends. In fact, there is at least one account of a stranger arriving on Blackbeard's boat wearing a dark cloak and a wicked grin. The mysterious figure appeared and disappeared at will, never spoke to any of the crew, and spent long hours in Blackbeard's cabin.

Legends also hold that Blackbeard still roams the earth because he is reluctant to enter Hell without his head. Although the pirate longs to enter the domain of pain and suffering, where he would surely become a lord of the fiery pits and a first-rate demon, he will not pass through the gates of the underworld until he is whole again. Blackbeard fears that until he recovers his head, he will not be recognized by his former mates and will therefore have no clout in Hell.

Unfortunately, Blackbeard may be forced to wander forever, as his head has been lost. In order to warn away other scoundrels, the pirate's head was mounted at the entrance of a harbor in North Carolina, where it was left to rot. After it was stripped of flesh by gulls, the bleached skull was sold to a wealthy plantation owner, who converted Blackbeard's massive head into a silver-sided punch bowl. This gruesome artifact eventually disappeared.

While vile and depraved in life, Blackbeard has become even more disturbed in death. He is completely driven to find his head and descend into Hell, but he also jealously guards his hidden treasures and his watery grave. By playing upon these deep-seated emotions, it may be possible to urge Blackbeard into appearing.

Blackbeard is most often found near Teach's Hole, which is on the western shore of Ocracoke Island, off the coast of North Carolina. When approaching this area, watch for the eerie green glow that Blackbeard's Ghost radiates. Oddly enough, Blackbeard's Ghost can also be spied at Teach's Hole on clear days as well. Because the pirate so enjoyed the ocean, it is likely that he resurfaces when the weather is splendid in order to bask in the sun once again. Fishermen in the area actually view any sighting of Blackbeard's headless corpse as a good omen signifying a successful and heavy haul.

When Blackbeard's Ghost is ashore, he almost always travels at night. His bright lantern is visible for many miles, but he can also be recognized by the sound of his boots and his deep, booming voice. Capable of speech, Blackbeard's Ghost often roars "Where's my head?" repeatedly. If you hear such screams, Blackbeard's Ghost will soon follow.

While it is exhilarating to spy Blackbeard's Ghost at a distance, avoid direct encounters with the ghoul. Like other headless ghosts, Blackbeard frequently attempts to claim the heads of others as his own. Death at the hands of Blackbeard's Ghost is slow and painful; if Blackbeard does attempt to take your head, rest assured that he will saw through your neck with a cutlass that is rusted and dull, and the last sound you will ever hear is his deep and brutal laughter.

WHITE HORSE PLAINS

VITAL STATISTICS

LOCATION: Saint François Xavier, Manitoba, Canada. The place where several ghost sightings have occurred is marked by a twelve-foot-tall statue of a white stallion near the TransCanada Highway.

NUMBER OF GHOSTLY RESIDENTS: One

IDENTITY OF GHOSTLY RESIDENT: A ghostly white horse believed to be the reincarnated spirit of a murdered Cree maiden

TYPE OF ACTIVITY: Phantom

DEMEANOR OF THE WHITE HORSE PLAINS GHOST: Free-spirited and wild. Although the ghost is wary of humans and does not take well to being pursued, it has never been known to charge mortals.

ENCOUNTERING THE WHITE HORSE PLAINS GHOST:

Virtually every region of North America boasts a large number of stories about spectral animals, almost always described as white, that cannot be caught or tamed. These range from wild white buffalo to elusive white deer and rabbits. Perhaps the most common of all the white animals are the white horses, viewed by many as the ultimate free spirits. Completely untamed, these supernatural steeds roam North American plains and prairies as they please. Almost all of the white horses and their kin are impossible to capture, kill, or subdue. Like many other ghostly white animals, white horses also pos-

sess supernatural powers enabling them to become invisible, pass through objects, heal rapidly, and run at speeds that defy nature.

The origins of the various white steeds vary, but many revolve around human reincarnation. The most famous of these tales relates the origin of the white horse of the White Horse Plains in Saint François Xavier, Manitoba. According to lore, long ago a Cree warrior brought an impressive white horse to a Cree chief in the hopes of winning the hand of the chief's daughter. The marriage was soon arranged, but a jealous Sioux rival organized a war party and descended upon the wedding.

In order to lead the Sioux away from the unarmed wedding guests, the bride and groom took to mounts, he on a gray steed and she on her beautiful white horse. The two riders soon found themselves on the open plain, without rocks or trees to provide camouflage. Tragically, the couple was quickly spotted, chased down, and slaughtered. The groom's mount was also killed, but the white horse managed to escape.

Immediately following the brutal murders, the magnificent white horse began appearing on the plains near Saint François Xavier, usually quite close to the site of the bride's death. Despite repeated attempts, the horse could neither be caught nor killed. Like the Cree who originally watched the horse in awe, supernaturalists now believe that upon her death, the bride's spirit fled her body and took possession of the horse. The union of the two transformed the steed into a specter capable of the supernatural feats. Today, the spirit of the White Horse Plains still roams free in memory of the blood spilled long ago, and a monument has been erected near the site in order to commemorate the horse's tragic origins.

Because of its speed and intelligence, the white horse of Saint François Xavier is very difficult to corner or even glimpse for more than a fleeting moment. Ghost hunters may be successful if they establish an observation post, complete with a comfortable chair and binoculars, near the statue of the white horse. Watch the horizon at dawn and dusk for any sign of the quickly moving stallion, but do not chase after the creature if you happen to spy it in the distance, as you will never be able to capture the beast. If, by some

> "[The White Horse's] fire, his grace, his beauty, his speed, his endurance, his intelligence were the attributes that men commonly admire most in horses, but in him they were supernal; his passion for liberty was the passion that his admirers and pursuers idealized most constantly, both in the abstract and in themselves."
>
> —J. Frank Dobie,
> *Tales of the Mustang*

Mike Grandmaison

The statue honoring the fabled White Horse of the White Horse Plains in Saint François Xavier, Manitoba.

Other White Horses

Several other prominent members of the "herd" of white horses have been reliably reported around North America. In the great plains, there are frequent sightings of the White Steed of the Prairies. The Southwest is home to the White Mustang, the Phantom Wild Horse, and the Ghost Horse of the Plains. The White Stallion of Vermont is believed to be the reborn spirit of American patriot Ethan Allen, who reportedly expressed his desire to be reincarnated as a wild white horse, the animal he most admired. Allen was devoted to Vermont and its people; this particular white stallion seems to have this same fierce loyalty, as it is never seen outside of the state.

Only one white horse has ever been captured, and the story surrounding that event is a lamentable tale. The Pacing White Stallion of Travis County, Texas, was long sought by cowboys, and it was eventually roped and brought to a ranch, where it was kept tied to a stake. The wranglers provided the horse with large amounts of food and water, both of which the animal completely refused. The horse languished for ten days before simply dropping dead. Like many animals born free and meant to live their lives in such a state, phantom horses clearly cannot bear captivity and readily choose a second death over a lifetime of imprisonment.

miraculous whim of fate, the horse actually approaches you, allow it to make the first gestures toward contact. Like all horses, this spectral steed is likely to be easily frightened and will flee if it feels at all threatened. Stand passively in front of the horse and do not reach out to touch the animal unless it offers its head or flank to you. Once you have established contact, try to communicate with the animal either verbally or psychically. If indeed the Cree maiden has been transformed into this wondrous spirit, she may be able to respond.

Other Natural Haunts

Even the smallest tracts of untouched land in North America can record ghostly phenomena. In fact, since the Native Americans ruled the continent well into the present, ghosts have been reported at natural sites throughout every U.S. state and Canadian province. Below is an abridged list of additional natural haunts.

- **Great Plains, Central North America:** This vast expanse of North American land is home to numerous ghosts, including a variety of phantom white horses, several ghostly locomotives, spectral wagon trains, and legions of warring Native Americans and U.S. soldiers. The most unusual of the Great Plains ghosts is the Ghost Wrestler, the spirit of a Native American brave who approaches lone campers. He is initially friendly, but enjoys challenging mortals to some sort of physical contest, usually a wrestling match. If the mortal wins, the Ghost Wrestler will grant the victor his wildest dream; however, if the spirit wins, he will claim his opponent's soul.

- **De Soto Falls, Mentone, Alabama:** This area is haunted by Nancy Dollar, known locally as Granny, who perished in January of 1931 at the age of 108. After her death, her beloved dog, Buster, was put to sleep and buried with the woman. Unfortunately, shortly before her burial, thieves stole Granny's savings, which the woman had been saving to buy a proper headstone. Her restless spirit rose in search of the lost money and was sighted so often that her neighbors finally bought the woman a headstone in 1973. Granny and her dog still appear, however, perhaps in order to thank her benefactors.

- **Coal Canyon, Arizona:** A glowing, giant woman known as the Eagle Woman of Black Mesa has been observed rising from this canyon, most often on clear summer nights. Hundreds of people have had encounters with the apparition, who Native Americans believe was a Hopi widow who committed suicide. Her spirit is said to lure people toward the canyon's rim, where they fall to their deaths.

- **Crooked Creek, Harrison, Arkansas:** On November 21, 1912, Ella Barham was murdered on the shores of this stream by Odus Davidson, who chopped the dead woman's body into seven pieces and hid them in a mine shaft. Davidson was convicted and hanged, but Ella's ghost still wanders the creek.

- **Mark's Mill, Warren, Arkansas:** One of dozens of Civil War battlegrounds haunted by the phantoms and disembodied moans of the men killed at the site. The ghosts here include a Confederate soldier looking for lost gold and several Yankee soldiers whose bodies were thrown down a well by their comrades.

- **Elfin Forest, Escondido, California:** One of several ghosts to appear in broad daylight, the White Lady of Elfin Forest is a friendly specter who has made physical contact with witnesses on several occasions. She is usually observed floating about fifteen inches from the ground and has been known to pass through solid objects.

- **Mount Shasta, California:** Aside from legends of an underground city inhabited by giants, Mount Shasta boasts stories of hooded phantoms and other spirits. The mountain also records frequent Bigfoot sightings.

- **Santa Cruz Island, Channel Islands, California:** This island is the home of a dead Chinese fisherman searching for his lost hand and the ghost of Mary Morrison Reese, who was married to a man notorious for brutally murdering Chinese immigrants.

- **Little Fountain Creek, Dead Man's Canyon, Colorado Springs, Colorado:** William Harkins, murdered by Mexican religious zealots in 1863, torments anyone who comes near this stream. He chases victims with uncanny speed, seemingly oblivious to the ax still protruding from his forehead.

- **Saybrook Woods, New London, Connecticut:** In the winter months, the spirit of young Lottie Enken manifests in this grove. In the early 1700s, the little girl was kidnapped by a deranged hermit known as Old Dreary. Shortly after her disappearance, she was seen skipping through the woods wearing a blue cape. Although she could never be cornered, she left behind a trail of bloody footsteps in the snow. Eventually, her battered and broken body was discovered in a cave, but the revelation did not put the spirit to rest and Lottie is still encountered regularly today.

- **Bethany Beach, Delaware:** Naval hero Eddie Rickenbacker wanders this stretch of coastline in a deranged and confused state, his clothes torn and tattered.

- **Fiddler's Hill, Lewes, Delaware:** This bluff receives its name from the haunting strains of fiddle music that can be heard floating through the area. Legend holds that in the late 1800s, two local men found themselves in love with the same woman. One of the men tried to frighten his rival away by making weird noises on his fiddle while hiding in a tree near the young lady's house. Although the plot worked, the victor, in his elation, fell from the tree, broke his neck, and died.

- **Everglades, Florida:** Along with the spirits of those killed in the Eastern Airlines crash of 1972 (see chapter 2), these swamps are haunted by the ghosts of those lost or murdered in the region. Many of these spirits have refused to travel to the afterlife. Frightening, hair-covered monsters are also reported here with surprising regularity.

- **Lost Island, Okefenokee Swamp, Georgia:** This mysterious island, hidden somewhere deep in the swamp, is home to a race of ghostly women known as the Daughters of the Sun, who have turned their island abode into a paradise. Many explorers have perished trying to find the island, and today numerous visitors to the swamp have

seen the glowing phantom women wandering through the trees at dusk.

- **Rock Oven, Altamaha Swamp, Georgia:** Long ago, numerous sacred rituals were conducted in this cave by Native Americans, who continue to appear in the area as phantoms or disembodied, chanting voices.

- **Lower Mesa Falls, Fayette County, Idaho:** The ghost of a Shoshone maiden, who tried to rescue her lover from the raging waters and drowned for her efforts, appears at the edge of the falls.

- **Wood River Camp, Baker Creek, Idaho:** Russian John, an immense immigrant miner who died in the early 1900s, still roams this riverbed in search of people to frighten. He frequently leaps from behind trees to terrify campers and hikers.

- **Lakey's Creek, McLeansboro, Illinois:** Mr. Lakey, a settler who was decapitated by unknown assailants on his property in this area, has searched for his lost head since his death in the 1840s.

- **Robinson Woods, Chicago, Illinois:** Ghost lights, phantom faces, and the moans of the murdered Alexander Robinson family plague this forest. The Robinsons were Native Americans who received the land as a gift in 1829 after saving a group of white settlers from the Fort Dearborn massacre. The Robinsons were butchered by jealous members of their own tribe.

- **Dunes State Park, Gary, Indiana:** A beautiful phantom woman named Diana of the Dunes, recently identified as Alice Mable Gray, makes her home here. After suffering undisclosed physical and emotional traumas during her youth, Gray decided to abandon society and live alone on the shores of Lake Michigan between 1915 and 1926. In 1920, she fell in love with a vagabond named Paul Wilson, and the couple spent six years in a shack on the beach. Unfortunately, in February of 1926, Alice was beaten to death, presumably by her violent lover.

- **Lover's Leap, Elkader, Iowa:** Long ago, White Cloud, a Native American maiden living near this spot, fell in love with a young white settler. Unfortunately, members of her tribe discovered the affair and attacked the white man. Although the settler escaped the assault without serious injury, the tribal elders told White Cloud that he had actually been slain. The distraught maiden then committed suicide at what is now known as Lover's Leap. A few days later, White Cloud's body was discovered by her true love, who buried her corpse atop the cliff. Today, White Cloud's translucent form can be seen pacing the edge of Lover's Leap as if contemplating another jump.

- **Saline River, Ellis County, Kansas:** Takaluma, an old Native American searching for his father's skull, haunts this area.

- **Sentinel Hill, Hays, Kansas:** Kansas's most famous ghost is Elizabeth Polly, also known as the Blue Light Lady or the Angel of Fort Hays. During a 1867 cholera epidemic that swept through the fort, Polly worked tirelessly to comfort the dying until she herself contracted the disease. As she passed away, she begged to be buried on Sentinel Hill, within view of Fort Hays. Her ghost, which appears wearing a blue bonnet and long blue dress, has been encountered since 1917.

- **Spooksville Triangle, Columbus, Kansas:** This vast stretch of land extending into Missouri and Oklahoma is said to be the home of numerous ghost lights. The spirits have been spotted for over 110 years.

- **Mississippi River, Saint Joseph, Louisiana:** A woman's voice can be heard screaming, "Help me, in the name of God. The men are hurting me!" from this spot along the Mississippi. The specter is believed to be the ghost of a passenger aboard the *Iron Mountain,* a steamboat that disappeared without a trace in 1872 and is believed to have fallen victim to river pirates.

- **Appledore Island, Maine:** The apparition of a woman with long blond hair wanders this island, especially near the area known as Golden Girl Point. She is thought to be the spirit of a woman who once fell in love with Blackbeard (see "Teach's Hole" on page 119), but was abandoned by the pirate when he left her on the island to guard his treasure. The forlorn phantom can be heard whispering, "He will come again."

- **High Point, Belfast, Maine:** Barbara Houndsworth, a woman driven to her death by witch hunters several hundred years ago, wanders the coastline here. After being unfairly sentenced to die as a witch, Barbara fled her captors, but was caught in a sudden rainstorm. In her haste to escape, she slipped on some rocks and plummeted to her death. Her screams are sometimes heard shortly before her glowing apparition emerges, and it is said that she travels with a flock of ghostly gulls.

- **Peddler's Rock, Port Tobacco, Maryland:** This site is haunted by a spirit known as Blue Dog, a spectral canine who once belonged to a wandering peddler. The salesman was robbed and murdered at the rock in the 1700s, but his dog continues to guard the area.

- **Monomy Island National Wildlife Refuge, Massachusetts:** A black stallion surrounded by a ghostly white aura swims in the rough waters just off shore at this park. The horse was once used by a pirate, who would tie a lantern to the steed's neck and force it to pace back and forth along the beach. The moving light attracted ships, which ran aground near the island and were subsequently pillaged by the pirate. Some say that today the black stallion attempts to warn ships of the unsafe conditions near the island, perhaps to atone for the misdeeds of its past.

- **Forester Campgrounds, Port Sanilac, Michigan:** Perhaps the most haunted campground in North America, this retreat is visited by the ghost of Minnie Quay. On May 29, 1876, the teenage girl heard news that her lover had been lost at sea. She threw herself from the Forester pier and drowned, but now appears at the edge of the campground, where she urges other young girls to follow her example. The ghost has been blamed for at least one death.

- **Castle Royal Caves, Saint Paul, Minnesota:** In 1933, these natural limestone caves were converted into an underground nightclub that catered to gangsters and other undesirables. Ever since three hoodlums were shot dead in the club in 1934, ghosts have been sighted here. Along with the dead hoods, the caves are haunted by a man and woman who appear very night at 3:00 A.M. and an unknown man in a Panama hat.

- **Slaughter Slough, Lake Shetek, Minnesota:** In the mid-1800s, settlers massacred scores of Native Americans at this site. Perhaps because they were buried without proper rights in a huge pit, the ghosts have reappeared as spirited ghost lights flying over the lake at night.

- **Natchez Trace, Natchez, Mississippi:** This notorious path, which stretches for hundreds of miles, is also known as the Witches Dance because it was once thought that witches and warlocks cavorted along the trail, causing the grass to wither and die. At least one witch is believed to have lived along the Trace; she was blamed for murdering outlaws and grinding their bones to make her wicked potions. Joseph Thompson, a bandit who killed over one hundred people while lurking along the Trace, confessed to encountering numerous spirits, including a spectral white horse. Thompson was hanged in 1818, but many believe he too has returned to the Trace.

- **Ozark Mountains, Missouri:** The so-called Ozark Madonna, a barefoot phantom, carries her ghostly infant throughout these mountains. The apparition is the spirit of Laurie May Maumsey, who lived with her drunken husband and beloved baby in a shack. One night, in a dreadful argument, the drunken Mr. Maumsey threatened to kill the couple's child, but Laurie grabbed the infant from him. In the ensuing struggle, the child slipped from Laurie's arms and was killed when its head struck the ground. Soon after, Laurie took her own life.

- **Black Horse Lake, Great Falls, Montana:** A road on the shores of this lake has been the site of numerous encounters with a phantom hitchhiker who stands in the middle of the street until he is struck by an oncoming car, at which point he vanishes. He appears to be a Native American man with long black hair wearing overalls and a denim jacket.

- **Blackbird Hill, Omaha Indian Reservation, Nebraska:** Every October 17, the anguished screams of a murdered woman echo throughout this site. In 1849, the woman asked her husband for a divorce, confessing that she was in love with another man. The husband lost his mind, stabbed his wife several times, and finally slit her throat. Shortly after, the dead woman's lover stole her corpse and buried it on Blackbird Hill.

- **Six Mile Canyon, Virginia City, Nevada:** In the 1860s, outlaw Jack Davis buried hordes of treasure in this stretch of canyon. After his death in 1877, he returned to jealously guard his loot. Numerous treasure hunters entering the canyon have been confronted by Davis's shrieking specter hovering in the air on huge wings.

- **Raccoon Mountain Road, Ossipee, New Hampshire:** The horse of Adam Brown, who was ambushed and murdered in the 1830s, still wanders this hill. While Brown was being butchered, the horse slid into a ravine, broke its leg, and slowly starved to death. Now, the spectral animal follows behind visitors to the area.

- **Toll Hill, Eaton Center, New Hampshire:** Another New Hampshire phantom horse haunts this area. The animal died during a blizzard in 1925 when it was trapped in an abandoned building at the site.

- **Chaco Canyon National Park, New Mexico:** This park courses with supernatural energies of every variety and is believed by some to be among the most powerful sacred sites in the entire world. Among the ghosts reported is a tall, naked man of unknown origin, who is often surrounded by a blue light or a strange mist.

- **Lake Pleasant, Albany, New York:** Mary Golden Rhinelander, whose husband built a large estate and sawmill here in the early 1800s, has haunted the site since her death in 1818. During the years following her demise, she appeared before numerous workers and was not afraid to walk abroad during the day. Her former home was destroyed in a fire in 1874, but she continues to stroll the shores of Lake Pleasant.

- **Thompson Park, Watertown, New York:** This park has recorded a number of unusual incidents, beginning in the 1930s, when several stone walls were built on a grassy hill in the area. Ever since, a huge number of visitors have been affected by the site's aura, which leaves many light-headed. Phantoms, disembodied voices, ghost lights, and spectral animals have also been witnessed. In the 1970s, a teenager standing atop the hill simply vanished before numerous astounded observers. He reappeared a full twenty minutes later at the bottom of the hill, totally confused and with no recollection of where he had been. Many people believe that the hill is a doorway to another dimension.

- **Hannah's Creek Swamp, Smithfield, North Carolina:** An island in this swamp is haunted by the spirits of the fifty members of David Fanning's Marauders, a pack of wild bandits who terrorized the area until they were cornered during the Civil War by Confederate troops. The soldiers were led by Colonel John Saunders, who had recently lost his parents to the Marauders. In an act of revenge, Saunders ordered that all of the bandits be hanged. Today, fifty ghostly forms can be seen hanging from the island's trees, moaning as they sway in the breeze.

- **Shut-in Creek, Hot Springs, North Carolina:** Disembodied voices, a rolling ghost light, and other strange happenings have occurred at this site since a man was overcome and killed by poison fumes from a nearby manganese mine in the early 1900s.

- **Black Butte, Amidon, North Dakota:** The spirit of Bob Pierce, a ranch hand known locally as Crazy Loon because of his reckless riding of horses, can be observed as he forces a spectral steed up the sides of the butte. He only appears on moonless nights and is often trailed by an eerie chorus of wolves howling.

- **Big Rock, Pike County, Ohio:** Old Raridan, a huge ghostly gray wolf, is said to guard this formation. In the late 1700s, the spot was known as a place where wolves came to die. In a phenomenon still unexplained by science, literally hundreds of the animals, most suffering from the effects of disease or old age, pulled themselves across miles of rough terrain until they reached the hill, where they finally allowed themselves to die. In the early 1800s, Old Raridan and his mate were mortally wounded

by hunters. With his last ounce of strength, Raridan dragged his bleeding mate to Big Rock, where they both perished.

- **Cherry Hill, Fayette County, Ohio:** Also known as Haunted Hill, this region is ruled by a headless horseman, believed to have been murdered by thieves seeking the man's gold. The victim's skeletal remains, save for his head, were uncovered in June of 1953, but the identities of the ghost and his killers remain unknown, as does the location of his skull.

- **Elk Mountain, Lawton, Oklahoma:** An underground cave in this mountain is said to house a fortune in gold, but the treasure is guarded by the hundreds of explorers who have lost their lives trying to find the hidden vault.

- **Forest Grove, Washington County, Oregon:** An angry and muscular phantom roaming these woods has been accused of several deaths and disappearances in the area. The ghost, known as the Phantom Bugler, was a woodsman who traveled around Forest Grove with a gold bugle around his neck. In 1910, he was savaged by a mountain lion. When his body was discovered, his battered bugle was lying beside him; in an act of desperation, he had evidently used his beloved instrument to fend off the animal. Beware: Death has greatly angered the Bugler, and he takes the life of anyone he encounters.

- **Gettysburg National Military Park, Gettysburg, Pennsylvania:** Over fifty thousand Americans died at this battleground on July 3, 1863, in the most devastating confrontation of the Civil War. The bloodshed has left a lasting impression, creating dozens of spirits who wander the area. The most commonly reported spirit is that of George Washington, who allegedly first appeared to lead the Union soldiers to victory.

- **Hawk Mountain Sanctuary, Berks County, Pennsylvania:** Numerous apparitions inhabit this area, including a glowing, ten-foot-tall phantom. Other ghosts include a few murdered settlers and the victims of Mathias Schambacher and his wife, who ran an inn at the peak where they robbed and murdered their guests.

- **Huntington Beach State Park, Myrtle Beach, South Carolina:** Whenever the tide rises, the phantom of a ten-year-old boy who died at this site can be heard screaming for help as he drowns in the surf. Locals have nicknamed the spirit Crab Boy, because the child perished when he was attacked by a huge stone crab while wandering the marsh. He could not free himself and drowned when the tide came in.

- **Stones River Battlefield, Murfreesboro, Tennessee:** Among the numerous Civil War soldiers still manifesting here is yet another headless ghost. Ironically known as Old Green Eyes, the spirit was decapitated by a cannonball. A distraught woman in white also roams the battlefield, searching for the corpse of her lover.

- **Stampede Mesa, Crosbytown, Texas:** Phantom longhorns, led by a ghostly man on a large spectral horse, run rampant across this bluff at night. The longhorns are the spirits of over fifteen hundred cattle who stampeded in 1889 and unwittingly rushed over a one-hundred-foot cliff. The next morning, a mob of cattlemen con-

victed a local man of causing the stampede, tied him to a horse, and sent the animal charging over the cliff as well. Both horse and rider were killed in the fall and have been cursed to ride along with the herd in death.

- **Old Rag Mountain, Winchester, Virginia:** A pair of female ghosts have been encountered along the slopes of this mountain since 1925. They are believed to be the spirits of Marie and Lucy Carwell, sisters who found themselves homeless after the Pheasant Hill Plantation burned to the ground in 1865. Lucy's fate is largely unknown, but Marie spent her remaining years alone in a cabin on the mountain, where she died in the 1880s. Lucy's ghost is always fashionably dressed, while Marie's seems to be wearing rags.

- **Green Lake, Seattle, Washington:** A dark wraith, said to be the soul of an unidentified serial killer, has been abducting and murdering victims in this area since the 1920s.

- **Ghost Hills, Morley, Alberta, Canada:** These mountains are home to the dead Stony Indian chief White Eagle, who is often spotted riding a spectral white horse. He emerges at night from a peak known as Devil's Head and scours the area in search of his enemies. He is often trailed by a spectral white terrier.

- **Pitt Lake, British Columbia, Canada:** The search for Slumach's Lost Mine, a hidden gold mine, has claimed the lives of over twenty people. The hoard was originally discovered by a Salish Indian named Slumach, who was known to bring a maiden with him to the mine each time he visited the site. Once at the mine, he would shoot or stab his guest in order to protect his secret and leave behind ghosts to guard his treasure. He was hanged in 1891 for murdering a prospector, but his soul has remained in the area well into modern times, ensuring that anyone who seeks the mine meets with tragedy.

- **Beaubears Island, New Brunswick, Canada:** This island is home to a headless French nun who was decapitated by a trapper shortly before she was to return to her homeland. Her ghost reappears in search of a way back to France.

- **Ile des Demons (Iles Harrington), Quebec, Canada:** Site of demonic apparitions and violent imps, the island was once the scene of great tragedy. In 1591, Jean-François de La Rocque de Roberval was traveling to the New World with his niece, Marguerite, when he discovered that the girl had taken a lover aboard the ship. In a fit of rage, Jean-François abandoned Marguerite and her maid, Damienne, on one of the Iles Harrington. Marguerite's lover jumped ship and swam to the island, where the three lived a difficult existence. Marguerite eventually gave birth, but the child

perished in days. Soon after, both her lover and maid died as well. Marguerite managed to hold onto life, but not her sanity, for three years. She was eventually rescued by fishermen and sent back to France. Today, it is unknown which island was the scene of Marguerite's trauma, but all of the Iles Harrington are considered haunted.

- **Ile d'Orléans, Saint Lawrence River, Quebec, Canada:** Jean-Pierre Lavallée, born to Indian and French parents, haunts this island. In life, he was believed to be a powerful sorcerer with complete control over the weather. When British ships attempted to attack Quebec City on August 24, 1711, Lavallee conjured a thick fog. The warships were forced to turn back, and Lavallée was heralded as a hero. Other spirits on the island include the spirits of dead sailors, who usually manifest as ghost lights.

- **Yorkton Crossroads, Saskatchewan, Canada:** The center of these paths is home of a very young ghost, estimated at about three- or four-years-old. She may be the spirit of a girl struck down by a wagon at the site. The girlish ghoul makes no sound, but stands for a moment in the middle of the crossroads and then suddenly vanishes.

5. OTHER HAUNTED SITES

THIS CHAPTER COVERS a variety of haunted sites that do not fit easily into any other category.

They run the gamut from the ghost-infested Alcatraz prison to a lonely street corner and a haunted highway. The only factors these places have in common is the presence of ghosts and, quite often, a tragic history. Although they offer few uniform rules, readers should note that many of the unorthodox sites contained in this section are considered among the most haunted locations in the entire world.

One subgroup of haunted sites included here and in need of special attention is the col-

lection of so-called haunted villages, small communities infested by ghosts. Haunted villages are usually located in isolated regions, far from the noise and activity of modern cities. Most haunted villages were founded by early settlers and were built near or directly atop supernatural sites of great power, usually dark and devious in nature. When this energy came into contact with mortals, it caused sweeping misfortune, such as the collapse of local industries, plagues, or constant attacks by Native Americans, often leading inhabitants to believe that the area was cursed. In Salem, Massachusetts, the disaster took the form of the Salem witch trials, while Connecticut's Dudleytown found itself surrounded by infertile land. In the majority of cases, the specific disaster causes the local populace to abandon their town. Today, most haunted villages are largely uninhabited by the living, but boast a healthy population of those who perished when the community fell victim to the whims of fate.

For the most part, the ghosts roaming a haunted village are merely lonely. Unless evil in life, few of these spirits are dangerous to the living. Unfortunately, haunted villages typically carry some form of curse that was responsible for the original community's downfall. Therefore, entering such a site can become hazardous if one is exposed to a supernatural aura of misfortune. To avoid the effects of these curses, one should never remain in a haunted village for more than a few hours. Also, it is essential that objects never be removed from the environs. Even a seemingly innocuous pebble or twig could carry a lingering hint of the town's powerful curse.

Another category of haunted sites are objects known to house a ghost. As odd as it may seem, everything from mirrors to cherished toys to a well-used hairbrush can become possessed by a spirit. Although the concept of a haunted toy or mirror may be strange, the theory behind this phenomenon is fairly simple.

Throughout our lives, we all become extremely attached to favorite possessions. We may have a special rocking chair or a guitar that seems to remain in perfect pitch; and we may fall in love with our cars or rely upon an old quilt for comfort. Subsequently, such items can become the focus of a spirit's haunting. A violinist, for example, might suddenly take up residence *within* his old instrument, while the spirit of a hardworking painter might choose to inhabit the artist's favorite piece.

Most object-bound ghosts reveal their presence through mild poltergeist activity centered upon the item they inhabit. Haunted instruments play themselves, haunted toys move about on their own, and a haunted rocking chair will rock endlessly. Because of the limitations of the object they inhabit, some ghosts are forced to be a bit more creative. As a general rule, the more unusual the object, the more unusual the manifestation becomes. A portrait housing a ghost might suddenly fade (as occurred at the **Haw Branch Plantation,** featured in chapter 1), while a haunted mirror is likely to warp or crack inexplicably.

Although often unsettling, haunted objects rarely pose a threat to the living. Exceptions to this rule include items that are dangerous simply by virtue of their original functions, such as a rifle, butcher knife, or lawnmower. When plagued by poltergeist activity, such objects may seem to come alive and attack innocent bystanders. In some cases, the presence of a ghost in an object can also create the illusion that the item is cursed. For example, fatal accidents may plague anyone who dons a pair of haunted skis, while the individual who possesses a haunted lighter is doomed to die in a horrible fire. In both these instances and in similar cases, the cause of death is undoubtedly the resident spirit, who may be unhappy that its former possession is now in the hands of another.

ALCATRAZ ISLAND

VITAL STATISTICS

LOCATION: San Francisco Bay, San Francisco, California; (415) 705-1042. Cell Blocks A, B, C, and D are all considered haunted. The former prison can be reached only by special tour boats moored at Pier 41; tour information can be obtained at (415) 705-5555, or contact the San Francisco Visitor's Bureau at (415) 391-2000.

NUMBER OF GHOSTLY RESIDENTS: Unknown, but probably over a dozen

IDENTITIES OF GHOSTLY RESIDENTS: Numerous former inmates, including Al Capone, George "Machine Gun" Kelly, Alvin "Creepy" Karpis, Arthur "Doc" Barker, bank robber Bernie Coy, murderer Rufe McCain, Abie "Butcher" Maldowitz, and Robert Stroud, better known as the Birdman of Alcatraz

TYPE OF ACTIVITY: Strange and unexplained noises, poltergeist disturbances, disembodied voices, phantom banjo music, hot and cold spots, eerie auras, and apparitions

DEMEANOR OF GHOSTLY RESIDENTS: Belligerent and criminal. Most of the ghosts were violent sociopaths in life, and there is no indication that their behavior or attitudes have changed in death. Fortunately, they seem content with casting their miserable aura over others, rarely escalating to physical attacks. However, the ghost in the laundry room should be considered a physical threat.

ENCOUNTERING THE GHOSTS OF ALCATRAZ:

The most notorious prison in the United States is also one of the country's most haunted historical tourist attractions. The Miwok Indians, who first named the site Alcatraz—or "island of the pelicans"—believed that the area was inhabited by several evil spirits. They refused to sail to the island for any reason, but the U.S. military did not heed these warnings and began using the large rock as a prison. In 1859, many of the Miwok were finally compelled to visit the island as Alcatraz's very first prisoners. By

Alcatraz Prison.

1868, the island had been given to the U.S. War Department for use as an internment camp for deserters and prisoners of war. In 1912, the military completed construction of a vast stone fortress, which was transformed into a federal prison in 1933.

Reserved for only the worst criminals from across the nation, Alcatraz soon became home to a host of gangsters and killers, including Al Capone and "Machine Gun" Kelly. Once locked in the prison, these thugs found that escape was largely impossible. Alcatraz was

staffed with one guard for every three inmates, a ratio far greater than any other prison on the continent. And even if a prisoner could somehow slip from his cell, sneak past the guards, and scale the prison's walls, he would never be able to make the long swim from the island to the mainland because of the San Francisco Bay's cold waters and strong currents.

Inmates also discovered that life within the Alcatraz, nicknamed "the Rock," was incredibly harsh. The convicts were not allowed to talk to one another and were forced to remain in their cells for up to fourteen hours each day. Unruly inmates were doused with powerful water hoses, beaten by clubs, chained to their cell bars by biting handcuffs, kept in solitary confinement for months at a time, or confined to straitjackets.

Despite its legendary status as "escape-proof," several escape attempts did occur on the island, most of which ended in death. Arthur "Doc" Barker, son of the criminal mastermind Kate "Ma" Barker, was gunned down while trying to flee the prison on June 13, 1939. In 1946, 46-year-old Bernie Coy, serving time for bank robbery, plotted another escape attempt. Joined by several other inmates, Coy rushed a group of nine guards, stole their weapons, and took control of the armory. After releasing almost all of Alcatraz's inmates, Coy and his allies incited a riot, hoping to slip from the island during the ensuing chaos. Unfortunately, they could not find a vital key and were trapped. Shortly after, the prison's authorities called in the marines to restore order. Coy and most of his accomplices were shot dead in the conflict.

Coy's bold escape attempt attracted widespread attention and caused the federal government to launch a full-scale investigation into conditions on the island. They were horrified to find that many of the prisoners had been brutally mistreated. Some had been beaten to the edge of death, and at least one man suffered seven years of sensory deprivation within the "hole," a dank, dark, and cramped pit used for solitary confinement. The prison eventually fell into disrepair and was officially shut down in 1963. The island subsequently became the property of the National Park Service, who reopened Alcatraz as a tourist attraction later that same year.

While the mortal prisoners were ultimately transferred from Alcatraz, those who had died at the site stayed behind as ghosts. In later years, many of the Rock's former inmates passed away while serving out their sentences in other facilities, but their spirits were inexplicably drawn back to Alcatraz, where they had suffered for so many years. Today, the prison seems positively overrun with specters, who roam the cell blocks in the company of chattering tourists.

Strange noises are the most common ghostly manifestation on Alcatraz. Visitors and park personnel have reported hearing screams, weeping, metal pans striking the bars, whispers, and phantom footsteps throughout Cell Blocks A, B, and C. A "dungeon" near Cell Block A is especially active.

At one point, authorities were compelled to hire psychic Sylvia Brown to investigate the staggering number of unexplained sounds and poltergeist activity emanating from Cell Block C. According to Brown, Block C is dominated by an extremely agitated and violent spirit calling himself Butcher. Butcher could not be calmed by Brown, who evidently established a psychic link with the vicious ghost. Later, investigators deduced that this spirit is actually the ghost of a mob hit man named Abie Maldowitz, who was renowned for his savagery and often went by the nickname of Butcher. While serving time in Alcatraz, Maldowitz was forced to work in the laundry facilities in Cell Block C, where he was eventually overpowered and murdered by another inmate. Today, his angry spirit has refused to leave the site of his violent demise.

Within Cell Block D, at least four separate cells are haunted by individual ghosts. Cells 11-D, 12-D, and 13-D produce three distinct

The Most Haunted State

There is much controversy as to which state boasts the most haunted sites. Many believe that the majority of haunts are located along the East Coast, particularly in New England. However, this simply is not the case, as evidenced by the numerous reports of hauntings from all across the continent. In fact, as of this writing, the most haunted state appears to be California, reporting in with well over a thousand confirmed haunted sites. The Golden State's spectral standing is admittedly due in part to its great size. However, California also has a long history of violence and hardship. It also appears to be the center of vast supernatural energy and boasts a number of very popular sacred sites and power points far more active than those in other states.

New York state follows immediately behind California (and, according to some researchers, may even rival it). Other ghost-infested states include Virginia, Pennsylvania, and Arizona. The least haunted state is Alaska, due to the small population and perhaps the cold, which may ward away ghosts. New Hampshire, Washington State, South Dakota, Rhode Island, and Idaho also possess relatively small ghost populations.

voices that often have conversations with one another. Cell 14-D was once used as the solitary confinement cell for murderer Rufe McCain, who spent more than three years in isolation. The torture inflicted on McCain has had a lasting effect on the cell, which is reported to have a chilling aura even during the height of summer. In one corner of the cell, where McCain undoubtedly spent many hours huddled in anguish, sensitives report being overwhelmed by sorrow and despair.

The strangest spectral occurrence is reported in the dilapidated shower room, where the eerie strains of banjo music can often be heard. Most ghost hunters suspect that music is the work of the infamous mobster Al Capone. Convicted on charges of income tax evasion in 1932, Capone spent the next seven years in Alcatraz. During this time, his brain and body were ravaged by unchecked syphilis. Upon his release in 1939, Capone was deranged and physically unable to care for himself. His remaining eight years were spent in seclusion in Miami Beach, where he finally wasted away.

Other candidates for the disturbances on Alcatraz include Bernie Coy and Doc Barker, the two men killed only minutes from freedom. Another spirit may be Alvin "Creepy" Karpis, who served one of Alcatraz's longest sentences. Karpis was one of Doc Barker's partners and spent twenty-six years on the Rock before being transferred to Washington's McNeil Island Penitentiary in 1962. He was finally released in 1969 and returned to Canada, where he eventually passed away.

George "Machine Gun" Kelly, who served a brief stint in Alcatraz before being transferred to Leavenworth in Kansas, where he died in 1954, might also be a permanent resident of the prison today.

Possibly the only peaceful inhabitant of Alcatraz is Robert Stroud, the world-famous "Birdman of Alcatraz." In 1906, at the age of nineteen, Stroud was self-employed as a purveyor of prostitutes in Alaska. When a bartender refused to pay Stroud a fee of ten dollars, Stroud attacked and killed the man. For this crime, he was sentenced to twelve years in prison. During this time, he became a voracious reader of ornithology texts and was eventually transformed into a skilled ornithologist. He even cataloged a number of previously unknown diseases that plague birds, merely by observing the birds that passed by the window of his cell.

Unfortunately, shortly before his release from Leavenworth, Stroud stabbed a guard through the heart and was sentenced to die. He was saved from the gallows by his mother, who wrote a compelling letter to Woodrow and Elizabeth Wilson. The first lady was touched by Stroud's devotion to birds and urged her husband to commute Stroud's sentence to life in solitary confinement.

From 1920 to 1943, Stroud was imprisoned in Leavenworth, where the guards expanded his cell to allow him to conduct his research. After writing and publishing *A Diary of Bird Diseases* in 1943, he was transferred to Alcatraz, where he received widespread notice as an eccentric and finally earned his nickname, "the Birdman of Alcatraz." After spending almost twenty years in Alcatraz, he was transferred to Springfield, Missouri, where he died in 1963. Yet even today, visitors can hear the Birdman calling to his pets in a high-pitched whistle near his old cell, 22-D.

Alcatraz can be visited only through guided audio tours that begin at Pier 41 in San Francisco. The tour covers all four haunted cell blocks, although it does not enter the showers where Al Capone plays his banjo. However, as you pass near this area, remove your headphones and listen carefully, for you may hear the warped music drifting through the hallways.

During the tour, you (and the rest of the group) will be asked to step into a cell for a moment. The cell will then be closed and locked temporarily in an attempt to convey the confinement that the prisoners endured. During this experience, many sensitives are overwhelmed by Alcatraz's aura of hopelessness. While most visitors should be content with a "normal" cell, ghost hunters are encouraged to request that they spend their momentary imprisonment in either Cell 11-D, 12-D, 13-D, 14-D, or 22-D. If you manage to squeeze into Cell 14-D, slowly explore each corner until you find the lingering remains of Rufe Mc-Cain's spirit.

Alcatraz should be considered fairly safe for ghost hunters, largely because it can be explored only during the day and in the company of a large number of other people. However, never forget that the island's many ghosts are all hardened criminals. These are the spirits of brutal and cold-blooded murderers who probably loathe the living. While the ghosts of Alcatraz have yet to rise up and use their supernatural powers to commit murder, there is no guarantee that they will not do so in the future. Ghost hunters should be extremely wary, especially of such ghoulish entities as Butcher and Al Capone.

BIRD CAGE THEATRE AND TOMBSTONE, ARIZONA

VITAL STATISTICS

LOCATION: The Theatre is a National Historic Site located on the corner of Sixth and Allen Streets in Tombstone, Arizona. Inquiries for more information should be sent to P.O. Box 248, Tombstone, AZ 85638.

NUMBER OF GHOSTLY RESIDENTS: Unknown

IDENTITIES OF GHOSTLY RESIDENTS: Several slain gunfighters; the ghost of a little boy who perished of yellow fever; a former owner; prostitutes, card players, and others who spent time in the Bird Cage; possibly one (or more) of the Clantons; and an elderly woman who passed away in 1958

TYPE OF ACTIVITY: Phantoms, place-memory spirits, strange smells and sounds, ghost lights, poltergeist disturbances, disembodied singing and laughter, phantom music and crowd noise, invisible footsteps, and virtually every other form of ghostly manifestation known

DEMEANOR OF GHOSTLY RESIDENTS: Varies. At least one of the phantoms is angry and destructive, but the other ghosts simply reenact an evening from a time long past.

ENCOUNTERING THE GHOSTS OF THE BIRD CAGE THEATRE: RIP RIP RIP RIP

T ombstone, Arizona, is one of those towns so marked by violence that almost every building in the small community has recorded some sort of spectral manifestation. The city sprang from the desert in 1877 when silver was discovered in the area, and from 1879 to 1889, Tombstone was considered a boom town, attracting hordes of prospectors seeking their fortunes in Arizona's mountains. With the miners came thieves, who were followed by bounty hunters and corrupt lawmen, creating an atmosphere of unchecked lawlessness. Among the gunfighters who spent time in Tombstone were Wyatt Earp and his kin, Doc Holliday, Johnny Ringo, Jesse James, Wild Bill Hickok, the notorious Clantons and McLaurys, Billy the Kid, and Calamity Jane. Tombstone's long history of bloody shoot-outs, including the brutal incident at the OK Corral, filled the infamous Boot Hill Cemetery to capacity. In fact, the bloodshed became so severe that in 1882, President Chester A. Arthur threatened to declare martial law on the outlaw town.

The violence that permeated Tombstone has had a long-lasting effect. Phantoms are spotted wandering the streets and in most of the older buildings. Tombstone's famous saloons, such as Big Nose Kate's, have had a number of ghostly experiences. At the OK Corral, the Earps, Clantons, McLaurys, and Doc Holliday reenact their historical gunfight. And Boot Hill is positively alive with spirits rising up from their graves.

Within this haunted town, one of the most ghost-infested in all the world, the heart of the spectral activity is considered to be the Bird Cage Theatre. Built as a burlesque hall in 1881, the Bird Cage was the Wild West's most sinful den of iniquity, offering a stage, dance hall, bar, and casino. But the Theatre's centerpiece was a collection of fourteen "bird cages," draped in red velvet and hanging from the ceiling, from which prostitutes solicited the Bird Cage's patrons. At the height of its grandeur, the Bird Cage offered everything a scoundrel could desire: booze, sex, raucous music, cigars, poker and other games of chance, fistfights, and the chance to rub shoulders with the great gunfighters of the day. Within a year of its grand opening, the Bird Cage's reputation had spread across the country, prompting the *New York Times* to call the club "the wildest, wickedest night spot between Basin Street and the Barbary Coast."

On many nights, the combination of drink and macho blustering led to confrontations between the various rogues who gathered at the site. Between 1881 and 1889, the year that the Bird Cage officially closed, the honky-tonk recorded at least sixteen fatal and fearsome gun battles that left the establishment pockmarked by over 140 separate bullet holes. Many of the victims of these shootouts were carried away to the Boot Hill Cemetery in the Black Mariah, the town's original hearse, which is currently on display at the Bird Cage Theatre.

While Tombstone is now a small community of scarcely two thousand people, those who enjoyed life and experienced death at the Bird Cage still inhabit the hall. Literally hundreds of witnesses have come forward with descriptions of the widespread haunting that has taken root in the building. The most common ghostly phenomena are auditory in nature; these include the sounds of laughter, music, talking, singing, and gunfire. Numerous people visiting the Bird Cage suddenly hear themselves surrounded by a loud, drunken crowd, despite the fact that the rooms remain empty.

The Bird Cage is also known for its olfactory spectral manifestations. Witnesses detect cigar smoke, gunpowder, spilled booze, and human sweat. In particular, an operating music box, ornately carved from rosewood, emits the strong smell of cigar smoke whenever it is opened.

Phantoms are a common sight within the Bird Cage as well. Most wear clothing fashionable in the late 1800s, and almost all of the male apparitions sport some sort of weapon. The most frequently encountered ghost is a man wearing a visor and carrying a clipboard. He is most often spotted walking quickly across the stage. Although his identity is unknown, he may have been in charge of the Bird Cage's entertainment.

On some occasions, several types of spectral manifestations come together to make those entering the Bird Cage feel as if they have been momentarily transported back in time: For a few seconds they hear, see, and even smell the Bird Cage Theatre as it was back in the 1880s. They are surrounded by phantoms and the noise of the crowded rooms. They glimpse the prostitutes swinging in their cages and hear these women calling out to prospective clients. Sometimes, they witness a gunfight or drunken brawl, experiencing the event as if it were actually happening.

The haunting is further intensified by the poltergeist activity that frequently plagues the Bird Cage. The ghosts performing this mischief are generally harmless, content to hide or move objects about, topple chairs, and the like. However, during at least one séance, Bill Hunley, the Bird Cage's owner, was nearly strangled to death by an unseen spirit. Some ghost hunters speculate that the assailant may have been the spirit of one of the Clantons, a group of gunslingers killed by the Earp brothers at the OK Corral. The Clanton ghost is also blamed for repeatedly toppling a statue carved to resemble Wyatt Earp.

Among the other ghosts believed to inhabit the Bird Cage are Bill Hunley's great-grandfather, who originally built the theatre. Hunley's aunt, who passed away in 1958, is also said to roam the premises. The youngest ghost at the site, however, is the spirit of a little boy who was struck down by yellow fever and died at the Bird Cage in 1882. He races through the building creating mild poltergeist disturbances and strange cold spots. Interestingly enough, the boy's mother committed suicide soon after her son's death and can now be spotted roaming the roads of Tombstone in a white dress. In many instances, she has even blocked traffic.

While visiting the Bird Cage Theatre, be sure to explore every room and spend as much time in the building as is feasible. Sometimes, phantoms of this variety are slow to manifest, but once they do so, their presence becomes overwhelming. Listen carefully and make sure you do not ignore the building's unique scents. If you detect cigar smoke, cheap perfume, or any sounds that seem out of the ordinary, be on guard for the emergence of a full-scale phantasmal display.

If you experience the place-memory haunting and suddenly find yourself transported back in time, you have little to fear. The ghosts will probably ignore your presence and you will only be in danger if you find yourself caught in the crossfire during a gun battle.

However, be much more wary of the isolated phantoms who appear outside of the larger place memory. The little boy killed by yellow fever and the man with the clipboard appear harmless, but the ghost of the slain Clanton could prove much more dangerous. Bitter and prone to violence in life, a dead Clanton who has been forced to watch as his murderer, Wyatt Earp, has been elevated to the status of local hero is probably a dangerous entity to encounter. As evidenced by Bill Hunley's experience, this is not a ghost with whom to trifle. If you encounter any violent spirits in the Bird Cage, leave immediately.

DUDLEYTOWN

VITAL STATISTICS

LOCATION: Cornwall, Litchfield County, northwestern Connecticut. The settlement is now on a private nature reserve near U.S. Highway 7, and can be reached via Dark Entry Road. However, the road ends at the edge of Dudleytown and therefore the haunted town must be entered on foot.

NUMBER OF GHOSTLY RESIDENTS: Unknown

IDENTITIES OF GHOSTLY RESIDENTS: Unknown, but possibly victims of misfortune, including Gershorn Hollister, murdered by an insane neighbor; Sarah Faye Swift, struck by lightning; Mary Cheney, a suicide; most of the Carter family, murdered by Indians; Dr. William Clark's wife, who went raving mad while living in Dudleytown; and many others

TYPE OF ACTIVITY: Phantoms, disembodied voices, cold spots, an aura of despair, bad luck, and poltergeists

DEMEANOR OF GHOSTLY RESIDENTS: Dreary and despondent. It is not known whether these specters have attacked humans in the past. While the ghosts themselves appear harmless, the site is incredibly dangerous because of the strong aura of misfortune that plagues everyone who visits.

ENCOUNTERING THE DUDLEYTOWN GHOSTS:

known to some, is an example of a haunted site that is plagued by malicious supernatural forces far beyond mortal comprehension. The sheer number of tragedies that have afflicted natives of the small hamlet (many of whom have returned to the area after death) clearly proves that some devious energy is at work in Dudleytown.

Over one hundred witnesses have come forward with reports of ghost sightings of some kind in Dudleytown. Most often, people experience moderate poltergeist activity, with some visitors being shoved to the ground, punched, or otherwise harassed. A phantom woman atop a white horse has also been spotted roaming the darkness; and in the 1990s, a film crew investigating the site encountered a black, amorphous shape that seemed to sap their very life energies. Other visitors have been followed by a mysterious raven or have been overwhelmed by an aura of cold despair. Finally, Dudleytown is well known for the proliferation of disembodied voices that float through the trees, whispering and laughing insanely. But it is the Dudleytown Curse that most often attracts supernaturalists to the site.

Connecticut's Dudleytown is one of the most often discussed and studied haunted villages in all of the Western world. Home to the legendary Dudley Curse, Dudleytown, or Owlsbury, as it has been

Dudleytown existed under bad omens from its earliest days. Founded in 1738 by Thomas Griffis, who bought the first parcel of land in the area, the town began slowly attracting scores of farmers. In 1747, the burg received its name when brothers Abiel, Barzillai, Gideon, and Abijah Dudley arrived in Connecticut and took up residence near the Griffis property. Unfortunately, the four Dudleys came from a long line of cursed folk. In their native England, the Dudleys of the sixteenth century had a bad habit of offending the reigning monarchs; several were decapitated as a result. At this same time, another Dudley returned from France the unwitting carrier of a terrible plague that killed thousands.

The Dudley Curse followed the Dudley family to Connecticut as well. Abiel Dudley, one of the village's founding fathers, eventually went quite mad and lost all of his money. He became a laborer, performing hard work for the townsfolk just to earn enough to survive until his death at the age of ninety. Meanwhile, the Dudley Curse mysteriously transformed the once-prosperous land into an infertile wasteland, forcing many of the Dudleys' neighbors to move away as the town slowly shriveled and died.

While Dudleytown shrank, insanity similar to the madness that plagued Abiel became a common affliction for those living in the village. Abiel's neighbor, William Tanner, lost his mind in 1792 after a man named Gershorn Hollister was murdered in the Tanner home. The killing was never solved (although some have argued that Hollister merely slipped and fell while helping Tanner repair his barn), but local gossip held Tanner responsible. Revolutionary war hero General Herman Swift lived in Dudleytown and went crazy as well; after his wife, Sarah Faye Swift, was tragically struck dead by a lightning bolt, the general slowly lost his grip on reality and died in a state of dementia.

Although Dudleytown was largely deserted by 1900, the few people who tried to maintain a life in the area continued to suffer the Dudley Curse. In 1901, a farmer named Calvin Brophy, whose thieving sons were chased from Dudleytown by authorities and whose wife succumbed to tuberculosis shortly after, was found walking around on all fours and bleating like the goats he had raised for years. Only a few years later, Dr. William Clark, a prominent physician from New York City, decided to build his summer home in deserted Dudleytown. Unfortunately, Dr. Clark returned from a business trip one evening to find his wife transformed into a wildly laughing lunatic. Dr. Clark returned his wife to New York City, but the poor woman committed suicide soon after.

Suicide, like insanity, has been another frequent manifestation of the Dudleytown curse. The most famous Dudleytown suicide is undoubtedly Mary Cheney, a woman who escaped the village for a better life. Once outside of the town, she met and married Horace Greeley, who would go on to become a leading presidential candidate. A week before Greeley's defeat in the presidential election, however, Mary took her own life.

Brutal murders are also a staple of the Dudley Curse. A staggering case in point is the tale of the Nathaniel Carter family, who tried to escape Dudleytown in 1763. The following year, their new home in Binghamton, New York, was raided by Cherokee braves when only Mrs. Carter and her four children were at home. Mrs. Carter's head was cleaved in half by a single blow from a tomahawk, and the youngest child was beaten against a wall until dead. Nathaniel Jr. and his two sisters were then spirited away by their assailants. The elder Nathaniel returned to find his home razed, his wife and infant child dead, and his three remaining children missing. But his grief was short-lived, for the braves returned and immediately killed and scalped the poor man.

The ordeal of the Carter family did not end with Nathaniel's death, however. Of the three kidnapped children, both of the girls were ultimately recovered. Unfortunately, both had been permanently traumatized. Sarah Carter died a madwoman, while Elizabeth Carter eventually married but was described as a lifelong invalid who needed constant care.

Clearly, there are dark forces at work in Dudleytown, which is today part of a private nature preserve and no longer boasts any inhabitants. Even animals seem afraid to enter the site, and the surrounding land is often described as a dead zone devoid of any sounds of life. More important, the Dudley Curse has continued to affect many of Dudleytown's former residents even long after their deaths.

Because of the dark forces present at the site, Dudleytown is an extremely dangerous destination for the uninitiated. Many who have been exposed to the Dudley Curse, even briefly, have never been able to escape its influence. Almost as frightening are the actual spirits inhabiting the village, most of which seem outright hostile. If you encounter such entities, snap a few photographs (for the Dudleytown phantoms have been known to appear on film), and then promptly flee.

To protect yourself from the curse, do not take *anything* from Dudleytown. Even a small rock, twig, or brick can carry the Dudley Curse into your life. Legion are the tales of visitors who unwittingly picked up souvenirs from the site, only to be plagued by a long string of tragedies until the object was returned.

Dudleytown is made more difficult to explore by the fact that the village's neighbors do not take kindly to ghost hunters. In fact, they are positively exasperated by the curiosity seekers who have trampled through the town. If you visit Dudleytown, be extremely respectful of any locals you might encounter. While they may not believe that Dudleytown is haunted, remember that everyone is entitled to their own opinion regarding such matters. Also understand that Dudleytown is located on private land controlled and maintained by members of the Dark Entry Forest Association, who have every right to refuse entry onto the property.

Finally, there are several mundane threats to be concerned with when visiting Dudleytown. Many visitors have experienced a high incidence of injuries, ranging from twisted ankles to broken limbs and concussions (no doubt a lingering effect of the Dudley Curse), so be careful where you tread. Also be wary of evil witches, satanists, or other cultists who have decided to use Dudleytown as a stage for their dark rituals. Bones of sacrificial animals, candles, graffiti, and other paraphernalia associated with black magic have been discovered within Dudleytown with surprising regularity, so be on guard.

HARVARD EXIT THEATER

VITAL STATISTICS

LOCATION: 807 E. Roy Street, Seattle, Washington 98122; (206) 323-8986

NUMBER OF GHOSTLY RESIDENTS: Three

IDENTITIES OF GHOSTLY RESIDENTS: Bertha K. Landis, Seattle's first female mayor; an unidentified woman wearing turn-of-the-century dress; and an unknown man known only as Peter, who may have died in an accident at the site

TYPE OF ACTIVITY: Poltergeist disturbances and phantoms

DEMEANOR OF GHOSTLY RESIDENTS: Ranges from giddy to stately and dignified. In either case, the spirits do not appear threatening in any way.

ENCOUNTERING THE HARVARD EXIT THEATER GHOSTS: RIP RIP

The building now known as the Harvard Exit Theater was originally built in 1924 as the headquarters of the Women's Century Club, a feminist organization founded by Bertha K. Landis. During this time, many of the Club's members lived in the house, but it was not until the building was converted into a movie theater in 1968 that the first reports of ghosts surfaced.

Almost as soon as the Harvard Exit Theater opened in the late 1960s, visitors and staff began experiencing mild poltergeist activity. Projectors would run by themselves, film canisters would mysteriously move about or disappear, and doors would suddenly prove impossible to close.

In the early 1970s, the Harvard Exit expanded by adding a second theater and screen on the third floor. At this point, the hauntings intensified dramatically and many staff members began encountering several phantoms at the site. At least three separate apparitions have been encountered in the theater, although only one has been conclusively identified.

The named phantom seems to be Bertha Landis, who, as mentioned earlier, founded the Women's Century Club. In 1926, Landis went on to become Seattle's first woman mayor, cementing her place in that city's history. Today, she appears as a translucent woman wearing clothes common in the mid-1920s. She often hovers a few feet above the ground and can float through walls. Although sometimes described as stern and a bit frightening, Landis has never shown any proclivity for violence.

The Harvard Exit Theater's other female phantom is much stouter than the Landis ghost. This pudgy woman may have been an actress at some point in her life, and she always appears wearing an elaborate dress from the Victorian era, which is believed to be a costume of some sort. She may have been murdered, perhaps even strangled, at the theater.

The third and final ghost is an unnamed man with a frivolous personality. He enjoys playing pranks and may be responsible for the vast majority of the poltergeist activity at the site. Some psychics have described him as portly or possessing a thick accent, but neither of these traits have been consistently reported by witnesses, who rarely glimpse the ghost for more than a few moments. Despite the lack of information surrounding this spirit, he has been nicknamed Peter, and it has been theorized that he perished at the site long before the current building was even constructed.

The best way to encounter ghosts at the Harvard Exit Theater is to actually watch a movie. Upon arriving, notify the staff that you intend to find a ghost at the site and politely ask them to notify you if anything weird occurs during your visit. Once the movie starts, sit in the back row and watch for any strange shapes, figures, or shadows passing through the screen or the audience. Also be alert for any ghosts toying with your hair, popcorn, candy, or clothing, as Peter has been known to do. Finally, continually glance at the exit doors and the aisles, where the phantoms most frequently appear.

THE HAUNTED ROCKING CHAIR

VITAL STATISTICS

LOCATION: Ash Lawn (James Monroe's cottage), Charlottesville, Virginia. The site is in Albemarle County near 1-64 and Castle Hill, and is in the shadow of Carter's Mountain.

NUMBER OF GHOSTLY RESIDENTS: One

IDENTITY OF GHOSTLY RESIDENT: James Monroe

TYPE OF ACTIVITY: Poltergeist activity limited to a rocking chair that moves of its own accord

DEMEANOR OF GHOSTLY RESIDENT: Relaxed and content. The ghost simply enjoys rocking back and forth in the chair.

ENCOUNTERING THE HAUNTED ROCKING CHAIR'S GHOST: RIP RIP

Ash Lawn was the favorite home of president James Monroe, largely because it offered him an escape from the pressures of his political life. Ash Lawn was also the site of many important meetings between Monroe and Thomas Jefferson. When these two men were together, conversation and ideas flowed easily. There is little doubt that monumental decisions regarding the fate of the country were formulated within this tiny cottage in central Virginia.

During Monroe's stays at the quaint home, it is said that he frequently sat in his beloved rocking chair for hours. Sometimes he would read, but most hours were spent lost in thought as he enjoyed the serenity and quiet of his surroundings. Today, well over a hundred and fifty years after Monroe's death in 1831, the fifth president of the United States frequently returns to Ash Lawn and his comfortable chair.

When Ash Lawn was converted into a museum, the wooden rocking chair was originally located in the main room. Because it was considered an antique, visitors were not allowed to sit in the inviting chair. Yet, although the rocking chair was always empty, scores of witnesses observed it slowly rocking back and forth at all hours of the day. If a mortal grabbed the chair, it would stop rocking, but the mysterious movements would commence again once the chair was released. Despite the wealth of evidence, the museum has denied any ghostly activity.

While the identity of the invisible entity inhabiting the haunted rocking chair can never be confirmed, it is widely accepted that the spirit is the contemplative ghost of James Monroe. He may return to the chair periodically to escape the activity of the afterlife,

where he is likely something of a celebrity. As always, it seems that he uses the chair to collect his thoughts and meditate.

Eventually, reports of the haunted rocking chair became too numerous to ignore and the site began attracting attention as a genuine haunted locale. Perhaps embarrassed or concerned that Ash Lawn's historical significance would be overshadowed by the haunting, the museum locked the rocking chair in the basement, where it has since collected dust. It is unknown whether Monroe continues to return to his rocking chair, as no one has been allowed to study the object since it was relocated to the basement. Whether or not the chair will be returned to the house remains to be seen, and ghost hunters should contact the museum before wasting a visit.

THE HAUNTED ORGAN

VITAL STATISTICS

LOCATION: Woolsey Hall, Yale University, 1502A Yale Station, New Haven, Connecticut 06520; (203) 432-1900

NUMBER OF GHOSTLY RESIDENTS: One or two

IDENTITIES OF GHOSTLY RESIDENTS: Either Frank Bozyan or Harry Jepson, former Yale organists

TYPE OF ACTIVITY: Unexplained music and malevolent aura

DEMEANOR OF GHOSTLY RESIDENTS: Unknown. If the haunted organ is indeed possessed by one or more ghosts, they appear to be extremely unhappy and have cast an aura of evil around the object. It is possible that, as time passes, they will become increasingly frustrated and may eventually escalate to poltergeist activity that could prove both destructive and dangerous.

ENCOUNTERING THE HAUNTED ORGAN'S GHOST:

The haunted organ, located in Yale's Woolsey Hall, was originally commissioned in 1903 by the university's organist, Harry B. Jepson, and financed by the wealthy Newberry family. After a brief series of alterations, it was finally dedicated in 1916. However, in 1926, the instrument was rebuilt to keep pace with technological advances and musical tastes. During the 1926 renovation, there was a great deal of tension between the two men working on the organ, which may have first imbued the instrument with the evil energy it possesses today.

More important to the organ's current status, however, was the forced retirement of Mr. Jepson from Yale in the 1940s. Although he lived a scant two blocks from Woolsey Hall, he was never invited to play his beloved instrument again. He died in 1952, still pining for the organ.

In the 1970s, Yale decided to abolish the post of university organist altogether and urged the man who currently held the position, Frank Bozyan, to retire. Reluctantly, Bozyan accepted his retirement offer, although he admitted to coworkers that he felt he was making a huge mistake. Indeed, the hold that the organ had over Bozyan proved insurmountable. Without access to the organ, Bozyan withered and died, passing away just six months after he left Woolsey Hall for the last time.

During the 1970s, Woolsey Hall was frequently used to host rock concerts, and the loud music that crashed down around the organ may have summoned the spirit of one of the instrument's former caretakers. Bozyan is the most likely culprit, as the hauntings began shortly after his death, but Jepson's love of the instrument could have drawn him back to Woolsey Hall as well.

Regardless of the identity of the organ's current tenant, the activities of the specter are well known to those working within the building. Witnesses report that the organ chamber has a heavy and menacing aura. Those who have entered the chamber often feel as if they are being watched by a sinister presence. The ghost (or perhaps ghosts) lurk directly behind visitors, peering over shoulders and crowding witnesses until they feel forced to flee the organ chamber.

Most important to this haunting is the organ's tendency to play by itself. Late at night, people passing Woolsey Hall have reported hearing ghostly organ music coming from within the building. Students, custodians, and others who spend a great deal of time in the hall have also heard the music while standing close to the organ, verifying that the instrument is indeed responsible for the disturbance.

While visiting Woolsey Hall, be sure to visit the organ chamber and open your mind to the aura present at this site. Make an attempt to visit the building in the late evening, but be warned that the Yale university authorities are not likely to take a ghost hunter seriously or talk openly about the haunting. Still, if you manage to arrange a thorough study of the organ, be sure to bring a tape recorder to preserve any strange noises you might hear rising from the instrument. Also, when you detect either the music or the disturbing presence in the organ chamber, try to communicate with the ghost responsible. Second to self-preservation, your top priority in this situation should be the discovery of the phantom organist's true identity.

HIGHWAY 666

VITAL STATISTICS

LOCATION: U.S. Highway 666 is a two-hundred-mile stretch of road running through Utah, southwestern Colorado, and northwest New Mexico. The junction between Highway 64 and Highway 666 at Shiprock, New Mexico, is considered a good starting point for exploring this haunted site.

NUMBER OF GHOSTLY RESIDENTS: Unknown

IDENTITIES OF GHOSTLY RESIDENTS: Probably the scores of people who have died along the road in accidents or whose bodies have been dumped near the highway. The most recognizable phantoms include a deranged trucker, at least one other phantom motorist, a phantom hitchhiker, and a pack of spectral hounds

TYPE OF ACTIVITY: Phantoms, poltergeists, ghost lights, and an aura of misfortune

DEMEANOR OF GHOSTLY RESIDENTS: Thoroughly evil and sadistic, for the most part. Among the most recognizable spirits, the only ghost known to be relatively harmless is the phantom hitchhiker. All others are devoted to mayhem.

ENCOUNTERING THE GHOSTS OF HIGHWAY 666:

RIP RIP RIP RIP

C onsidered the most haunted stretch of asphalt in the world, U.S. Highway 666 is known by many as the Highway to Hell, Satan's Speedway, and the Devil's Dragstrip. The highway's numerical designation, 666, is purported to be the "number of the beast," Satan's personal bar code. According to some sources, the child of the Devil can be identified by a birthmark reading 666, and all of Satan's minions wear the number somewhere on their bodies.

The number fits Highway 666 well. First and foremost, Highway 666 is incredibly dangerous, responsible for a record number of fatal accidents each year. The portion that runs through New Mexico is considered among the most dangerous in the state, if not the nation. Furthermore, an abnormally high number of corpses are found alongside the highway. Many are likely to be unidentified murder victims, possibly runaways, thrown from passing cars or vans.

But it is the ghostly apparitions that are cause for concern along Highway 666. One of the most frequently sighted phantoms is a skinny girl with pale skin wearing a white nightgown. Upon spotting the barefoot child, numerous motorists have pulled over to offer aid, only to watch in horror as the phantom vanished.

A phantom vehicle known as Satan's Sedan has also been encountered virtually hundreds of times along Highway 666. The car, of indeterminate make and model, manifests only at night and only during a full moon. It often plays chicken with other vehicles, rushing headlong toward oncoming cars. Dozens of motorists have been forced from the road by the hikers who run afoul of the trucker are never seen again.

Even more disturbing than either of the phantom vehicles, however, are reports of demon dogs roaming Highway 666 in large, vicious packs. The dogs appear out of nowhere and, quite incredibly, chase down fleeing cars. While moving at speeds in excess of one hundred miles per hour, the Highway 666 demon dogs tear through their prey's tires with their teeth and claws. When the disabled car pulls to the roadside, the vehicle is immediately buried beneath the pack of bloodthirsty curs, who break through the windows and pull screaming passengers into the desert.

Highway 666's demonic denizens and terrible reputation have attracted widespread media attention.

Adriel Heisey/Photographers Aspen

Highway 666.

hell-bent apparition, and at least five deaths have been connected to this diabolical car.

One of the nation's notorious phantom truckers calls Highway 666 home as well. The crazed trucker drives a black (or sometimes blood red) rig and enjoys crushing pedestrians beneath his vehicle. Stranded motorists who flag the truck usually find themselves plastered against the phantom vehicle's grill, and hitch-

The infamous highway terrified Arizona's motorists, who complained loudly about the highway's designation. Today, the small portion of Highway 666 that runs through Arizona has been renamed Highway 191, but it remains to be seen whether or not the stretch of road will be free of the spectral manifestations that affect the rest of the highway.

For those with immense and unfaltering

courage, Highway 666's ghosts can be encountered by simply driving the road, preferably at night. Only ghost hunters with excellent driving skills and a strong understanding of mechanics should attempt this trek. Practice changing your tires before you leave, and repeatedly check your brakes and engine.

The only phantom along Highway 666 who has (thus far) shown no signs of hostility is the unidentified girl in the white night-gown, who merely stands at the side of the road until forced to disappear by a stopping vehicle. All other apparitions (and probably most of the other motorists traveling this road at night) should be given a wide berth. Unfortunately, if you are targeted by any of the hostile ghosts of Highway 666, you can expect to be driven from the road, in a violent and possibly deadly accident, as these spirits have yet to be outrun.

KWJJ RADIO STATION

VITAL STATISTICS

LOCATION: 931 S.W. King Street, Portland, Oregon 97205; (503) 226-3699

NUMBER OF GHOSTLY RESIDENTS: Approximately four

IDENTITIES OF GHOSTLY RESIDENTS: An unknown servant girl, an unidentified musician, an indistinguishable phantom in the basement, and Theodore Wilcox, Jr.

TYPE OF ACTIVITY: Phantoms, ghostly music, and poltergeists

DEMEANOR OF GHOSTLY RESIDENTS: Detached. Only the gray ghost in the basement has been known to terrorize mortals. The remaining spirits seem content to go about their business without disturbing the living.

ENCOUNTERING THE KWJJ GHOSTS:
RIP RIP RIP

KWJJ, the nation's haunted radio station, currently resides in one of Portland's most distinguished buildings—the Wilcox Mansion. Built in 1893 by Theodore Wilcox, a banking giant, the house remained within the family until World War II. During the war, it was leased by the Soviet government, and then was purchased by a Russian émigré named Ariel Rubestein. Rubestein was a concert pianist and used the mansion to open a school of music and dance. Finally, in 1959, the building was converted into a radio station by KWJJ owners Rod and Betty Johnson.

Despite its long and varied history, the three-story building did not begin to exhibit any spectral activity until KWJJ moved in. However, within weeks, disc jockeys, executives, the cleaning staff, and visitors began experiencing ghostly phenomena.

The mildest form of phantom

incursions manifest as short-lived and harmless poltergeists. The playful ghosts within the building have been known to swing on a large crystal chandelier, throw open or lock doors, shift papers, turn hanging photographs upside down, and leave behind mysterious artifacts, such as a plastic statuette of the Virgin Mary. One of the poltergeists is fond of running amok through the bathroom, slamming stall doors and throwing toilet paper rolls about. Curiously, none of the ghosts have ever interfered with the broadcast booth or the daily operations of the radio station.

Aside from the poltergeist activity, KWJJ has recorded numerous encounters with fully formed phantoms. One such apparition is a man dressed in a white suit and hat who only manifests near the building's elegant grand piano. The man, believed to be a former musician or one of Rubestein's students, spends his time walking in endless circles around the instrument. However, late at night, when he is not being watched, the ghost enjoys playing the piano. Several of the station's employees have reported hearing the ghostly music, even when they were quite certain that no one else was in the building.

Another ghost appears to be a young woman dressed in a servant's outfit consisting of a black dress and white hat. She may have worked for Theodore Wilcox, Jr., during the 1920s, shortly before the building was leased to the Russian government. Now, she silently strolls up and down the stairs, continually performing some unknown errand. Wilcox probably shares the house with this servant as well. There have been numerous encounters with an elderly, well-mannered gentleman in the attic. He wears dark, fairly informal garb and has white hair. The ghost has also been met in the downstairs hallways and lower rooms on occasion, and has been held responsible for much of the poltergeist activity. Finally, the basement seems to be occupied by a gray, shapeless apparition. Of all the ghosts at the radio station, only this phantom has caused any trouble, at one point chasing a visitor from the room.

The KWJJ ghosts are almost always encountered after dusk, usually by those who have spent a great deal of time at the station during the dead of night. Due to these conditions, DJs and the cleaning staff are the most likely witnesses. The radio station once offered tours, but does so only rarely now because news of the hauntings began to attract undesirables. Therefore, conduct yourself with dignity and use discretion when revealing your true purpose for investigating the site. If you do manage to wander the Wilcox mansion, pay special attention to the building's grand piano, the attic, and the basement. In most areas of the house, you can be relaxed and comfortable, but raise your guard before entering the basement, where the frightening gray specter resides.

MICHIE TAVERN

VITAL STATISTICS

LOCATION: Old Black Mountain Road, Charlottesville, Virginia. The mailing address is Michie Tavern, Route 6 Box 7A, Charlottesville, VA 22901. Call (804) 977-1234 for more information.

NUMBER OF GHOSTLY RESIDENTS: At least a dozen

IDENTITIES OF GHOSTLY RESIDENTS: Unknown, but believed to be patrons of the tavern from the late 1700s

TYPE OF ACTIVITY: Disembodied voices, music, and footsteps

DEMEANOR OF GHOSTLY RESIDENTS: Festive and generally happy. There are a small group of ghosts involved in a heated argument, but these spirits ignore mortals. The bulk of the phantoms at this site simply enjoy having a party, again and again and again.

ENCOUNTERING THE MICHIE TAVERN GHOSTS:

The Michie Tavern, one of Virginia's most historic sites, was originally built in 1784. It attracted travelers, statesmen, socialites, musicians, and a host of other visitors during its day. Andrew Jackson, Thomas Jefferson, and James Monroe all entertained and ate at the tavern during their lifetimes. Currently, the building serves as a restaurant, coffee shop, and museum. And it is also the home of several ghosts.

Michie Tavern's ghostly residents are typically heard, rather than seen or sensed. Two hundred years ago, the tavern hosted the first waltz ever danced in the New World, and that joyous gathering is continually relived in the building today. Visitors often report hearing the sounds of laughter, music, conversation, and dancing on the top floor. Others have overheard snippets of an argument between two men and a woman. According to some sources, the conversation concerned the woman's social standing, which had been marred when she danced a waltz with a young man from France. Other witnesses have encountered Thomas Jefferson on the stairs, or suddenly felt transported back in time to the era when the Michie Tavern rollicked with music.

The ghosts of Michie Tavern appear to be extremely selective about when and to whom they appear. The most successful ghost hunters to enter the site have been psychics. If you have consistently seen or detected phantoms that those around you are incapable of observing, Michie Tavern may yield an encounter. When you visit, ask for permission to sit in one of the tavern's original chairs, which visitors are forbidden to touch. By doing so, you may pick up the psychic energies of the era long past and find yourself in contact with the ghosts of this remarkable building.

NOB HILL

VITAL STATISTICS

LOCATION: California Street, between Jones and Powell, in San Francisco's Nob Hill district, California. The ghost is most often sighted within view of the Fairmont Hotel.

NUMBER OF GHOSTLY RESIDENTS: One

IDENTITY OF GHOSTLY RESIDENT: Flora Sommerton

TYPE OF ACTIVITY: Phantom

DEMEANOR OF GHOSTLY RESIDENT: Lost, dazed, and confused. The ghost of Nob Hill may be searching for something, including her estranged family, or she may be reenacting the night she fled her home in 1876. Regardless, she avoids any human contact and has not been blamed for any injuries or death.

ENCOUNTERING THE NOB HILL GHOST:

I n 1876, Flora Sommerton, the daughter of a wealthy couple living in one of San Francisco's richest neighborhoods, was preparing to emerge into the public eye. It was the eve of her eighteenth birthday, and her parents were showering her with gifts and a sumptuous gala meant to serve as her debutante ball. At the ball, the Sommertons also planned to announce to their socially elite friends that Flora would soon be wed to an upstanding, well-to-do young man from San Francisco's growing aristocracy.

Unfortunately, Flora had been suffering from a terrible melancholy. Neither her parents nor her fiancé had realized that she simply did not love her future husband, and her impending fate began to weigh upon her tremendously. Finally, on the night of the debutante ball, she simply snapped. No longer able to maintain her facade, she went rushing from her mansion shortly before the first guests arrived. She quickly faded into San Francisco's streets, penniless but still wearing her ball gown.

Flora's parents were distraught and offered a $250,000 reward for any information about their daughter. The story gripped the press and became one of San Francisco's most notorious scandals. Yet, despite the attention Flora's case generated across the country, the Sommertons and the authorities made little progress in finding the girl. As numerous false leads poured into San Francisco, Flora remained hidden.

After months without word, authorities began to fear that Flora had met misfortune. Within a year, the nearsighted media had forgotten about the case, and even her parents eventually began to avoid any mention of the girl. It seemed that Flora Sommerton had truly and completely vanished.

However, fifty years after her disappearance, Flora Sommerton again achieved nationwide fame when her corpse was found in a flophouse in Butte, Montana. Flora had survived into her late sixties, but had evidently died alone and impoverished, her body wracked with disease. Strangely enough, she was discovered wearing a nineteenth-century ball gown covered with literally thousands of crystal beads. Her mortal remains were transported back to San Francisco, where she was buried in the family plot, and her story became a legend.

In recent years, Flora Sommerton has yet again managed to achieve headlines. Her phantom, wearing a beautiful ball gown, has been spotted numerous times wandering California Street in Nob Hill. She always appears as a spectral young girl who is confused, upset, and determined to escape some unseen pursuer. Unfortunately, she is only glimpsed for a brief moment before she disappears into the crowded streets.

While San Francisco is an incredibly active city at all hours of the day and night, the area of Nob Hill where Flora is most often encountered can become surprisingly quiet between about one and four in the morning. Flora's section of California Street, which is in the shadow of the posh Fairmont Hotel, is also fairly safe, and ghost hunters should feel comfortable strolling along the sidewalk even at the witching hour. Repeatedly walking California Street and the surrounding blocks should eventually produce a sighting of this phantom. Riding the cable car, which passes the spot where Flora manifests regularly, is also a wise course of action.

If you encounter Flora, you must question her on the details of her life. Very little is known about Flora's adventures between her disappearance and death. Did she ever wed or have children? How did she earn enough money to survive? Where did she live? And, most important, was she happy?

OLD SALEM

VITAL STATISTICS

LOCATION: Old Salem, formerly Salem—the site of the infamous Salem witch trials—is a popular tourist destination in Massachusetts. General tour information can be obtained at (800) 441-5305.

NUMBER OF GHOSTLY RESIDENTS: At least two dozen

IDENTITIES OF GHOSTLY RESIDENTS: Giles Corey, Bridget Bishop, Sarah Osborne, Rebecca Nurse, Susanna Martin, Elizabeth Howe, Sarah Good, Sarah Wildes, George Jacobs, Martha Carrier, George Burroughs, John Proctor, John Willard, Martha Corey, Margaret Scott, Mary Easty, Alice Parker, Ann Pudeator, Wilmott Redd, Samuel Wardwell, Mary Parker, and others tormented by the witch trials; Judge Nathaniel Ropes and his wife Abigail; and several other spirits

TYPE OF ACTIVITY: Phantoms, disembodied screams and voices, and poltergeists

DEMEANOR OF GHOSTLY RESIDENTS: Alternates between bewildered and driven. The ghosts of those murdered in the witch trials are sometimes unsure of their plight, but other times they appear to be seeking justice. A mass uprising could be extremely disturbing, but in general the ghosts are harmless to everyone save witch hunters.

ENCOUNTERING THE OLD SALEM GHOSTS: RIP

Salem, Massachusetts, will live forever in infamy as the site of the Salem witch trials of 1692. The hysteria began when two young girls began justifying their strange behavior, which included sudden seizures and the spouting of foul language, as the work of local witches. The pair identified several women whom they disliked as the culprits, and the frenzy of accusations soon swept through the village. In less than a year, the Salem court had tried and executed twenty suspected witches as well as ensured the death of Sarah Osborne, who sickened and died in prison. As a result of this carnage, today the entire village of Old Salem is thoroughly haunted.

During the course of the trials, all but one of the executions were carried out through public hangings on Gallows Hill. Not surprising, this site near Salem Hospital is overrun with phantoms. The ghosts of all nineteen victims can sometimes be seen swaying from invisible gallows, and the apparitions have been known to wander the vicinity in a confused daze. Among the assembled spirits is the Reverend George Burroughs, who earned Salem's

The House of Seven Gables, a building in old Salem that author Nathaniel Hawthorne believed to be haunted.

wrath when he wrote an essay denying the existence of witchcraft. Sarah Good, Rebecca Nurse, and all the others are also present, and their appearance is said to foretell disaster for the living.

Old Salem is frequently plagued by the terrible screams of Giles Corey, the alleged warlock who was slowly tortured to death through the archaic means of "pressing." Essentially, Corey's tormentors pinned the poor man to the ground and systematically piled rocks atop his chest in the hopes that he would confess to dealings with the Devil. Corey refused to implicate himself and was eventually crushed beneath the great weight, horrible shrieks escaping his lips even as his lungs collapsed. Corey is also known to appear near the Old

Jail. His phantom is regarded as an omen indicating something dreadful will soon occur within the town.

Along with Gallows Hill and the Old Jail, all of the "witches" have been known to visit the former home of Jonathan Corwin, a site now known as the Witch House. Corwin was a judge during the trials and used his home to examine the accused. Many of the witches were condemned by the judges assembled within the Witch House well before trial. Today, the executed witches may be seeking Corwin's ghost in order to exact revenge.

While the Salem witches are the most notorious ghosts in the old town, they are not the only supernatural entities roaming the village. The Ropes Mansion is haunted by the spirits of Judge Nathaniel Ropes and his wife, Abigail. Nathaniel was killed by incensed colonists, who stoned the judge after he revealed his Tory loyalties. Some time later, Abigail's nightgown caught fire when she passed an open fireplace and she burned to death. For the most part, Mr. and Mrs. Ropes try to maintain a normal life, even in death, but on occasion Abigail emerges from one of the upstairs bedrooms totally engulfed in flames and screaming for help.

The most recent ghost to join the spectral community of Old Salem haunts the Salem Hospital, which overlooks Gallows Hill. The ghost is believed to be the spirit of a woman who died in the late 1980s during a painful and complicated childbirth. She is encountered in the hospital's delivery room, where she may be searching for her child, and has been witnessed by doctors, nurses, and several patients.

Old Salem is one of the most important supernatural sites in North America, and all ghost hunters *must* visit the village at least once, preferably early in their careers. The ghosts of Salem are invaluable learning tools because they appear frequently and in predictable locations. They are also important because their experiences span two hundred years, representing both colonial and modern times. Finally, as every good student knows, we study history to avoid repeating the mistakes of the past, and the Salem witch trials were definitely a result of heinous human error that should be prevented from happening again.

In order to gain the most from your time in Salem, take a walking tour of all the historical sites and immerse yourself in the town's rich history. Visiting during October and November is especially rewarding because the town stages numerous celebrations and activities revolving around the rituals of Halloween. When you feel prepared, visit Gallows Hill and the Old Jail at night, watching for any phantoms that might appear. Do not fail to devote some time to the Ropes Mansion and the Salem Hospital, sites often overlooked by ghost hunters.

Library of Congress

The Witch House, Salem, Massachusetts.

QUANTUM LEAP CAFÉ

VITAL STATISTICS

LOCATION: 88 West Third Street, New York, New York 10012 (corner of West Third and Sullivan Streets in Greenwich Village).

NUMBER OF GHOSTLY RESIDENTS: One

IDENTITY OF GHOSTLY RESIDENT: Aaron Burr

TYPE OF ACTIVITY: Phantom

DEMEANOR OF GHOSTLY RESIDENT: Sad and desperate. Aaron Burr's ghost is searching for his lost daughter, whom he will probably never find. Unless he encounters a mortal he mistakes for a political enemy, he should be considered innocuous.

ENCOUNTERING THE GHOST OF THE QUANTUM LEAP CAFÉ: RIP RIP

The building housing the Quantum Leap Café in New York City's Greenwich Village is a three-story edifice built before the Revolutionary War. It was originally owned by a British colonial family, but eventually became the property of the politician and one-time vice president Aaron Burr. During Burr's possession of the land, the lower floor where the Quantum Leap is currently located formed part of the statesman's stables. Burr retained the stables until near his death in 1836, at which point the building changed hands several times. At one point, the lower floor became the Café Bizarre, at which time the building's ghost was first noticed.

Café Bizarre's ghost was first noticed by a waiter and the wife of the establishment's owner. Both described the phantom as an intense man wearing a shirt with white ruffles. He had a short black beard and dark, piercing eyes that unsettled the witnesses. Since the apparition's first appearance, it has been sighted on dozens of occasions, but is always described in the same dramatic fashion.

Although the phantom remained unidentified for quite some time, today the ghost has been positively identified as the spirit of Aaron Burr, whose life was accentuated by tragedy and sorrow. Burr reached a level of infamy when he killed Alexander Hamilton during a fair duel. Despite testimony to the contrary by witnesses, Burr was blamed for murdering Hamilton, who was extremely popular and viewed as one of the country's most promising politicians. Although he was eventually cleared of any crime, Burr's presidential aspirations were crushed.

Later, Burr tired of politics and moved west, but his enemies accused him of attempting to create a new country along the frontier. Again, he was cleared of these charges, but the constant attacks drained him considerably. He was further wracked by grief over the loss of his beloved daughter, Theodosia, who was mysteriously lost at sea aboard a ship that simply disappeared.

Today, Aaron Burr has returned to his stables for reasons he alone fully understands. It

Hatteras Beach, North Carolina

While Aaron Burr searches for Theodosia in New York, his lost daughter comes ashore at Hatteras Beach to look for her father. Theodosia Burr Alston, who was married to the governor of South Carolina, left Georgetown aboard the *Patriot* in 1812. The sound sailing vessel was bound for New York City, where Theodosia was to be reunited with her beloved father, but the boat never reached its destination. During the relatively short journey, the *Patriot* was blown off course and became hopelessly lost. Some claim that it fell victim to pirates, while others believe it eventually wandered south toward Florida, where it was lost forever in the Bermuda Triangle. Given the fact that Theodosia now walks the shores of Hatteras Beach, it is probable that the *Patriot* sank somewhere near the mouth of Cape Hatteras.

is clear that he is still upset over the loss of his political career and his daughter, and is somewhat confused by his plight. When contacted by psychics, he expressed anguish and a desire to find Theodosia, but he has yet to acknowledge that he knows he is dead or that his time has long since passed.

It is unclear whether or not the site has experienced any spectral phenomena since becoming the Quantum Leap Café, but it is unlikely that Burr's ghost would simply leave after all these years. If he is indeed still present, as is probable, Aaron Burr is best contacted by a small group of psychics who strongly believe in his existence. A séance or similar ceremony should be held to summon the spirit, and he should be invited to express his sorrow. At no time should you or your companions mention Hamilton's death or the loss of Theodosia unless Burr himself gravitates toward these topics. In any event, express your respect for the much-maligned statesman, commenting on the good deeds he performed. Perhaps this will ease Burr's conscience and allow him to find true peace at last.

6. GHOST HUNTING

IN ORDER TO address the concerns of novice ghost hunters, those trying to cope with a new spectral presence in their lives, and anyone simply wishing to avoid a real encounter with a spirit, this chapter covers a wide variety of topics.

Most important is the first section, which offers advice for identifying a haunted site. The chapter will go on to discuss successful methods for studying ghosts in their natural habitats, investigating allegedly haunted sites, and interacting safely with spirits. Finally, the chapter closes with a course on combating violent ghosts while offering techniques for living in harmony with less offensive phantoms.

Identifying a Haunted Site

It must be acknowledged here that for every known haunting recorded in North America, there have been dozens of suspected hauntings that were ultimately attributed to natural causes, hoaxes, or confusion on the part of witnesses. However, by following the steps listed below one can confidently confirm or disprove a site's haunted nature. The advice is given in no particular order and, although written with the assumption that the site is a suspected haunted *house,* most of the tactics can be easily translated to cover all other haunted sites.

- **Investigate the geography of the area.** Sometimes, during the course of an investigation into ghostly phenomena, it is discovered that the afflicted house rests atop a cave, mine, underground stream, fault, ore deposit, or other unusual geographical incident. Any such natural occurrence can cause a wide range of disturbances within a home that, although unsettling, are not the work of ghosts. In particular, ore deposits cause magnetic fields that disrupt televisions and other appliances. A frequently moving fault creates the illusion of poltergeists, as does a sinkhole or similar unsound foundation. Caves, underground streams, mines, and the like can echo with bizarre noises that rise into the "haunted house," creating the illusion of disembodied voices floating through the home.

- **Study the landscape.** In particular, look for large power lines, train tracks, nearby airports or subway lines, power plants, radio towers, or other manmade structures. Passing trains, landing planes, or even large trucks driving past the site could be responsible for alleged poltergeists. Erratic radio or television waves, toxic waste, and energy emissions of any kind can also cause people to see "phantoms" or experience other strange visions.

- **Check the plumbing.** A burst or leaking pipe that has gone unnoticed for any length of time can cause a host of problems often associated with ghosts, including strange noises resembling disembodied moans and weird stains or ominous cracks on the ceilings and walls.

- **Search for rats and other vermin.** Raccoons, rabbits, stray cats, skunks, mice, and rats can infest attics, basements, crawl spaces, and hollow walls with surprising ease. The movements of the creatures, as well as their incessant chattering and chewing, have often been misinterpreted as ghostly phenomena. In addition, many of these animals are prone to sneaking into

homes and stealing, breaking, or moving objects, activities commonly blamed on poltergeists.

- **Interview neighbors.** Typically, a true haunted house's problems do not spill over to affect the homes nearby. By tactfully asking neighbors about any possible disturbances, it may be possible to determine whether or not the "haunting" is an isolated incident. If neighboring homes are indeed experiencing similar phenomena, it is unlikely that a ghost is at work, and investigators should search for natural causes, including those listed above. However, if the haunting simply cannot be explained and is, in fact, influencing a large number of homes, consider the possibility that you have stumbled across a haunted village or town.

- **Investigate the house's history.** A house that has been remodeled, rebuilt, or otherwise altered extensively can have many quirks easily misinterpreted as a haunting, such as frequent settling, creaking supports, electrical abnormalities, and the like. The same is true for any house forced to endure a natural disaster, including a tornado or flood. However, the house's history can also suggest a ghost's presence. Obviously, if a murder or similar tragedy occurred at the house, the supernatural is very likely to be at work.

- **Bring animals into the house.** Almost all animals are incredibly sensitive to the manifestation of ghosts. Dogs are among the most vocal upon sensing an invisible spirit and will typically bark ferociously at the unseen visitor, whine pathetically, attack the air, or flee from the house altogether. Cats become increasingly nervous when in the presence of ghosts and are known to hiss or spit at the apparitions before ultimately fleeing as well. If you bring an animal into the house and the creature exhibits any of the above behavior, the home is probably haunted.

- **Observe the behavior of children.** Children will often feel a ghost's presence, and even a spirit's personality, long before anyone else, although they are often reluctant to reveal the phantom's existence. Watch for children who talk to empty rooms or play with invisible companions. Alternately, be aware of children who are constantly upset, nervous, or paranoid, for they may have sensed a far more malign entity within the house. If you believe that a child has detected a ghost, ask if he or she has met any new friends or recently suffered recurrent nightmares. Also, be sure to explore the child's feelings about entering certain rooms in the house.

- **Search for hot or cold spots.** Temperature fluctuations are usually the first sign of spectral manifestation. On a mild day, wander the house in the hopes of stumbling across an area that is inexplicably much warmer or colder than the other parts of the house. However, once such a spot is discovered, be sure to check any heating or air-conditioning systems, as well as nearby appliances, for problems. Next, assess the integrity of the walls, floor, and ceiling near the spot, as a broken vent, cracked wall, or loose floor

board can easily alter the temperature in the area.

- **Call in a psychic.** Many people balk at this suggestion, but a professional medium, sensitive, or psychic should be able to detect whether or not a house is being visited by a spirit. You can find psychics in your area through the phone book, the Internet, or local stores that sell occult paraphernalia. When you first contact a prospective psychic, only reveal that you are experiencing unusual phenomena at the site, but do not give specifics. Furthermore, while leading the psychic through the haunted site, reveal very little information about the house. The psychic's observations about the location's history and current troubles should reveal the extent of his or her abilities. If the psychic is unable to sense *anything* relevant about the house's past or present, you have probably hired a fraud.

- **Invite in a skeptic.** If all else fails and you are still unable to determine the forces behind a suspected haunting, ask for aid from a logical skeptic. Good candidates for this role include police detectives, lawyers, scientists, university professors, medical doctors, and others who must rely on logic to perform well in their chosen professions. Skeptics provide the detached, objective viewpoint necessary to adequately explore all possible explanations for the unusual phenomena. An impartial observer will also bring a new range of experiences and knowledge to the investigation, and prevent the research team from jumping to conclusions.

General Advice for Novice Ghost Hunters

Once you have determined that a given site is indeed haunted by a supernatural presence, you can prepare to seek out the ghostly inhabitants. This is not an endeavor to be undertaken lightly; spectral encounters can be dangerous and traumatic. To ensure eventual success and avoid misfortune, adhere to the following guidelines.

- **Know your physical limitations.** Carefully assess your physical strengths and weaknesses, and research your target location in order to ascertain the type of physical skills you will need to navigate the site successfully. Fortunately, ghost hunting is an endeavor that only rarely places physical demands upon its practitioners, but there are some potentially dangerous environments that should only be explored by those with the proper training. For example, if you are not experienced at exploring caves, do not begin your ghost hunting career searching for spirits in **Mammoth Cave** or some similar location.

- **Never travel alone.** Solitary ghost hunters place themselves in great danger, as even a mundane accident (such as breaking one's leg while hiking through a haunted grove) could result in death. Working with a partner provides essential backup and aid should one of you become injured. Most important, when a ghost appears, four eyes will prove far better than two for observing and preserving the moment.

- **Use caution.** Some ghostly environs, including caves and urban dwellings, can present numerous dangers. Be mindful that exposure to natural and criminal elements, attacks by wildlife, and becoming lost are occupational hazards that ghost hunters face. Moreover, many of the ghosts in this book have shown some proclivity for violence, further increasing a ghost hunter's risk. It is each individual ghost hunter's personal responsibility to exercise caution and common sense.

- **Be patient.** In general, ghosts do not manifest regularly or with any great frequency, even at the most haunted sites. Therefore, it is extremely important that you remain patient and calm throughout any extended investigation. Documenting ghosts requires months, often years, of dedicated research and field study. There are numerous ghost hunters who have searched for spirits their entire lives only to collect a handful of sightings and concrete encounters. Much of the information contained in this book may increase your likelihood of an encounter, but it would be impossible to guarantee results. Therefore, it is essential that you develop the invaluable virtue of patience.

- **Always gain permission.** This should be the mantra of the ghost hunter, as nothing angers those plagued by ghosts more than insensitive investigators who tramp through haunted sites without fair warning. Always, always, always gain permission before visiting any privately owned haunted site. When exploring a public site, including most of the locations in this book, be sure to confirm hours of operation and pay any appropriate fees. While at a public site, never enter any area marked as off limits or private unless you

The 15 Most Haunted Sites in North America

Below is a list of the most active haunted sites contained in this book, organized by chapter and in alphabetical order. All have received four RIP in the "Encountering . . ." section of the Vital Statistics Box. Novice ghost hunters should visit all of the sites on this list as an introductory course on haunted locales.

- **Lalaurie House**, New Orleans, Louisiana (chapter 1)
- **Spy House**, Port Monmouth, New Jersey (chapter 1)
- **Whaley House**, San Diego, California (chapter 1)
- **White House**, Washington, D.C. (chapter 1)
- **USS** *Constellation*, Baltimore, Maryland (chapter 2)
- *Queen Mary*, Long Beach, California (chapter 2)
- **Bachelor's Grove Cemetery**, Midlothian, Illinois (chapter 3)
- **Silver Cliff Cemetery**, Silver Cliff, Colorado (chapter 3)
- **Grand Manan Island**, New Brunswick, Canada (chapter 4)
- **Little Bighorn Battlefield National Monument**, Custer Battlefield National Park, Montana (chapter 4)
- **Mammoth Cave**, Mammoth Cave National Park, Kentucky (chapter 4)
- **Alcatraz Island**, San Francisco, California (chapter 5)
- **Bird Cage Theatre**, Tombstone, Arizona (chapter 5)
- **Highway 666**, New Mexico/Utah/Colorado (chapter 5)
- **Old Salem**, Salem, Massachusetts (chapter 5)

have obtained express *permission* to do so. Furthermore, do not attempt to be sneaky or surreptitious in your investigation, never resort to illegal activity in order to gain entry into a site, and always check with authorities regarding any areas that might prohibit your visit.

Interviewing Witnesses

Early in your ghost hunting career, you must master the art of the interview. When conducted properly, an interview can yield invaluable information regarding a ghost's appearance, habits, and demeanor, all of which can lead the ghost hunter into an encounter with the spirit.

In order to hold a thorough interview, follow a detailed questionnaire, such as the sample list of questions provided in Appendix A. When interviewing groups, question each witness separately to prevent observers from altering their stories to conform to another witness's account of the event.

Both before and after the interview, consider the type of witness involved. An observer's educational background, level of sobriety, mental and physical state, degree of retention, age, personal agenda, and history could taint his or her recollection of the encounter. Be sure to spend at least a portion of each interview assessing the factors listed above.

Experiencing Spectral Phenomena

Of course, the point of visiting a haunted site is not necessarily to visit with a witness, but to become a witness yourself. Night is usually the best time to explore a haunted location in search of ghosts (although some sites may have ghosts that appear at specific times of the day, month, or year). When a ghost finally appears, follow these rules:

- **Keep your distance.** Until you can assess a ghost's demeanor and/or identity, do not approach. Although the phantom may not attack outright, many carry powerful auras that could do great harm. They may also curse you with bad luck. Headless ghosts, other phantoms seeking new body parts, and those apparitions known to seek revenge or bloodshed should be avoided.

- **Remain still and silent.** Many ghosts vanish as soon as they realize that they are being watched. For this reason, it is best if you observe the phantom in silence until you have memorized its appearance. Once you have gathered sufficient data, you can try to establish communication with the spirit to glean even more information, but realize that you risk frightening the entity away (or, even worse, inciting its wrath).

- **Be observant.** Make mental notes regarding everything you see, feel, hear, smell, think, or even taste (some ghosts have an aura that can actually be detected by a witness's tongue) throughout the encounter. At the first possible moment, commit your memories to paper.

- **Record the event.** Oddly enough, a small fraction of video recorders, still cameras, movie cameras, and tape recorders are capable of preserving spectral manifestations. Although rare, you can discover these devices, known as "psychic cameras" or "psychic recorders," through trial and error. First, purchase some basic equipment—a standard still camera and a handheld video recorder will do. Next, whenever you visit a haunted site, take numerous snapshots and several minutes of video of areas where ghosts have been reported. If you are fortunate, the film or video will reveal a phantom or other spectral manifestation, even if you did not observe such phenomena while exploring the site. Obviously, if you do witness a ghost, attempt to take some pictures or footage as well.

- **Protect your evidence.** In a staggering number of cases, evidence linked to a haunting has simply vanished. It is unknown who, or what, is responsible for stealing, mangling, or destroying haunting evidence, but the forces at work are quite nefarious. For this reason, never send original photographs, videotapes, or films through the mail. Always develop photos yourself or entrust them to a loyal and lifelong friend. Make multiple copies of everything, including your personal notes, and lock the originals in a safe place.

Hoaxed Hauntings

Even after you have experienced a ghostly occurrence, be on guard, as a great many hauntings have later been revealed to be nothing more than hoaxes perpetrated by teenagers, glory hounds, or the disturbed. To protect yourself from a hoax, follow these simple steps:

- **Videotape everything.** Often, hoaxers are reluctant to ply their trade if they know that their activities might be captured on video. Also, taping any spectral phenomena allows you to study the alleged haunting again and again, searching for fishing wire, suspicious-looking bystanders, or other revealing clues.

- **Use masking tape.** In a common trick used by hoaxers, one of the alleged witnesses leads the ghost hunter into a supposedly haunted room, where the witness claims the ghost will manifest once the lights have been turned off. Then, a coconspirator dressed in black sneaks into the room through a window or door and moves some objects, makes an eerie moan, or does something else that could be construed as a ghostly manifestation. To prevent this, seal all doors and windows in a haunted room with masking tape after you have entered. After the phenomena cease and the lights come back on, check your tape: If it is broken at any point, you know that you have been the victim of a hoax.

- **Use salt.** A more elaborate variation of the scam described above requires the second hoaxer to sneak into the room via a secret passageway. To identify hidden doors, ring the room in a thick line of salt near the walls. If a hidden passage is used in the hoax, the secret door will disturb the salt as it swings open. The salt will also reveal any footprints left behind by a fraudulent ghost.

- **Use colored flashlights.** Along with one normal flashlight, you should carry a flashlight equipped with a black-light bulb and another fitted with a red bulb. Both are capable of revealing thin laser lights, fishing line, holograms, transparencies, and other devices used to stage a haunting.

- **Watch for static phenomena.** Truly impressive ghostly manifestations are extremely difficult to hoax. Stationary ghosts or those that repeat a brief action over and over again are probably images projected from a hidden camera. An object that only moves up and down, or left to right, at a uniform speed may be connected to a fishing line or similar source. Fake phantom voices also tend to utter the same phrases endlessly.

Interacting with Spirits

If you are quite sure that a ghost is real and safe to approach, you may be ready to attempt communication. As already mentioned above, ghosts are often flighty and easily startled, and thus any approach should be made slowly and with great care. A detailed questionnaire for interviewing ghosts is provided in Appendix B, but even when using those sample questions, you should always adhere to the following rules:

- **Speak calmly and coherently.** A great many ghosts are terribly confused by their plight. Begin your conversation by introducing yourself, and then clearly ask the ghost its name.

- **Do not mention death.** Unless you clearly realize that the ghost knows it is dead, do not broach the topic. For a ghost who has yet to realize it is, in fact, dead, the shock of hearing it from you could be traumatic for the specter.

- **Do not take anything from the spirit.** Aside from earning the wrath of the ghost, taking any object belonging to the phantom is likely to bring a heavy curse upon your head at best.

- **Avoid physical contact.** There is no way to gauge how a ghost will react if you attempt to touch it, nor how such contact will effect a mortal. You may be killed outright by the supernatural energies coursing through the phantom, or you may so offend the spirit that it decides to leave immediately.

- **Follow proper customs.** The majority of the ghosts you will encounter are not of this era and thus have different notions about the conventions of polite conversation. To avoid offending the spirit's sensibilities, try to remain formal and polite in your speech and action unless the ghost takes on an informal and friendly tone.

- **Leave if asked to do so.** When the ghost decides the conversation is over, back away amiably and allow the spirit to depart.

- **Leave if you feel threatened.** Whenever you sense that you might be in danger, flee the scene immediately (see the following section for more details on dangerous ghosts).

Recognizing a Threat

While ghost hunting or living in a suspected haunted house, there may come a time when you begin to feel threatened by a spectral presence. Although the vast majority of ghosts are completely harmless, and many are actually friendly and outgoing, a number of malevolent spirits do exist. The following list identifies some of the early warning signs that could indicate a potentially violent haunting:

- **Escalating poltergeists.** Mischievous spirits who are content to steal small objects or occasionally slam doors are of little concern. However, when poltergeists steadily increase their level of violence, one should be prepared for an eventual assault. A poltergeist that graduates from opening drawers to shattering dishes is well on its way to throwing bricks at visitors and slapping children.

- **Mysterious fires.** Another frequent poltergeist activity associated with violent ghosts is the sudden appearance of small fires. They usually erupt in trash cans, attics, or garages and are initially nothing more than a minor nuisance. However, the fires will undoubtedly increase in intensity and frequency until the haunted house burns to the ground.

- **Bedroom assaults.** Any ghost who molests a sleeping occupant of a haunted house is definitely dangerous. Initially, the attacks will not seem to be attacks at all, but mere pranks. The ghost may pull victims from bed, overturn mattresses, or "playfully" hit sleeping mortals with pillows. Eventually, however, the ghost will begin battering victims while they sleep, possibly even attempting to smother its prey beneath a pillow.

- **Invisible voyeurs.** People visiting or inhabiting haunted houses frequently feel as if they are being watched, which is understandable given the fact that a ghost could be standing anywhere, unseen. While this feeling of being watched is not always a bad omen of things to come, if you begin to experience the sensation during private and vulnerable moments—while taking a shower, making love, undressing, or trying to fall asleep—your ghost may have low moral standards. Such spirits often go through a series of increasingly perverse behaviors, beginning with "innocent" voyeurism and ending with all-out sexual assault. And lest male ghost

hunters think they have little to fear from such lecherous spirits, reported attacks indicate that men and women are equally victimized in this manner.

- **Incomplete ghosts.** Any phantom missing any part of its anatomy is potentially dangerous, largely because these ghosts are extremely preoccupied with regaining whatever it is that they have lost. In many cases, they strive to claim their missing body parts by killing mortals. Headless ghosts are the most dangerous of the incomplete phantoms, but all of these spirits should be avoided.

- **Verbal abuse.** A disembodied voice that curses, makes threats, speaks lewdly, spouts satanic verse, frequently hisses or spits, or laughs wickedly probably belongs to a deranged ghost of some sort. Such entities are clearly capable of physical violence and often make good their threats once they have thoroughly terrorized their victims.

- **Violent past.** If you manage to identify the ghost (or ghosts) responsible for the haunting, be sure to investigate the spirit's history, details of its death, and personality during its life. Clearly, if you discover that you are sharing a home with a psychopathic ax murderer who was gunned down by police after hacking up a series of teenage girls, you are probably in danger. However, even ghosts who lived innocent lives may be dangerous under the right circumstances. For example, if your troublesome ghost was once a respected local businessman who lost his fortune and committed suicide when the stock market crashed, the spirit may become violent on the anniversary of that terrible day. A generally kind Confederate ghost may not take kindly to a Yankee inhabiting his former home, and a Native American maiden who never harmed a soul during her lifetime could attack whites on general principle.

- **Loved ones feel threatened.** In some cases, ghosts take a liking to one of the living residents of the haunted house, but then become intensely jealous and overprotective. If you find the ghost extremely agreeable, be wary when your family begins reporting any misgivings about the phantom.

Putting Ghosts to Rest

Even if your personal spook is not remotely violent, you may find it difficult to go on living in a haunted house. This is a totally understandable and quite common reaction. If you decide that the living arrangement is simply unbearable, yet you do not want to leave your home, there are a few methods for removing the ghost or decreasing the level of spectral activity.

- **Remove attracting objects.** Ghosts are often linked to their old homes through familiar objects, such as old furniture, photographs, or even carpet. If you can identify and remove the items that were important to the ghost (which usually requires some knowledge of the spirit's personality and history), the spirit may follow suit.

- **Remodel and decorate.** By completely remodeling your house, you may be able to convince the ghost that the building is no longer the ghost's home. As soon as the site ceases to be familiar, the phantom is likely to leave.

- **Start a family.** If you are single, find a partner; if you are married but childless, have a few kids. The introduction of a family to the haunted house may, yet again, force the ghost to realize that new tenants belong at the site.

- **Send the kids away.** If you already have children, the ghostly manifestation may, in fact, be centered upon your offspring. Poltergeists are especially prone to this type of selective haunting. If you suspect this phenomenon, send your children to live with relatives or enroll them in boarding school: Your house will suddenly become extremely quiet, regardless of the ghost's current whereabouts.

- **Perform an exorcism.** Either with the aid of the Catholic church or some other organization, attempt to cleanse the house. Blessings, prayers, holy water, sacred artifacts, and other devices might be used in this manner to push the ghost from the house.

- **Bury the body.** If the ghost was a murder victim whose body was never properly buried, you need to find the corpse (or the skeletal remains) and have it interred in sacred ground, as per the customs of the deceased. This is a difficult task, but begin by searching for the body on your own property. The corpse may be hidden in the garden or buried in the basement.

- **Break any reenactments.** Some ghosts are doomed to repeat their final moments throughout eternity. The spirits of a murdered woman and her killer, for example, may be forced to reenact the murder every night for years on end. However, you may be able to intervene and stop the apparitions. In the above example, you might be able to intersperse yourself between the attacker and victim, saving the young woman's "life" and freeing her to travel to the Land of the Dead. A phantom who falls from a second-story window every night may only need to be caught once before he departs forever, while a ghostly suicide will probably fade if it hears a kind word.

- **Confront the ghost.** If all else fails, you can try to persuade the ghost to leave. This usually requires a great deal of courage and patience, and you must be firm yet sympathetic. First, acknowledge that the house did not always belong to you and thank the ghost for taking such good care of the dwelling. Then, gently but persistently, remind the ghost that you and your family now own the home.

Living with Ghosts

Finally, for those who have made the monumental decision to actually live with a ghost, life can be made much simpler if you decide to make the spirit part of the household in the following manner:

- **Give the ghost a name.** Preferably, you will want to call the ghost by its original name, but if this is unknown to you, simply make one up. Consult the other residents for suggestions, attempting to gauge whether you believe the ghost to be male or female (the vast majority of people who have lived with an invisible presence claim to know the ghost's sex). If you cannot determine the spirit's sex, apply a unisex name, such as "Chris," "Bobby," or "Pat."

- **Talk to the ghost.** Whenever you sense its presence, greet the ghost. Invite it to sit with you when you have a spare moment, then talk about the weather or the latest news. Thank the ghost if it does chores around the house or opens the door for you. However, if the ghost is becoming a nuisance, ask it to leave you alone for a short time, much as you would a bothersome spouse or child.

- **Give the ghost a room.** Set aside a portion of the house specifically for use as the ghost's private quarters. The attic, a spare bedroom, or the basement are prime locations for this type of arrangement. Keep the area tidy and frequently spruce it up with flowers or music to raise the phantom's spirits.

- **Set limits.** Let the ghost know what you will and will not tolerate. If the ghost is never to appear in your bedroom at night, inform it of that rule when you sense its presence in that room. If you'd prefer that the phantom did not unload the dishwasher or lift the baby into the air, politely ask it to avoid such antics.

- **Find a method of communication.** While you will be able to talk to the ghost, it may not be able to talk to you. Therefore, it is essential that you develop a means by which the spirit can make contact and relate its needs, emotions, or thoughts. Despite the superstitious paranoia surrounding Ouija boards, they are actually a perfectly safe and reliable method for conversing with spirits. Other techniques could involve the ghost rapping on walls in a type of Morse code or writing messages on a chalkboard. One inventive couple established contact with their resident ghost by leaving a pile of Scrabble game pieces on the dining room table every night before they went to bed; in the morning, they would always wake to find a short message from their spectral housemate.

- **Include the ghost during family functions.** At family meals, set a place for the ghost. On holidays (and especially the ghost's birthday, if the date can be determined), have a little gift for the spirit. If you sit down to watch a movie, leave a space on the couch. All of these gestures will be greatly appreciated by the lonely spirit.

A Final Word

Although the existence of ghosts has been widely known and accepted for hundreds of years, the related fields of ghost hunting and supernaturalism are still in nascent stages. In order for ghost hunters to expand our knowledge of our quarry, we must devote ourselves to countless hours of scholarly research, bolstered by tireless months of fieldwork. Even when encounters are separated by decades, we must never relent in our pursuit of the spectral entities living alongside us all. We must never stop collecting the random and bizarre reports of ghostly phenomena, never cease interviewing witnesses, never prop up our feet when they should be treading haunted ground.

Most important, we must never forget that the vast majority of these phantoms and poltergeists, spirits and apparitions, disembodied voices and ghost lights, were once mortals likes ourselves. We must have compassion for even the most horrible of spirits we may meet and learn to recognize the humanity not only in the tragic murder victims and forlorn vanishing hitchhikers, but in the headless horsemen and crazed killers as well. Only then will we truly be able to begin to understand the wonders of the paranormal world.

APPENDIX A: SAMPLE QUESTIONNAIRE FOR GHOST WITNESSES

It is important that you interview each witness of supernatural phenomena thoroughly. Following is a sample list of questions to help you ensure consistency and obtain a detailed description of the haunting.

Sample Questionnaire

1. Witness Data:
Name:
Current age:
Age at time of encounter (if different):
Sex:
Current occupation:
Occupation at time of encounter (if different):

2. Describe the details of the encounter, including:
Exact location of encounter:
Type of haunted site (e.g., house, cemetery, forest, etc.):
Time and date of encounter:
Weather conditions:
Duration of encounter:
Number of witnesses:
Number of ghosts encountered:
The distance between the witness(es) and ghost(s):

3. Was the ghost visible? If so, describe its:
General shape and appearance:
Coloration:
Any visible aura:
Other outstanding features:

4. Was the ghost in motion?
If so, how did it move?
How fast, and in which direction?
Did it pass through any objects, including walls or closed doors?
Did it pass through any people?

5. Did the ghost move any objects around it?

6. Did the ghost make any noise? If so, describe:
Did the ghost speak? If so, what did it say?

7. How did the ghost interact with humans?
Did it attack, flee, or remain indifferent?
Did it attempt any form of communication with you?

8. Were you frightened by the ghost?

9. Do you consider yourself psychic?

10. Do you know anything about the history of the site? If so, describe:
The site's previous owners or residents (if applicable):
Any deaths that have occurred at the site:
Any previously reported ghostly manifestations or encounters:

11. Did the ghost seem limited to a certain geographical location or specific area?
If so, describe the ghost's evident range.

12. Did you experience any other weird phenomena while in the presence of the ghost?

13. Did the ghost exhibit any special abilities or powers?

14. Were there any animals present during the manifestation?
If so, how did they react to the ghost's presence?

15. Did the ghost leave behind any physical evidence, such as footprints or ectoplasmic slime?

16. Did you experiment with a Ouija board, satanic rituals, witchcraft, Voodoo, heavy metal music, or role-playing games before the encounter?

17. Describe your emotional state directly before and immediately after the sighting:

18. Were you experiencing any emotional trauma or ordeal in the months or weeks before the sighting?

19. Have you suffered any misfortune or a string of bad luck since the sighting?

20. Did you ingest any form of alcohol, medication, or drug prior to the sighting?

21. Are you in good physical and mental health?

22. Have you ever been convicted of a crime?

23. Have you ever been accused of perpetrating a hoax?

24. Is this your first ghost sighting? If not, describe your previous encounter(s).

Upon completing the above two dozen questions, the ghost hunter/interviewer should take a moment to assess the type of ghost encountered and then proceed as follows:

For **phantoms** and other humanoid apparitions, continue with questions 25–29.

For **poltergeists** or invisible entities, continue with questions 30–34.

For **ghost lights**, continue with questions 35–40.

For **spectral animals**, continue with questions 41–46.

For **phantom craft**, continue with questions 47–49.

For **haunted objects**, continue with questions 50–53.

For **hot or cold spots** or weird auras, continue with questions 54–58.

For **unexplained noises**, including disembodied voices, continue with questions 59–62.

For Phantoms Only

25. How tall was the phantom?
Did it seem abnormally tall or short?

26. If possible, identify the ghost's sex:

27. Describe the phantom's facial features:
Did you recognize the phantom?

28. Was the phantom missing any body parts?

29. What was the phantom wearing?
Can you identify the time period or era when the phantom's clothing might have been fashionable or common?

For Poltergeists Only

30. Describe the objects affected by the poltergeist.

31. Has the poltergeist ever thrown anything at you?

32. Does the house have a history of inexplicable fires?

33. Did the poltergeist make any form of hostile gesture?

34. Was the poltergeist disturbance centered upon a single individual? If so, identify

the subject(s) and describe his or her age, sex, mental state at the time of the haunting(s).

Did the haunting(s) cease when the subject was no longer present at the site?

For Ghost Lights Only

35. Did you observe more than one light? If so, how many did you see?

Did the lights seem to travel on individual courses, or did they move together as a whole?

36. Did the ghost light(s) buzz or hum?

37. Did the ghost light(s) pulsate or change colors?

38. Did you feel compelled to follow the light(s)?

39. Have there been any reports of unusual disappearances in the area where you observed the ghost lights(s)?

40. Did the ghost lights seem
Playful?
Indifferent?
Or aggressive?

For Spectral Animals Only

41. What type of animal did you observe?
Is the species common or native to the area?

42. What color was the animal?

43. Did the ghost animal seem translucent and intangible, or solid and tangible?

44. Did you attempt to capture or kill the animal?
If so, describe your efforts and the outcome:

45. Did the animal seem to move abnormally fast?

46. Was the ghost animal accompanied by any other entities, including other ghosts or real, living creatures?

For Phantom Craft Only

47. Identify the type of vessel.

48. Did you see any passengers?

49. Did the craft reenact any type of disaster?

For Haunted Objects Only

50. Describe the haunted object in detail.

51. Can you identify the previous owner?

52. Has misfortune afflicted those who have come into contact with the object?

53. Do you consider the haunted object dangerous?

For Hot and Cold Spots Only

54. How many hot or cold spots were encountered at the site?

55. Were the spots predominately hot or cold?

56. Did the spots move about?

57. Are there any unusual stains, noises, formations, or other anomalies near the spots?

58. To your knowledge, are the spots still present?

For Unexplained Noises

59. Describe the noises in as much detail as possible.

Can you compare the noises to any other sounds with which you are familiar?

Did the noises seem to come from a human voice?

Were you able to discern any words, phrases, or sentences?

60. Did you attempt to record the noises?
If so, what were the results?

61. Did the noises seem to come from far away or from the immediate vicinity?

62. Were the noises followed by an echo of any sort?

APPENDIX B: SAMPLE QUESTIONNAIRE FOR GHOSTS

Interviewing ghosts can be a delicate process, and most spirits are emotionally unstable and prone to flee rather than face unpleasant memories or difficult questions. However, using tact and a series of questions that slowly increase in intensity, you may be able to glean invaluable information. If possible, attempt to conduct the various stages of the questionnaire over the course of several encounters. Be sure to tailor each question to the ghost's age, era, and sensibilities.

Stage One: Identifying the Ghost

Questions 1–13 should be asked during a first encounter (but only if the ghost is friendly) and are designed to give you information about the ghost's identity. After you have completed this portion of the questionnaire, you should conduct independent research at the library, on the Internet, or in the county clerk's office to learn more about the ghost and its family.

1. What is your name?

2. How old are you?

3. Do you have any relatives? What are their names?

4. Are you married? What is your spouse's name?

5. Where do you live?

6. Where do you work (or go to school, if the ghost is young)?

7. What are your hobbies or favorite pastimes?

8. Who are your close friends?

9. Where do you most like to visit?

10. Where were you born?

11. What is your fondest memory?

12. Do you have a favorite possession?

13. Have you ever spent any time in a government institution, such as an asylum, prison, or military installation?

Stage Two: Assessing a Ghost's Mental State

These questions are essentially geared toward determining whether or not the ghost realizes that it is dead. A ghost who still believes it is alive will still believe that it is the year of its death and will have little knowledge about events in the real world. Those with weak psyches, or alternately those ghosts on the verge of realizing that they are actually dead, may express confusion when faced with some of the questions below. Stage Two also reveals how the ghost is coping with the afterlife. Some ghosts may reveal hostile feelings or tendencies, while others may express a healthy acceptance.

14. How do you feel at this moment?

15. How do you feel in general? Are you generally happy or sad?

16. Physically, how do you feel?

17. Are you frequently tired, weak, or cold?

18. Do you consider yourself forgetful?

19. Do you miss your loved ones?

20. Do you consider yourself normal and well-adjusted?

21. What year is it? Do you know today's exact date?

22. Where are you?

23. Who is the president of the United States (or king of England, or chief of the local tribe depending upon when and where the ghost died)?

24. Are you hungry or thirsty?

25. Do you have any violent thoughts?

26. Have you committed any violent actions recently?

27. Does my manner of speech or dress seem strange to you?

28. What is your worst memory or experience?

29. Do you have nightmares?

30. Do you ever feel trapped, confused, or lost?

Stage Three: Confronting the Ghost with Death

Stage Three questions are meant to coax a ghost into the realization that it is, in fact, dead. Be very careful when pursuing this line of questioning, as reluctant ghosts may violently deny their undead state. If the ghost appears delicate, you should probably warn it that the interview may take an emotional turn to prepare the spirit for the revelations to come. Stubborn but otherwise psychologically sound ghosts who refuse to admit that they are dead may be convinced of this fact if they are presented with evidence, such as a photograph of their own headstone (or the headstone itself), a copy of their obituary, or intimate details of their last years of life.

31. Do you ever have dreams in which you die?

32. When was the last time you had anything to eat? If it has been quite some time, does that seem unusual to you?

33. When was the last time you saw your family, friends, or spouse? If it has been quite some time, does that seem unusual to you?

34. Have you ever walked through a wall by accident or felt invisible? Does this seem strange to you?

35. Do you recognize anything around us? Does that seem unusual?

36. Do you know what a "ghost" is? (If the ghost answers with a negative, define the term).

37. Have you ever considered the possibility that you may be a ghost?

38. I believe that you are a ghost. How does that make you feel?

39. Can you prove that you are alive?

40. Do you accept that you are, in fact, a ghost?

Stage Four: Learning About the Afterlife

This stage is only for those ghosts who know that they are dead and have had some time to contemplate their plight. Any ghost who answers yes to question 40 above should be open to the questions in this section.

41. Can you fly, move through walls, or become invisible?

42. Do you feel that you have returned from

the dead because you have a mission to complete?

43. Do you feel that you have returned from the dead because you are searching for someone or something?

44. How did you die?

45. [If the ghost was murdered] Who do you think was responsible for your death?

46. [If the ghost was a suicide] Why did you take your own life?

47. [If the ghost died in a tragic accident] Do you know of others who perished with you?

48. What do you enjoy most about being a ghost?

49. What do you like least about being a ghost?

50. What do you miss most about being alive?

51. Do you know any other ghosts?

52. When you are not visible to me, where do you go?

53. Do you ever remember a moment, perhaps as you died, when you consciously chose to become a ghost?

54. Do you know where your body is buried?

55. Have you visited your old home?

56. Do you enjoy frightening people?

57. Have you ever attacked anyone using your ghostly powers?

58. Why have you allowed me to conduct this interview?

59. Are you tired of being a ghost?

60. [If the ghost answers yes to question 58] Is there anything I can do to help you find peace?

APPENDIX C: STATE AND PROVINCE LISTING

This supplemental section arranges the haunted sites found throughout this book as they appear by U.S. state and Canadian province. Please note that for every haunted location named in this text, there are perhaps a hundred others within each given state or province.

Alabama: Bladon Springs Cemetery, De Soto Falls, Interstate 65, McConnico Cemetery, Rocky Hill Castle

Alaska: Gakona Lodge and Trading Post

Alberta: Devil's Head Mountain, Ghost Hills

Arizona: Bird Cage Theatre, Coal Canyon, Phantom Train of Dragoon, San Carlos Hotel, Superstition Mountains and the Lost Dutchman Gold Mine

Arkansas: Crooked Creek, Mark's Mill

British Columbia: Oak Bay, Pitt Lake

California: Alcatraz Island, Diablo Valley, Elfin Forest, Hotel del Coronado, Los Angeles Pet Cemetery, Mission San Antonio de Padua, Mount Shasta, Nob Hill, the *Queen Mary*, Santa Cruz Island, Stagecoach Inn, Westwood Memorial Cemetery, Whaley House, Winchester Mystery House

Colorado: Cheesman Park and City Cemetery, Grand Junction Dread 107, Grant-Humphreys Mansion, Highway 666, Little Fountain Creek and Dead Man's Canyon, Silver Cliff Cemetery

Connecticut: Devil's Footprint, Dudleytown, Franklin's Haunted Orchards, Phelps Mansion, Saybrook Woods, Union Cemetery, Yale Haunted Organ

Delaware: Bethany Beach, Fiddler's Hill, Governor's Mansion/Woodburn, HMS *deBraak*, Port Mahon

Florida: Artist House, Everglades, Ghosts of Flight 401 (who also appear across the country), Huguenot Cemetery

Georgia: Lost Island and Okefenokee Swamp, MacKay's Trading House, New Enterprise Freewill Baptist Church Cemetery

Idaho: Lower Mesa Falls, Wood River Camp

Illinois: Bachelor's Grove Cemetery, Devil's Back Oven, Devil's Kitchen, Hull House, Lakey's Creek, Midlothian Turnpike, Resurrection Cemetery, Robinson Woods

Indiana: Dunes State Park, Hannah House, Park Cemetery

Iowa: Lover's Leap, Oak Hill Cemetery

Kansas: Great Plains, Hangar 43, Phi Gamma Delta House, Saline River, Sentinel Hill, Spooksville Triangle, Stull Cemetery

Kentucky: Liberty Hall, Mammoth Cave

Louisiana: Lalaurie House, Mississippi River, St. Louis Cemetery

Maine: Appledore Island, Captain Fairfield Inn, High Point, Old York Cemetery

Manitoba: Oldman River, White Horse Plains

Maryland: USS *Constellation*, Peddler's Rock, Poe House

Massachusetts: Boston Public Garden, Coffin House, Hockomock Swamp, Monomy Island National Wildlife Refuge, Old Salem

Michigan: The *Edmund Fitzgerald*, Forester Campgrounds, the *W. H. Gilcher*

Minnesota: Castle Royal Caves, Loon Lake Cemetery, Saint Mary's College, Slaughter Slough

Mississippi: Mississippi River, Natchez Trace

Missouri: Devil's Promenade, Ozark Mountains, Phantom Steamboat of the Missouri River, Spooksville Triangle

Montana: Black Horse Lake, Little Bighorn Battlefield National Monument

Nebraska: Blackbird Hill, Great Plains, Hat Creek Battleground

Nevada: Bee Hive Whorehouse, Devil's Hole, Six Mile Canyon

New Brunswick/Nova Scotia: Beaubears Island, Cox House, Grand Manan Island, Merigomish, Northumberland Strait, Pleasant Bay, Teazer Light

New Hampshire: Devil's Den, Raccoon Mountain Road, Sise Inn, Toll Hill

New Jersey: Laurel Grove Cemetery, Spy House

New Mexico: Chaco Canyon National Park, Highway 666, Hoyle's Castle

New York: Amityville "Horror" House, Conference House, Devil's Hole, Elm Lake, the *Half Moon*, Niagara Falls, Quantum Leap Café, Thompson Park

North Carolina: The *Adventure*, Andrew Johnson Home, Devil's Stairs, Devil's Tramping Ground, Hannah's Creek Swamp, Hatteras Beach, Shut-in Creek, Teach's Hole

North Dakota: Black Butte, Great Plains

Ohio: Big Rock, Camp Chase Confederate Cemetery, Cherry Hill, Tiedeman Castle

Oklahoma: Apache Cemetery, Elk Mountain, Great Plains, Spooksville Triangle

Ontario: The *Bannockburn*, Devil's Hole, the *Edmund Fitzgerald*, the *Griffin*, Lost Seven Shore, Niagara Falls, Phantom Train of Wellington

Oregon: Forest Grove, Hot Lake Hotel, KWJJ Radio Station

Pennsylvania: General Wayne Inn, Gettysburg National Military Park, Hawk Mountain Sanctuary

Quebec: Devil's Garden, Ile des Demons, Ile d'Orléans

Rhode Island: Chestnut Hill Cemetery, the Palatine Light

Saskatchewan: Qu'Appelle River, Yorkton Crossroads

South Carolina: All Saints Waccamaw Cemetery, Huntington Beach State Park

South Dakota: Great Plains

Tennessee: Bell House, Stones River Battlefield

Texas: Galveston Bay, Stampede Mesa

Utah: Highway 666, Utah State Historical Society

Vermont: Farr House

Virginia: Haunted Rocking Chair, Haw Branch Plantation, Michie Tavern, Old Berkeley Cemetery, Old Rag Mountain

Washington: Green Lake, Harvard Exit Theater, The Mansion

Washington, D.C.: The White House

West Virginia: Big Bend Tunnel, Shue House

Wisconsin: Devil's Lake and Devil's Lake State Park, the *Griffin*

Wyoming: Devil's Tower, Platte River Ship of Death, Saint Mark's Episcopal Church

GLOSSARY

Apparition: Any semitransparent form, often (but not always) human in appearance.

Aura: An energy field surrounding all objects and living creatures. Auras, which are invisible to most people but can be seen by psychics and other sensitive individuals, vary widely in hue and intensity depending upon the mental, physical, and moral state of the aura's owner. Auras can also emit odors and affect one's emotional well-being.

Cold Spot: A spectral phenomenon in which a certain section of a haunted site always records a significantly lower room temperature than the surrounding areas. Usually, cold spots are found in hallways or the corners of rooms.

Collective Spirit: The result of several different souls or spirits joining together into a unified whole and manifesting as a spectral being. A collective spirit is often composed of several people who died in a uniform cause or pursuit or share some experience or history. An object associated with this event is often incorporated into the phantom's appearance. For example, if the souls of those who drowned aboard a sinking ship were to become a collective spirit, they would be likely to take the form of the vessel upon which they all perished.

Devil: The immensely powerful and completely evil ruler of Hell, also known as Lucifer or Satan. It is believed that the Devil has allowed many immoral or vile people to return to the land of the living as vicious ghosts.

Ectoplasm: A spectral "trail" left behind by ghosts. In its primary form, ectoplasm is a gossamer, weblike fog that follows behind ghost lights, phantoms, and other ghosts. Another variety of ectoplasm is a sticky goo that oozes from many evil spirits and can be found on doors, walls, or windows touched by these ghosts. In either form, ectoplasm is most often green in color, but can also be black, red, white, or a sickly yellow.

Exorcism: A ritual meant to cleanse a person, place, or object of a supernatural presence. The most familiar exorcisms are conducted by Catholic priests with the intention of purging demons from a possessed victim's body. Exorcisms are frequently used to force ghosts from haunted houses as well. In all cases, exorcisms are generally arduous and are only a temporary solution, as the ghosts eventually escape the effects of the ritual and return with a vengeance.

Exorcist: Anyone trained to conduct an exorcism, but usually a Catholic priest.

Fetch: An apparition of someone who will soon die, usually within a year from the sighting. Fetches usually do not interact with humans and are totally oblivious to the surrounding world. They are most often spotted by the ill-fated individual's relatives or loved ones, who will recognize the fetch. In some instances, the fetch is encountered by the person whose death the phantom foretells. These spirits may be accompanied by another type of ghost, such as a phantom ship.

Ghost: The spirit of one who has died but, for numerous reasons, has refused to leave the land of the living.

Ghost Hunter: Anyone who spends time seeking out ghosts. Usually ghost hunters have mild psychic abilities (such as a nagging "sixth sense") or are naturally sensitive to spectral manifestations. They must also have resilient nerves, keen senses, and a belief in the spirit world.

Ghost Light: A type of ghost that appears as a bobbing, radiant ball of light floating through the darkness. Ghost lights are frequently blamed for mesmerizing and misleading witnessses. Also known as will-o'-the-wisps, jack-o'-lanterns, *ignis fatuus* (foolish fire), and by a host of other names.

Ghost Ship: A phantom taking the form of a vessel, usually a sailing ship, lost at sea.

Haunted House: Any human dwelling shared by one or more ghosts.

Haunted Site: Any place, manmade or natural, occupied by one or more ghosts.

Haunted Vessel: Either a vessel inhabited by one or more ghosts or a phantom vehicle.

Haunted Village: A town, usually abandoned, that is inhabited by numerous ghosts of its former residents.

Hell: A commonly reported underworld to which the souls of the damned are destined. Reserved for sinners, Hell is believed to be ruled by the Devil, a creature of great evil

power. Some ghosts are thought to be the spirits of those who refused to enter Hell.

Hot Spot: A somewhat rare spectral phenomena in which a certain section of a haunted dwelling always records a significantly higher temperature than the surrounding areas. Usually, hot spots are found in hallways or the corners of specific rooms.

Incomplete Ghost: A phantom missing a limb, its head, eyes, ears, or other readily noticeable features. Most often, the ghost lost the missing organ or limb shortly before death and may be returning from the land of the dead in search of a replacement body part.

Intangible: Lacking physical form. Almost all ghosts are capable of rendering themselves intangible (or "immaterial"), thus avoiding physical injury.

Land of the Dead: A common generic term for the afterlife, described in a variety of ways and called by a number of different names in various religions, literature, and stories around the world. Simply, the land of the dead refers to the place where all souls journey upon death.

Ley Line: An invisible band of supernatural energy. Ley lines encircle the earth, and the point where two (or more) ley lines intersect is known as a nexus. It is believed that a ley line nexus releases supernatural energy, causing strange phenomena.

Magic: The art of tapping into supernatural forces in order to produce a host of effects. Those who use magic are known by a vast number of terms, including sorcerers, witches, magicians, and priests. The most vile form of magic, known as black magic, petitions dark and evil supernatural powers and is practiced only by immoral individuals.

Medium: One who can contact and communicate with ghosts.

Night Spirit: A type of ghost, usually evil, found abroad only at night.

Ouija Board: A type of divining device used by mediums and others to hold dialogues with unseen spirits. A Ouija board is adorned with the entire alphabet and the words "Yes," "No," and "Good-bye." The medium lightly places her hands on a pointer and asks the ghost questions. The ghost can answer simple queries by moving the pointer to the "Yes" or "No" icons, or can spell out a longer explanations using the alphabet. When the spirit tires of conversation, it simply moves the pointer to "Good-bye" and vanishes.

Paranormal: Any event or object that defies current scientific knowledge. Interchangeable with "supernatural," although usually used to describe occurrences that are more firmly rooted in the physical world, such as telepathy.

Phantasm: An apparition.

Phantom: A ghost with an identifiable form. Most phantoms appear as humans, but phantom animals and planes, ships, or trains are not uncommon. Many phantoms appear completely real until approached.

Phantom Craft: A ghostly vessel of any sort.

Place Memory: A recurring image, mirage, or event from the past. Those who encounter place-memory spirits often feel as if they are peering through a window in time. Place-memory spirits do not acknowledge the living (although the beings in a place memory will interact with each other), and seem to repeat the same scene again and again.

Poltergeist: An invisible ghost that delights in throwing objects, slamming doors, and turning appliances on and off. Poltergeists usually limit their activities to mere annoyances, but more malicious poltergeists may strike the living, set fires, kill small pets, or kidnap children.

Psychic: A person with a strange "sixth sense" that detects auras, spectral visitors, and other invisible energy fields. Many psychics can also mentally communicate with spirits and can become accomplished mediums.

Psychical Research: The investigation of a wide range of phenomena, from psychic powers to ghosts, but generally concerned with hauntings and the spirit world. Proponents of psychical research are often skilled mediums, and the séance is a favorite device used by the investigators.

Séance: A ritual performed to contact spirits. Séances take a wide range of forms and adhere to no set rules, but generally consist of several participants. The leader of the séance is usually a medium who serves as the intermediary between the living and the dead for the other members of the séance. Many séances involve candles, incense, crystal balls, special chants, potions, or other trappings often associated with witchcraft.

Second Sight: The ability to detect, and often "see," invisible entities, including ghosts. The term is also used when describing the ability to peer into the future or glance into the past.

Sensitive: Anyone capable of detecting any element of the supernatural world. Some sensitives are adept at detecting auras, while others frequently encounter ghosts or can mysteriously divine the emotions of those around them. The vast majority of children are considered to be sensitives, but most lose their special "second sight" or "sixth sense" as they are indoctrinated by society's rules, standards, and rigid beliefs. Trained sensitives who manage to retain their gifts often become accomplished psychics or mediums. Oddly enough, many animals, including domestic dogs and cats, are considered sensitives as well.

Sixth Sense: A powerful ability, believed to be increased intuition, that allows some people to sense the presence of ghosts, detect auras, or predict the future.

Spirit: The disembodied inner essence of an individual. The spirits of those who have died manifest as ghosts.

Spirit World: A common term for the realm inhabited by those who have died. In many traditions, the spirit world exists alongside the mortal world and can be detected only by sensitives or psychics.

Spiritualism: Another term for the study of ghosts and the spirit realm.

Spook: Another term for a ghost, but usually reserved for malicious spirits or prankster poltergeists.

Supernatural: Anything beyond current scientific understanding. Interchangeable with "paranormal," although usually used to describe events or entities that deal with the occult, magic, mysticism, and otherworldly powers.

Supernaturalism: The study of supernatural events, conducted by supernaturalists.

Supernaturalist: Anyone who studies the world of the supernatural and paranormal. Such investigators may devote their attentions to a wide range of subjects, including monsters, ghosts, aliens, UFOs, angels, and anything else conventional sciences have yet to explain.

Undead: Any creature that should be dead but still maintains a semblance of life. The term covers vampires, living mummies, zombies, and ghosts.

Undeath: A state between life and death. Undead creatures, such as vampires and ghosts, exist in a state of undeath.

Urban Legends: Also known as "friend-of-a-friend stories," tales that are a modern form of folklore perpetuated through oral tradition. Like campfire yarns, they often relate a horrible event, and are told as if the event actually occurred. Famous urban legends tell of encounters with vanishing hitchhikers and bogeymen.

Vanishing Hitchhiker: A type of apparition that manifests as a seemingly normal human, usually a waifish teenage girl, alongside lonely roads at night. When the ghost is picked up by a passing motorist, the spirit appears alive in almost every respect. However, when the driver arrives at the phantom's destination, the hitchhiker has invariably vanished.

Warlock: A male witch.

Witch: A practitioner of one of several hundred religions associated with magic and spell-casting. Not necessarily evil, but capable of wielding devastating supernatural power.

Zombie: An undead human, usually lacking any intelligence or ability to communicate coherently, but extremely resistant to pain or injury.

SELECTED BIBLIOGRAPHY

The data for this book have been collected over a period of years from a wide variety of sources. Movies, Internet Web sites, comic books, magazine articles, television specials, documentaries, firsthand reports, campfire tales, local urban legends, and a host of other sources have provided invaluable information about specific haunts and ghosts in general. Below is a truncated list of the most valuable text resources for further research.

Blackman, W. Haden. *The Field Guide to North American Monsters.* New York: Three Rivers Press, 1998.

Botkin, B.A., ed. *The American People: In Their Stories, Legends, Tall Tales, Traditions, Ballads and Songs.* London: Pilot Press, 1946.
———. *A Treasury of American Folklore.* New York: Crown Publishers, 1944.
———. *A Treasury of Western Folklore.* New York: Crown Publishers, 1951.

Brunvand, Jan Harold. *The Vanishing Hitchhiker: American Urban Legends & Their Meanings.* New York, London: W.W. Norton, 1981.

Burland, Cottie, et al. *Mythology of the Americas.* London: Hamlyn Publishing, 1970.

Calkins, Carrol C., ed. *Mysteries of the Unexplained.* Pleasantville, N.Y.: Reader's Digest Association, 1982.

Cavendish, Richard, ed. *Man, Myth & Magic: The Illustrated Encyclopedia of Mythology, Religion & the Unknown.* North Bellmore, N.Y.: Marshall Cavendish, 1995.
———. *The World of Ghosts and the Supernatural.* New York: Facts on File, 1994.

Clark, Jerome. *Encyclopedia of Strange and Unexplained Physical Phenomena.* Detroit: Gale Research, 1993.

Clark, Jerome, and Nancy Pear, eds. *Strange and Unexplained Happenings: When Nature Breaks the Rules of Science.* Detroit: UXL/Gale Research, 1995.

Coleman, Loren. *Mysterious America.* London and Boston: Faber & Faber, 1983.

Colombo, John Robert. *Mysterious Canada: Strange Sights, Extraordinary Events, and Peculiar Places.* Toronto: Doubleday Canada, 1988.

Dane, Christopher. *The American Indian and the Occult.* New York: Popular Library, 1973.

Drury, Nevill, and Gregory Tillett. *The Occult Sourcebook.* London: Routledge & Kegan Paul, 1978.

Fitzhugh, William W., and Susan A. Kaplan. *Inua: Spirit World of the Bering Sea Eskimo.* Washington, D.C.: Smithsonian Institution Press, 1982.

Fleming, Robert Loren, and Robert F. Boyd. *The Big Book of Urban Legends.* New York: Paradox Press, 1994.

Gray, Louis Herbert, and Alexander Hartley Burr, eds. *The Mythology of All Races,* vol. X, *North America.* New York: Cooper Square Publishers, 1964.

Guiley, Rosemary Ellen. *Atlas of the Mysterious in North America.* New York: Facts on File, 1995.

Haining, Peter. *Ghosts: The Illustrated History.* London: Treasure Press, 1987.

Hardin, Terri, ed. *Supernatural Tales from Around The World.* New York: Barnes and Noble Books, 1995.

Hauck, Dennis William. *The National Directory of Haunted Places: Ghostly Abodes, Sacred Sites, UFO Landings, and Other Supernatural Locations.* New York: Penguin Books, 1996.

Holzer, Hans. *Where the Ghosts Are: The Ultimate Guide to Haunted Houses.* New York: Citadel Press, 1995.
———. *Ghosts: True Encounters with the World Beyond.* New York: Black Dog & Leventhal Publishers, 1997.

Innes, Brian. *Ghost Sightings.* New York: Barnes and Noble Books, 1996.

Jacobson, Laurie, and Marc Wanamaker. *Hollywood Haunted: A Ghostly Tour of Filmland.* Santa Monica, Calif.: Angel City Press, 1994.

Kurland, Michael. *A Gallery of Rogues: Portraits in True Crime.* New York: Prentice-Hall, 1994.

Lambert, R.S. *Exploring the Supernatural.* London: Arthur Barker, 1955.

Leach, Maria, ed. *Funk & Wagnalls Standard Dictionary of Folklore, Mythology and Legend.* New York: Harper & Row, 1984.

May, Antoinette. *Haunted Houses of California.* San Carlos, Calif.: Wide World Publishing, 1990.

Myers, Arthur. *A Ghosthunter's Guide: To Haunted Landmarks, Parks, Churches, and Other Public Places.* Chicago: Contemporary Books, 1993.

Norman, Michael, and Beth Scott. *Haunted America.* New York: Tor, 1994.

Opie, Iona, and Moira Tatem, eds. *A Dictionary of Superstitions.* Oxford, England: Oxford University Press, 1992.

Page, Michael, and Robert Ingpen. *Encyclopedia of Things That Never Were.* New York: Penguin Books, 1987.

Phillips, David E. *Legendary Connecticut: Traditional Tales from the Nutmeg State.* Willimantic, Conn.: Curbstone Press, 1992.

Polley, Jane, ed. *American Folklore and Legend.* Pleasantville, N.Y.: Reader's Digest Association, 1978.

Robinson, Herbert S., and Knox Wilson. *Myths and Legends of All Nations.* Garden City, N.Y.: Garden City Books, 1960.

Rogozinksi, Jan. *Pirates! An A–Z Encyclopedia.* New York: Da Capo Press, 1996.

Rovin, Jeff. *The Fantasy Almanac.* New York: Dutton, 1979.

Todeschi, Kevin J. *The Encyclopedia of Symbolism.* New York: Berkley Publishing, 1995.

Underwood, Peter. *Dictionary of the Supernatural: An A to Z of Hauntings, Possession, Witchcraft, Demonology, and Other Occult Phenomena.* London: Harrap, 1978.

Warren, Ed and Lorraine, and Robert David Chase. *Ghost Hunters.* New York: St. Martin's Press, 1989.

White, Gail. *Haunted San Diego: A Historic Guide to San Diego's Favorite Haunts.* San Diego, Calif.: Tecolote Publications, 1996.

ABOUT THE AUTHOR

W. Haden Blackman is a corporeal, embodied spirit haunting portions of San Francisco, where he manifests to serve a prominent computer game company. He rarely appears during the day, cannot be photographed, and is easily repelled by the sight of religious artifacts.